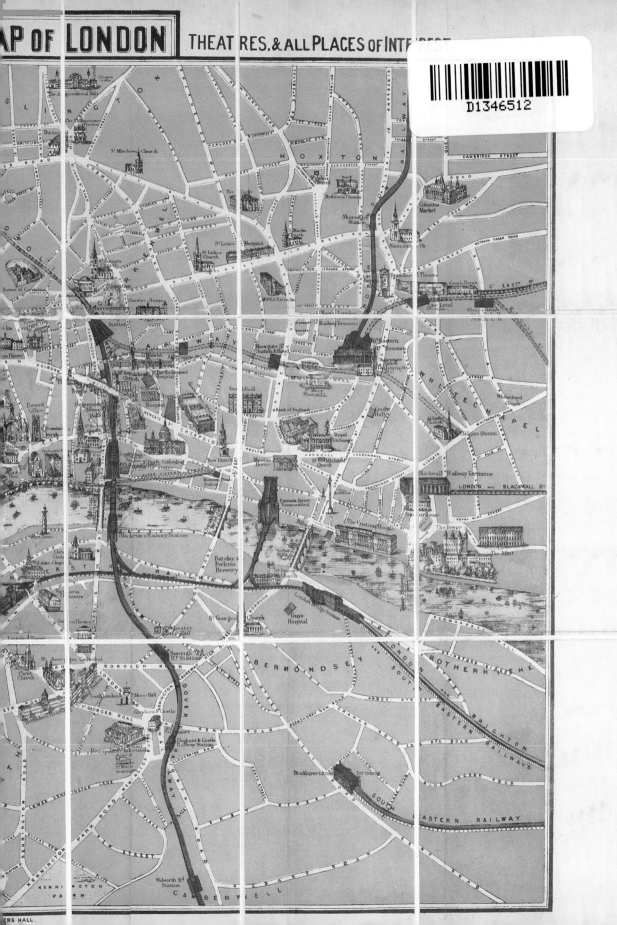

SHERLOCK
HOLMES

The Man Who Never Lived
and Will Never Die

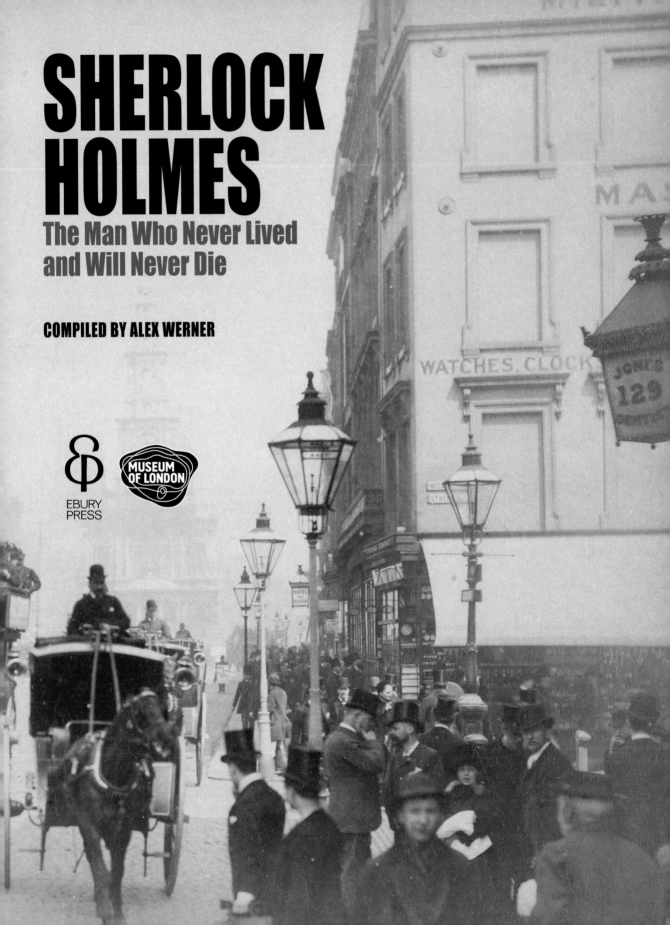

SHERLOCK HOLMES

The Man Who Never Lived and Will Never Die

COMPILED BY ALEX WERNER

EBURY PRESS

MUSEUM OF LONDON

1 3 5 7 9 10 8 6 4 2

Ebury Publishing
20 Vauxhall Bridge Road
London, SW1V 2SA

A Penguin Random House Company

Addresses for companies within Penguin Random House can be found at:
global.penguinrandomhouse.com

Published in 2014 by Ebury Press, an imprint of Ebury Publishing

www.eburypublishing.co.uk

A CIP catalogue record for this book is available from the British Library.

Designed by Peter Ward

ISBN 9780091958725

Printed and bound in Italy by L.E.G.O S.p.A
Colour reproduction by Altaimage

Penguin Random House is committed to a sustainable future for our business,
our readers and our planet. This book is made from Forest Stewardship Council®
certified paper.

Endpapers: Illustrated Map of London, c.1880, C. Smith & Sons; *Frontispiece:* Fleet Street,
c.1890; *Title page:* The Strand, c.1890, The London Stereoscopic and Photographic
Company Ltd; *This Page:* Piccadilly, c.1900, William Gordon Davis

CONTENTS

Collier's

Household Number for March

VOL XXXII NO 22   FEBRUARY 27 1904   PRICE 10 CENTS

PREFACE

As SHERLOCK HOLMES is one of the world's most famous fictional characters, it is surprising that there has not been a major exhibition on him in Britain for over sixty years. Yet, with the recent success of the BBC's *Sherlock*, together with Robert Doherty's *Elementary* and the two big-budget films directed by Guy Ritchie, starring Robert Downey Jr. and Jude Law, Holmes is arguably now at his most popular. The films combined have grossed around one billion dollars.

It is evident that Arthur Conan Doyle's iconic stories have the capacity to be reworked abundantly for new adaptations, whether set in a Victorian past or in a contemporary locale. Fresh audiences are constantly being drawn to Sherlock Holmes. This book investigates and reveals just why the detective and his world have endured. Important facets of his characters are discussed alongside the backdrop of Victorian and Edwardian London, that metamorphosing vast city with a rapidly expanding population and extremes of wealth and poverty.

This collection of essays aims to understand why Sherlock Holmes has become emblematic of much more than just a straight set of detective stories. Created at a time when modern life was becoming more complex and fast-moving, Sherlock Holmes was presented as the one person who could make sense of it all. Described as a 'magician', he solved complex problems by the power of his intellect, exceptional observational skills and forensic methods – often where everyone else had failed.

In developing a concept for the exhibition at the Museum of London, it was clear that there were a number of key subjects that needed to be examined in depth. Firstly, the long filmic history of Sherlock Holmes was unique, as no other fictional character has been the subject of so many interpretations (with the possible exceptions of Dracula and Frankenstein). It is necessary to chart and strip away the many layers of interpretation and portrayal if one is to understand how Holmes has come to dominate popular culture in such a commanding way. And it is not just Holmes, but Dr Watson also, as the two characters are inseparable when one thinks of their adventures. Even minor figures such as Mrs Hudson, Professor Moriarty, Irene Adler and Inspector Lestrade play important roles in supporting and establishing this very particular and special world. Actors, scriptwriters and directors alike have all drawn inspiration from earlier productions. One thinks especially of Jeremy

LEFT: COLLIER'S MAGAZINE COVER FOR 'BLACK PETER', FREDERIC DORR STEELE, FEBRUARY 1904

Brett and Basil Rathbone as two leading interpreters of the role of Sherlock Holmes in the twentieth century, but there were a number of fine earlier portrayals on film from actors such as Arthur Wontner, John Barrymore and Eille Norwood. Perhaps the most influential of all was William Gillette, who performed the role 1,300 times on the stage and made a film in 1916 based on his theatre play – now sadly lost.

Even before the early silent films, two very accomplished illustrators brought the stories to life in the late nineteenth and early twentieth centuries. In the United States, Frederic Dorr Steele, working for *Collier's Weekly* magazine, captured the suave confidence of Sherlock Holmes in a series of colour cover illustrations. In Britain, it was Sidney Paget's drawings which fixed the appearance of Holmes and Dr Watson in the public's mind's eye for the first time.

Secondly, another important element to consider was the context of London itself. Sherlock Holmes's London is both real and imaginary. His world radiates out from 221B Baker Street, a fictional address in a real road. It takes in the West End – where many of the detective's clients reside – and extends further out to the suburban fringes of the metropolis. Hansom cabs carry Holmes and Dr Watson around the capital as well as to the mainline railway stations, from where they travel on to distant parts of England on their many adventures.

London was a city in transition at the time the Sherlock Holmes stories were first published. Old buildings were being pulled down and streets widened. Nowhere was this more marked than in Westminster, where enormous government offices were springing up on either side of Whitehall. Nearby, around Trafalgar Square and along the Embankment, palatial hotels accommodated visitors to the imperial capital. These new city quarters promised dramatic possibilities – such as lost government documents, or even foreign dignitaries compromised in some awkward personal situation. Such circumstances required the services of Sherlock Holmes, the world's only consulting detective.

Late-nineteenth-century London was a city with a strong visual character of its own. The first film makers captured its hustle and bustle in a haunting way. Photographers recorded all the prominent landmarks, as well as the detail of its street life. Artists struggled to capture the capital's unique atmospheric mood, colour and light. The fog and smoke that so often shrouded the streets added an edge of threat and ambiguity to London's visual mood. Such atmospheric pollution also combined with the city's eerie nights, its gas-lit, cobbled streets seeming to invite danger to take a midnight stroll. Life and art alike compounded the intimidating milieu. Just at the time that Arthur Conan Doyle was writing his first Sherlock Holmes stories, the horrific Jack the Ripper murders were taking place in Whitechapel, a district of East

London – and on the stage each evening in the West End, Robert Louis Stevenson's *Dr Jekyll and Mr Hyde* was shocking London audiences.

As part of the exhibition, we also wanted to explore the origins of Sherlock Homes. A number of early jottings and notebooks have survived that give an insight into how Conan Doyle began to set out his ideas for a new sort of detective. In a single sheet of notes dating from 1885 to 1886, he jotted down 'Sherrinford Holmes' and 'Ormond Sacker', revealing that the characters' names were still not fully formed. However, there was a very precise concept, from the start, of a 'consulting detective' who used 'the Laws of Evidence'.

Conan Doyle also had in mind the skills of Dr Joseph Bell, who had been one of his tutors at Edinburgh University when he was reading medicine. Conan Doyle acted as Bell's outpatient clerk, which allowed him to study Bell's remarkable ability to assess a patient's background and condition just from close observation. He based the physical appearance of Sherlock Holmes on the surgeon as well. The first description of the detective noted especially his 'thin, hawk-like nose'. When Robert Louis Stevenson first read the stories in Samoa in 1893, he wrote to Conan Doyle asking: 'Can this be my old friend Dr Joe?' The response was: 'He's a bastard between Joe Bell and Poe's Monsieur Dupin (much diluted).*

Edgar Allan Poe was very influential both in the nature of the short-story form as well as in his invention of the detective genre. Poe's 'The Murders in the Rue Morgue' has been called the 'world's first detective story'. Intriguingly, both Poe's protagonist and Sherlock Holmes have amazing analytical powers and employ detailed investigation of the crime scene.

One of the aims of the Museum of London exhibition was to unpick Holmes's complex and unusual character and personality. He shuns all emotional feelings and has virtually no friends with the exception of Dr Watson and Mrs Hudson. Today, we might suspect him of having a mild form of autism or a bipolar condition. But whatever the cause of his behaviour, Sherlock Holmes remains a captivating figure. His cold, calculating mind with its remarkable powers is countered by a bohemian streak where dark moods and boredom can lead to drug-taking. His astonishing analytical brain can work out incredibly complex problems that defeat mere mortals. He employs the latest forensic methods to solve crimes and has a profound knowledge of obscure subjects such as cyphers and tobacco ash. He is also a master of disguise and goes undercover in the city. He is not afraid to break the law and sometimes acts as judge and jury on those who have committed crimes.

---

* Ernest Mehew (ed.), *Selected Letters of Robert Louis Stevenson* (New Haven, 1997), p. 540.

Sherlock Holmes and Dr Watson are, above all, true Englishmen – as their close friendship and distinctive gentlemanly dress make clear.

Conan Doyle wanted to kill off Sherlock Holmes not that long after he had created him. He thought that the detective took him away from what he considered his more serious writing. In the December 1893 issue of the *Strand* Magazine, Professor Moriarty and Sherlock Holmes plunge to their deaths at the Reichenbach Falls, a denouement which stunned and devastated readers in Britain and America. They pressed the author for Holmes's return and, after holding out for eight years, Conan Doyle wrote the detective's most famous adventure, *The Hound of the Baskervilles*, in 1901. However, the novel was set before the fatal scuffle with Moriarty. Finally, in 1903, Conan Doyle relented and resurrected the detective. Readers discovered that Sherlock Holmes had miraculously survived.

In the later stories, all attempts on his life fail – though he does grow old. His last appearance is just before the outbreak of the Great War when he comes out of retirement to outsmart a German spy.

Sherlock Holmes lives on and still endures to this day. Hopefully, these essays will add to the understanding of why this iconic detective still resonates with readers as strongly today as he did over a century ago.

SHERLOCK HOLMES

The Man Who Never Lived
and Will Never Die

INTRODUCTION

'A Case of [Mistaken?] Identity':
Conan Doyle, Sherlock Holmes and Fin de Siècle London[1]

DAVID CANNADINE

THE LATE 1880s were a remarkable and transformative era in the history of London, which suddenly attained an unprecedented prominence (but also an unrivalled notoriety) as the national capital, as the imperial metropolis, and as the one place on the globe that was uniquely and incomparably (yet also worryingly and troublingly) *the* 'world city'; and that pre-eminence would last until the outbreak of war in 1914.[2] There was a new awareness of its imperial, royal and historic associations, as exemplified by the popularity of the Colonial and Indian Exhibition held at South Kensington in 1886, by the successful staging of Queen Victoria's Golden Jubilee in the following year, and by the starring part given to the venerable fabric of the Tower of London in Gilbert and Sullivan's *The Yeoman of the Guard* (1888). There were major changes in the government of the metropolis, most of which would henceforward be administered by the newly established and democratically elected London County Council (LCC), which was created in 1888, even as the ancient City preserved its traditional autonomy and successfully fended off reform, in part by scaling up the glitter and the pageantry associated with its Lord Mayor.[3] But there was also a growing concern about what seemed to be the widening gap between the affluent and aristocratic West End, and the impoverished and indigent East End; and these anxieties were intensified and reinforced by the Trafalgar Square riots of the unemployed in 1886 and 1887, by the notorious 'Jack the Ripper' murders of 1888, and by the great London dock strike of 1889.[4] There were two revealing and contrasting responses to these varied events and developments. The construction of New Scotland Yard was undertaken as the headquarters of the rapidly expanding London Metropolitan Police force, and, in the same year as the London dock strike, Charles Booth published the first volume of what would become his monumental investigation into *Life and Labour in London*, which concluded that one third of the inhabitants of the world's greatest city were, in fact, living in poverty.[5]

Booth was one of many writers and thinkers, pundits and critics, journalists and commentators from Britain and far beyond who,

Left: QUEEN VICTORIA'S GOLDEN JUBILEE (DETAIL), 1887, DUDLEY HARDY. THIS WATERCOLOUR SHOWS CROWDS GATHERING IN TRAFALGAR SQUARE ON THE EVENING OF 21 JUNE 1887.

beginning in the mid-1880s, began to describe the metropolis as the place where both the challenges and the possibilities of contemporary urban living were displayed in their most extreme and exaggerated forms.[6] From one perspective, London debased and degraded humankind in new, troubling and horrifying ways; from another, it offered redemptive scope for personal fulfilment and individual achievement; and the young Arthur Conan Doyle embraced both these developing conventional wisdoms in two early writings that date from this time. In *A Study in Scarlet*, published in 1887, Dr Watson returned home, invalided from the army, with limited funds and knowing scarcely anyone, and he naturally – but reluctantly – gravitated to the nation's capital, which he described and deplored as that 'great cesspool into which all the loungers and idlers of the Empire are irresistibly drawn'. But a year later, Conan Doyle produced a very different piece, entitled 'The Geographical Distribution of British Intellect', in which he argued that in recent decades, London had 'clearly produced very much more than its numerical share of the intellect of the nation'. This was, he went on, 'as might be expected when one takes into account the centralization of wealth in London, and the way in which for centuries back the brightest intellects in every walk of life have been drawn towards the metropolis'.[7] Here were two contrasting images of London that would significantly inform Conan Doyle's Sherlock Holmes stories – the city as a great wen or 'Modern Babylon', which harboured and attracted dangerous undesirables who had to be sought out and apprehended; and the city as a great wonder or the 'New Jerusalem', which offered unprecedented possibilities and limitless opportunities, and which nurtured and drew in people of spirit and distinction, such as Sherlock Holmes himself, who would spend the whole of his professional life based in *fin de siècle* London.[8]

I

IT HAS OFTEN BEEN CLAIMED that there are three principal characters in the Holmes and Watson stories: the great detective, the good doctor and the ever-present metropolis, and up to a point (although only up to a point) this is true. Like the Tower of London in *The Yeoman of the Guard*, so this argument goes, the city was more than just the passive backdrop or the inert setting for Conan Doyle's fiction. It was for him, 'as it was for Dickens, a condition of possibility for the form and content of the tales'.[9] Yet London was not where Holmes started out, for his background was rural and gentrified. He was descended from a long line of country squires, he had attended a 'college' in a small university town, and his first two cases, 'The *Gloria Scott*' (set in 1874) and 'The Musgrave Ritual' (set in 1879) took him respectively to Norfolk and Sussex.[10] But sometime in-between, he decided to make a career as the world's first 'consulting detective', establishing himself in London, initially in Montague Street, near the British Museum, and subsequently at 221B Baker Street. There he settled, in 1881, with Dr Watson, as recounted in *A Study in Scarlet*, and there he practised for ten years until he disappeared, presumed dead, after his encounter with Professor Moriarty at the Reichenbach Falls in 'The Final Problem' (set in 1891).[11] Holmes later returned to Baker Street, as described in 'The Empty House' (set in 1894), and he detected for almost another decade, until late in 1903, as explained in 'The Creeping Man' (set in that year). At that point, he left London for good, and retired to 'that little farm of my dreams' on the South Downs near Eastbourne, to keep bees and study philosophy, and his last two recorded cases took place, like his first two, in out-of-town locations – 'The Lion's Mane' (set in 1907) on the coast near his home in Sussex, and 'His Last Bow' (set in 1914) near Harwich.[12] But during the 1880s, the mid and late 1890s, and on into the early 1900s, Sherlock Holmes was permanently residing in Baker Street, and it is with the London of those years that he has always been subsequently regarded as synonymous.[13]

Yet this close connection between the sleuth and the city was in several ways a misleading literary sleight of hand. Unlike his fictional detective, whose 'knowledge of the byways of London was extraordinary', Conan Doyle's personal acquaintance with the great metropolis was relatively limited, for the time he lived there was of brief duration, and he never became a 'London' novelist in the close, intimate and well-observed way that Dickens had been before him, or that George Gissing or H.G. Wells were during his own era.[14] His forebears were Irish (hence both 'Conan' and 'Doyle'), but he was born in 1859 in Edinburgh, and he was educated as a Catholic at Stonyhurst College in Lancashire and subsequently at Feldkirch in Austria, before returning to his home town to study medicine. While a student, he worked as a medical assistant in Birmingham; he went on two extended (and Joseph Conrad-like) voyages as a ship's surgeon to the Arctic and to west Africa; he was briefly a partner in an ill-fated Plymouth practice; and later he transferred to Southsea, near Portsmouth, where he was more successful (and married in 1885). It was while he was living on the south coast that Conan Doyle wrote his first Sherlock Holmes stories, but not until 1891 that he and his family moved to London, where he hoped to make a career as an eye specialist. Initially, they lived at Montague Place (his consulting rooms were at 2 Devonshire Place at the top of Wimpole Street) and subsequently in the suburb of South Norwood,

by which time he had abandoned his medical ambitions for full-time writing.[15] But the metropolitan sojourn was brief. In 1893 Conan Doyle's wife contracted tuberculosis, and after two years' travelling in warmer climes, the family left London for the country, settling at Hindhead, in Surrey, in 1896. The departure was permanent, and on the death of his wife ten years later, Conan Doyle remarried and moved to Windlesham Manor in Sussex where he lived for the rest of his life. Although by then he had become a member of the London literary, social and political establishments, and kept a small flat in town for overnight stays, he was never again a full-time city resident.[16]

This helps explain why Conan Doyle's familiarity with the *fin de siècle* metropolis was nothing like as detailed or as commanding as that which he claimed for his greatest fictional creation, or as that which Dickens or Gissing or Wells displayed. When he wrote *A Study in Scarlet* and *The Sign of Four*, he had visited London briefly and infrequently.

His knowledge of the city during the late 1880s was largely derived from the perusal of contemporary street atlases; and his subsequent four years' residence in the great metropolis did not deepen his close acquaintance all that much. Conan Doyle never became a committed, let alone a lifelong, Londoner. The Holmes and Watson stories were littered with descriptive and topographical errors, and he had little feel for what Henry James called the city's 'inconceivable immensity', or for particular neighbourhoods or buildings, which he often enumerated but rarely described. Indeed, on one occasion, late in his life, Conan Doyle claimed that he had never even set foot in Baker Street. This cannot have been literally true, since in 1874 he had visited Madame Tussaud's when it was located there; but although that famous thoroughfare loomed so large and so central in the Holmes and Watson stories, Conan Doyle never embellished or evoked it with any residential specificity or architectural details.[17] Such limitations and lacunae lend support to Owen Dudley Edwards's contention that Sherlock Holmes's London of the 1880s and 1890s was not, in fact, the great metropolis at all, but was instead a thinly disguised version of Conan Doyle's Edinburgh of the 1860s and 1870s, with its narrow alleys, its close juxtaposition of the grand and the squalid, and a strong sense of cohesive community that did not exist in the larger and more dispersed world city. In the same way, the Baker Street Irregulars were not so much a late nineteenth-century London gang; rather, they were modelled on a bunch of Edinburgh youths with whom Conan Doyle had for a time gone about.[18]

Conan Doyle's brief and superficial acquaintance with the metropolis also helps explain why Holmes undertook so much of his work outside London, often in Sussex and Surrey, and sometimes in the West Country and Birmingham, which were the parts of England that he knew better than he did the capital city. Of the four novellas, *A Study in Scarlet*, although set in London, had a substantial American back story; *The Sign of Four* was also located in the metropolis, but was much concerned with prior events in India; *The Hound of the Baskervilles* took place predominantly in the West Country, albeit with London interludes; and *The Valley of Fear* unfolded in Sussex with another lengthy American subplot. Among the fifty-six short stories, more than one third were primarily set outside London. These included such renowned episodes as 'Silver Blaze' (the West Country), 'The Speckled Band' (Surrey), 'The Crooked Man' (Aldershot) and 'The Priory School' (the north of England). Many of Holmes's clients journeyed from the provinces up to the city, seeking his help in solving a rural problem, often centring on a remote country house, such as Baskerville Hall, and he went back with them to investigate, which was why he and Watson were so often heading to or from the great metropolitan railway stations. It was on just such a train journey, in 'The Copper Beeches', that Holmes observed, drawing on his own experience, that 'the lowest and vilest alleys of London do not present a more dreadful record of sin than does the smiling and beautiful countryside'. There were also frequent allusions in the stories to Holmes's many continental cases, undertaken on behalf of such clients as the ruling houses of Holland and Scandinavia, the pope and the Sultan of Turkey. His brilliant exposure of Baron Maupertius as 'the most accomplished swindler in Europe' left him triumphant but prostrated in a Lyon hotel, and it was in Switzerland at the Reichenbach Falls, not in London, that Holmes allegedly fell to his death. In the three-year 'hiatus' that followed, he travelled extensively in Europe, Asia and North Africa.[19]

To be sure, many of the stories, wherever they eventually led and ended, did begin in the heart of central London, with Holmes and Watson comfortably ensconced at 221B Baker Street, and with the gaslamps and hansom cabs – and often the next, anxious, footpath-pacing client – indistinctly glimpsed through the windows. Here is one such opening, from 'The Copper Beeches':

> It was a cold morning in the early spring, and we sat after
> breakfast on either side of a cheery fire in the old room at Baker
> Street. A thick fog rolled down between the lines of dun coloured
> houses, and the opposing windows loomed like dark, shapeless
> blurs through the heavy yellow wreaths.[20]

In thus describing London's dense, yellow, pea-soup fog, and the feelings of mystery and menace that it conjured up, Conan Doyle rightly recognised a metropolitan phenomenon, which had become increasingly oppressive during the 1880s and 1890s, and which preoccupied contemporary meteorologists and environmentalists, and also such writers as Henry James and Oscar Wilde, and such artists as Whistler and Monet.[21] James loved London's 'atmosphere, with its magnificent mystifications, which flatters and superfuses, makes everything brown, rich, dim, vague'. 'Without the fog,' Monet once remarked, 'London would not be a beautiful city. It's the fog that gives it its magnificent breadth.'[22] Yet Conan Doyle never wrote about London fog so rhapsodically or so evocatively. In fact, he rarely wrote about it at all, for a cursory search of the Holmes and Watson texts throws up just thirty-five references to fog, of which the majority come from one single story ('The Bruce-Partington Plans'), set in London, and from one novella (*The Hound of the Baskervilles*), set in Devon. Indeed, the Holmes and Watson stories paid scant attention to what might be termed London's atmospherics. Not only the fog, but also the stench of the smoke and the horse droppings, the squalor of the pavements and the streets, the unrelenting noise of horses' hooves on the cobblestones and the almost intolerable traffic congestion were rarely mentioned.[23]

But his treatment of fog was not the only limitation to Conan Doyle's metropolitan vision. As G.M. Young once observed, the metropolis of the 1880s and 1890s, which was quintessentially Holmes's London, was gradually being transformed from 'the vast and shapeless city which Dickens knew – fog bound and fever haunted, brooding over its dark, mysterious river' into 'the imperial capital, of Whitehall, the Thames Embankment and South Kensington'.[24] Yet the fevers, like the fogs, received little notice from Conan Doyle. Their only significant mention was in 'The Dying Detective', when Holmes claimed to have contracted 'a coolie disease from Sumatra', which was 'infallibly deadly and horribly contagious', as a result of working on 'a case down at Rotherhithe, in an alley near the river'. And the evocation of the 'mysterious' Thames in *The Sign of Four* was little more than another catalogue of names and places, as Holmes and Watson went on a 'wild chase ... through the pool, past the West India Docks, down the long Deptford Reach, and up again after rounding the Isle of Dogs', in pursuit of the villains and their misbegotten 'Agra treasure'. Nor was 'imperial' London much in evidence in the stories, since most of that metropolitan transformation took place after Holmes had retired, early in the first decade of the twentieth century (of which more later).[25] Apart from one reference to the Royal Albert Hall, the museum complex of South Kensington barely rated a mention; and although Holmes and Watson regularly crossed the Thames, they never did so by Tower Bridge, which had been completed in 1895, shortly after Holmes's 'return'. As for Whitehall, Holmes's brother Mycroft was employed there, and the Foreign Office was mentioned in 'The Naval Treaty'; but Owen Dudley Edwards has argued that the description of the interior was not based on Sir George Gilbert Scott's recent, expansive neo-classical creation, but was modelled on the cramped and dingy chambers of Edinburgh lawyers.[26]

Not surprisingly, the parts of the great metropolis that appeared most frequently were the two areas of the city where Conan Doyle lived during his brief period of residence in the early 1890s. The first was in central London, extending from Bloomsbury to Marylebone, which was bounded (for Holmes) by Montague Street and Baker Street, and (for Conan Doyle) by Montague Place and Wimpole Street, bisected by the two major thoroughfares of Tottenham Court Road and Oxford Street. Such was their shared metropolitan heartland. The second, reflecting Conan Doyle's subsequent move to Norwood, was the sprawling suburbia south of the Thames, 'the monster tentacles which the giant city was throwing out into the country'. This encompassed not just Norwood itself, and such neighbouring communities as Sydenham and Streatham, but also Lambeth and Kennington, Lewisham and Woolwich, Blackheath and Greenwich, Brixton and Croydon, Wimbledon and Wandsworth.[27] Other parts of London were also frequently alluded to – the City, the

BIRD'S-EYE VIEW OF LONDON AS SEEN FROM A BALLOON, 1884, WILLIAM LIONEL WYLLIE AND HENRY WILLIAM BREWER

A CASE OF [MISTAKEN?] IDENTITY

21

THE GRAND HOTEL FROM
TRAFALGAR SQUARE, C.1890

docks and the East End; Clerkenwell and Covent Garden; Mayfair, St James's and Pall Mall; Regent Street and Piccadilly; Trafalgar Square, Fleet Street and the Strand; Kensington, Hyde Park and Notting Hill; Chiswick, Hammersmith and Fulham; and (but rarely) Hampstead and Harrow. Railway stations were the most significant buildings, especially Paddington, Charing Cross, Waterloo, London Bridge and Victoria (most of Holmes's out of town adventures took place to the south or west of London). Also mentioned were the British Museum, the Royal Albert Hall, the Foreign Office, the Houses of Parliament and Westminster Abbey, St Paul's Cathedral and the Crystal Palace; an assortment of theatres, hotels and restaurants, some of which were real (the Haymarket, the Langham and Simpsons), some not; St Bartholomew's, Charing Cross and Kings College Hospitals (in part in homage to Dr Watson); and Waterloo, Hammersmith and Vauxhall Bridges (though London Bridge, like Tower Bridge, was ignored).[28]

This wearying list of names (and, indeed, addresses) accurately reflects the limitations of Conan Doyle's mode of metropolitan evocation, and also it raises a further point often overlooked. While some of Holmes's London was genuinely old, such as Westminster

SHERLOCK HOLMES

Abbey and the British Museum, the great aristocratic estates in Covent Garden, Bloomsbury and Mayfair, and John Nash's Regent Street, much of his city had been constructed immediately before or during his own lifetime (Holmes, like Conan Doyle, had been born in the 1850s). Waterloo Station had opened in 1848, Paddington was completed in 1854, and Victoria and Charing Cross followed in 1860 and 1864. The underground Metropolitan Railway was inaugurated in 1863, linking King's Cross, Euston and Paddington Stations; and it was outside Aldgate Station, its eastern terminus, that the body of Arthur Cadogan West was discovered in 'The Bruce-Partington Plans'.[29] Among other buildings mentioned in the stories, the Crystal Palace at Sydenham had been put up in Hyde Park for the Great Exhibition of 1851, the Palace of Westminster and the Foreign Office were completed during the 1860s, and the Royal Albert Hall was opened in 1871. Charing Cross Road, Shaftesbury Avenue, Clerkenwell Road, Victoria Street and the Thames Embankment were mid-Victorian developments, while Northumberland Avenue and Rosebery Avenue were both laid out during Holmes's time in London. Most of the sprawling suburbia extending some eight or nine miles from Charing Cross was built during the second half of the nineteenth century, and was serviced by horse-drawn omnibuses and trams and commuter railway lines. Hotels, restaurants and theatres became a pronounced feature of the central London scene only from the 1870s. As one contemporary observed in 1888: 'This monster London is really a new city.' That may have been an exaggeration, yet the most striking feature of the great metropolis of Holmes and Watson was not (as it has since become) its nostalgic antiquity but its pervasive *modernity*.[30]

To be sure, for much of its history London had been the home of the royal court, the government, the judiciary and the legislature; it was also the hub of commerce and culture, politics and society, and literary and scientific endeavour; and it was a great port, a thriving manufacturing locale, and a major financial centre. But during the late nineteenth century, all these activities (with the exception of manufacturing) expanded and up-scaled, as London reasserted its dominance over the rest of the United Kingdom, and also became the financial and imperial capital of the world in ways that had never been quite true before.[31] Hence the dramatic increase in its population during the years Sherlock Holmes resided there. In the area governed by the LCC it rose from 3.8 million in 1881 to 4.5 million twenty years later, and across greater London as a whole, from 4.7 million to 6.6 million. Hence the arrival of immigrants and workers from all over Britain, from Europe, North America and the rest of the world. Hence the massive proliferation of clerks and office workers, who were employed in the City, but lived

CRYSTAL PALACE, SYDENHAM, KENT. 7915

CRYSTAL PALACE,
SYDENHAM, C.1890, GEORGE
WASHINGTON WILSON

in the new lower-middle-class suburbs (*vide* Mr Pooter).[32] Hence the unprecedented expansion in the numbers of middle class businessmen and professionals, and the influx of visitors and residents from the Empire and the United States. Thus enlarged and extended, the great metropolis became more varied and diverse than ever, as Conan Doyle acknowledged when he described how Holmes and Watson once passed, in rapid succession, 'through the fringe of fashionable London, hotel London, theatrical London, literary London, commercial London and, finally, maritime London'.[33] Yet as a depiction of the great, multifunctional world city, this was a characteristic combination of precision, vagueness and selectivity, for while fashionable, commercial and maritime London might be exactly located, the same could hardly be said of the others. If Conan Doyle, or Holmes and Watson, had ordered the driver of a hansom cab to take them to 'hotel London' or 'literary London', he would not have had the faintest (or even the foggiest) idea where it could be found.

II

SUCH WAS CONAN DOYLE's idiosyncratic image of late-nineteenth-century London, which was every bit as selective and impressionistic as Monet's contemporary canvases. But what, more substantively, lay behind this highly personal metropolitan vision, which Conan Doyle had created and Sherlock Holmes inhabited? As many contemporaries recognised, the answer was less than straightforward. To begin with, London may have been the one authentic and undisputed world city, but it was far from clear that its global supremacy would last, for the United States and Germany were both industrialising at prodigiously rapid rates. They would soon overtake Britain in manufacturing, and they seemed set to do so in finance as well; and New York, with its multi-ethnic energy, its massive territorial consolidation of the five boroughs, and (following Chicago) its pioneering skyscrapers, seemed to offer a very different and more challenging version of the urban future, as Conan Doyle recognised on his first visit there in 1894.[34] Moreover, London's position as the pre-eminent imperial metropolis was not quite as it seemed. The 'Scramble for Africa', the creation of the Australian Commonwealth and the conquest of the Boer Republics meant imperial euphoria was at its zenith, especially in the great metropolis; but the murder of General Gordon at Khartoum, the agitation for Home Rule in Ireland, the creation of the Congress Party demanding independence for India, and the humiliating defeats Britain suffered in South Africa, told a very different story. By 1900, many young Africans and Asians, who would later become nationalist leaders, were gaining a legal education in London. As a royal capital, London was certainly *en fête* and on parade during these years Victoria's Golden Jubilee was followed by her Diamond Jubilee in 1897 and, four years later, by her funeral, and then by the coronation of Edward VII – an innovative sequence of royal pageants celebrating a newly apotheosised monarchy.[35] But among those in the know, there was an underlying concern about royal scandal, resulting from the gambling and extra-marital liaisons of the Prince of Wales (later Edward VII), and from the delinquencies of his eldest son, Prince Eddy.

Here were crosscurrents and complexities aplenty in *fin de siècle* London, and there were others that were equally significant. The ethos of British government, as exemplified by those two late-Victorian titans, Lord Salisbury and Mr Gladstone, remained masculine, high-minded, public-spirited, incorruptible – and heterosexual. But the 1880s and 1890s were also an era of moral panic, of growing concerns about decadence, decay, disintegration and degeneracy, of anxiety about the 'new woman'

A photogravure of William Gladstone,
c.1893, from a painting in the National
Liberal Club by John Colin Forbes

Archibald Primrose, 5th Earl of Rosebery, 1894,
Henry T. Greenhead

and the threat she presented to conventional gender relations, and of fears that London high society was mired in scandal, as instanced by the trial of Oscar Wilde for 'gross indecency', and the revelations concerning a homosexual brothel in Cleveland Street, which it was alleged (probably mistakenly) was frequented by Prince Eddy.[36] Nor were the next generation of political leaders men of unimpeachable reputation or standing. It was rumoured in well-informed social and political circles that Gladstone's successor, Lord Rosebery, was homosexual while his Eton contemporary, Arthur Balfour, who was Lord Salisbury's nephew and political heir, was known in the same quarters as 'Fanny' or 'the hermaphrodite'.[37] In terms of party politics, it was the Conservatives and the Unionists, led by Salisbury and then by Balfour, who were the dominant force in government and national politics for most of Holmes's period of residence in London, and they were pledged to uphold the British monarchy, safeguard the British Empire and preserve the Union with Ireland. But the local politics of the great metropolis ran along very different lines for while the Conservatives had set up the LCC, until 1907 it was run by a left-of-centre 'Progressive' alliance of Liberals, Fabians and Socialists, with a more radical agenda. This was not the outcome Salisbury's government had wanted, and in an effort to rein in their non-compliant creation, they established a new tier of twenty-eight metropolitan boroughs in 1899, as a counterweight.[38]

There were many other contrasts and contradictions in late-nineteenth-century London, of which the greatest seemed to remain that between those whom Disraeli had earlier termed 'the rich' and 'the poor'. The Prince of Wales presided over a glittering and gaudy alternative court at Marlborough House, frequented by fast aristocrats, rich Jewish bankers and serial adulterers. Landowners lucky enough to enjoy extensive income from shares, mineral royalties and urban estates still kept up spectacular state in London during the season, whereas peers and gentry who depended solely on their farm rents were less lucky, as agricultural prices tumbled during the 'great depression'. Elsewhere, in Park Lane and Mayfair, South African 'Randlords' and American millionaires mingled with home-grown plutocrats, such as Edward Guinness (Lord Iveagh), Alfred Harmsworth (Lord Northcliffe) and Weetman Pearson (Lord Cowdray), and their opulent presence reinforced the conventional view that late-Victorian London was the richest city in the world. Yet what struck many observers during the 1880s and 1890s was the continued co-existence, amid so much plenty, of so much poverty. The particular sense of social crisis and division, associated with the riots and strikes of the late 1880s, was soon averted, but the awareness that London was the pre-eminent social problem remained. Charles Booth produced a second edition of *Life and Labour in London* in nine volumes between 1892 and 1897, and a third version in seventeen volumes between 1902 and 1903. His namesake, General William Booth, the founder of the Salvation Army, published *In Darkest England and the Way Out* in 1890, depicting London as an urban jungle, parts of which were inhabited by 'savages' who were physically deformed and spiritually decayed. The General's co-author, W.T. Stead, had earlier drawn attention to the scandal of child prostitution in London; and during and after the Ripper murders, the increasingly sensationalist – and increasingly national – press repeatedly described Holmes's London as the global capital of crime and vice.[39]

Yet while the facts of poverty and prostitution were undeniable, the London of Sherlock Holmes was actually becoming *much safer*, as all the reliable indices of crime began to fall from the 1850s, and continued to do so until the outbreak of the First World War. The *Report of the Commissioner of Police of the Metropolis* for 1882 declared London to be 'the safest capital for life and property in the world', and fifteen years

An illustration of 'the
seventh horrible murder
by the monster of the
East End' (Jack the
Ripper), *Illustrated Police
News*, 17 November 1888

later the criminal registrar at the Home Office, surveying trends during the Queen's reign, flatly announced that 'crime has immensely decreased since 1836'.[40] There were many causes and consequences of these developments. By the 1880s, the uniformed police force stood higher in public esteem than at any earlier time. They were widely thought to be decent, fair, brave and incorruptible, if not over bright, and they were affectionately parodied in Gilbert and Sullivan's *The Pirates of Penzance*.[41] The men in blue were joined by plain clothes detectives working for the new Criminal Investigation Department, who shared their colleagues' positive if plodding characteristics, while the scientific study of crime was also being initiated by a new breed of international experts known as criminologists (who created a growing body of literature to which Holmes himself contributed 'several monographs'). As policing and detection changed, so did the nature of crime. In the London of Dickens, it had been public, brutal and violent. Robbery and murder had been its visible and often horrific manifestations, and criminals were deemed to belong to the 'dangerous classes', who presented a systemic threat to social order. But in the London of Sherlock Holmes, crime was more likely to occur in private and in ostensibly 'respectable' dwellings; to be less violent because it was often concerned with fraud or embezzlement or blackmail; to require brain power rather than physical strength to uncover its perpetrators; and to represent less of a threat to the social order because wrongdoers were increasingly regarded as flawed individuals and criminal 'professionals' rather than as belonging to some generic, ill-defined and lawless underclass.[42]

Such was the *fin de siècle* metropolitan environment in which Conan Doyle briefly established himself, and although he was no Londoner,

he was very much a product of those times, reflecting in his own life and attitudes many of their contradictions and ambiguities. From one perspective, he appeared to be a quintessential late-Victorian conservative – conscious and proud of his race's innate superiority, unswervingly loyal to the British throne, devoted to the British Empire and deeply patriotic. He rejected his Irish heritage and Irish nationalism, and for most of his life was a fervent opponent of Home Rule, which he saw as portending the break-up of the British Empire. He idolised Queen Victoria ('the very heart of our lives . . . the dear mother of us all') and was a staunch admirer of Edward VII (he was overwhelmed by the 'majesty . . . colour . . . and variety' of his funeral). He volunteered for medical service in South Africa and wrote books justifying Britain's conduct during the Boer War, for which he received a knighthood. He stood (unsuccessfully) as a Unionist candidate at the general election in 1900 and again six years later, opposed giving votes to women and was a fervid supporter and chronicler of Britain's war effort between 1914 and 1918.[43] Indeed, with his love of sport, his adherence to a chivalric code of gentlemanly conduct, his military bearing and his handlebar

moustache, Conan Doyle might well have been Colonel Blimp before his time. It was a non-Blimpish version of this image that his family later sought to cultivate and embellish, via their commissioned biography by John Dickinson Carr, which (somewhat implausibly) insisted that Conan Doyle was in many ways his own Sherlock Holmes, as embodied in the phrase 'steel true, blade straight', which was engraved on his tombstone. Some recent commentators have also accepted this interpretation, although with the very different aim of denouncing Conan Doyle as an unreconstructed racist and diehard imperialist.[44]

Yet Conan Doyle was far from being sympathetic to many of the conventional conservative pieties of late-Victorian Britain and its Empire. He was a European cosmopolitan, at ease in the cultures and languages of Germany and France. He set many of his historical romances on the Continent rather than in Britain and admiringly intruded thinly disguised versions of Gladstone ('austere, high-nosed, eagle-eyed and dominant') and Lord Rosebery ('endowed with every beauty of body and mind') as Sherlock Holmes's clients in 'The Second Stain'. He was 'gladdened' that the Progressives won control of the newly established LCC, and disapproved of the hereditary House of Lords as a second chamber and of the 'bad monopoly' of the 'unearned increment' of the great ground landlords of London; he favoured the reform and liberalization of the 'deplorable' divorce laws, and he eventually came round to supporting Irish Home Rule. He rejected the Roman Catholicism in which he had been brought up and educated, and with it all other forms of Christianity, and from early adulthood he was drawn to Spiritualism.[45] His father was an alcoholic, he wrote about

syphilis in his Edinburgh MD dissertation and he explored such issues as homosexuality in some of his (non-Sherlockian) stories, and he admired and knew Oscar Wilde and thought his imprisonment unjust. He maintained a long-term liaison with another woman, Jean Leckie, while his first wife was ill with tuberculosis, he gave a thinly-disguised account of their relationship in his novel, *A Duet* (1899), and he married Jean as soon as he decently could once he was widowed.[46] He was also an admirer of the American anti-slavery campaigner, Henry Highland Garnet; he feared that on occasions Britain was too intrusive and interfering in its imperial mission; he opposed (as did Joseph Conrad) the selfish and exploitative conduct of the Belgian monarch in the Congo (where his allies included Roger Casement and E. D. Morrel); and in campaigning against miscarriages of justice in the British legal system, he intervened on behalf of a South Asian and a German-born Jew.[47]

Like his creator, albeit in different ways, Sherlock Holmes was also, in the complexities and contradictions of his character, very much a creature of the 1880s and 1890s. In one guise, Conan Doyle made him almost superhuman, a 'wizard' invested with 'special knowledge and special powers' that seemed to verge on the miraculous and meant he could 'outwit any adversary, however cunning, and solve any puzzle, however bizarre'. His mind constituted the most perfect reasoning machine ever created, his clients marvelled at his capacity for observation and deduction, and his handling of his greatest cases, such as 'The Bruce-Partington Plans', was astonishingly skilful. 'A masterpiece,' Watson told him. 'You have never risen to greater heights.' Holmes was also exceptionally

brave, strong, bold, fearless, resourceful, masterful, commanding and audacious; he was a chivalrous and patriotic 'knight-errant', adhering to a strict gentlemanly code of honour and conduct; he rebuked aristocrats and plutocrats when he believed they had behaved improperly or inappropriately; and as 'a benefactor of the race' he repeatedly restored order in a world constantly threatened by subversion.[48] To this end, he saw himself as being above the law: he burgled private residences without a qualm (and could clearly have been a first-class criminal had he so chosen); he acquitted murderers he had detected if he thought their cause was morally just; he could count, whenever needed, on the influence and support of people in the very highest of places; he never appeared in dock, either as a witness or defendant; and he was the self-appointed and self-constituted 'last and highest court of appeal' who 'represented justice'. As such, Sherlock Holmes was an early version of superman, the character introduced by Nietzsche as Ubermensch in *Thus Spoke Zarathustra*, initially published in 1883 in German (a language Conan Doyle read widely and well) and translated into English in 1896.[49]

But in an alternative guise, which was so utterly contradictory as to be almost completely inconsistent, Sherlock Holmes was not so much a reassuring superman but his very antithesis – a self-indulgent, drug-addicted Bohemian, a *fin de siècle* aesthete and decadent, and an isolated and alienated intellectual, who might have stepped straight from the pages, not of Nietzsche, but rather of Oscar Wilde.[50] For much of the time, he suffered from boredom and ennui. His sexuality was unclear – he had few, if any, friends apart from Watson, and he had an 'aversion to women'. He took heroin and cocaine (albeit only a 'seven per cent solution'); he enjoyed pipes, cigars and cigarettes, and 221B Baker Street was often wreathed in foul and impenetrable smoke; he played the violin, tunelessly, at all hours of the day and night; he was neurotic, lethargic and frequently depressed; and in such moods he was not a man of action and affairs, but 'an introspective and pallid dreamer'.[51] And for all his claims to be a cold and calculating reasoning machine, Holmes also possessed a strong artistic and theatrical streak, and he could have been a great actor (as well as a great criminal). He loved producing dramatic denouments to his cases, he relished the applause of his admirers, and it was both a professional necessity and a personal pleasure for him to dress up, put on make-up, and disguise himself as another man – or as a woman. 'With Vaseline upon one's forehead,' he told Watson in 'The Dying Detective', as if proclaiming a decadent manifesto, 'belladonna in one's eyes, rouge over the cheek bones, and crusts of beeswax around one's lips, a very satisfying effect can be produced.' What, then, was it about *fin de siècle* London that Sherlock Holmes found alternately, and contradictorily, so stultifying yet also so stimulating, and what were the circumstances under which, as Dr Watson so frequently observed, Holmes changed 'in an instant . . . from the languid dreamer to the man of action'?[52]

III

AT FIRST GLANCE, the answer to those questions is obvious, for during the 1880s and 1890s, 'the dark jungle' of criminal London was widely regarded as a place of squalor, danger, evil and wrongdoing on a uniquely massive and unrivalled scale, which meant it offered greater investigative opportunities and criminological possibilities than Holmes could ever have found in the 'stagnant' provinces, in Glasgow or Cardiff or Birmingham or Bristol, or in any other European town or continental capital. Hence his wholly understandable decision to set up, as the world's first consulting detective, in the first city of the world. 'He loved to lie,' Dr Watson observed at the beginning of 'The Resident Patient', 'in the very centre of five millions of people, with his filaments stretching out and running through them, responsive to every little rumour or suspicion of unsolved crime.' 'Amid the action and reaction of so dense a swarm of humanity,' Holmes told the good doctor on another occasion, 'every possible combination of events may be expected to take place.'[53] But in practice, and all too often, such high Holmesian expectations went un-met, for in an era of falling crime rates and enhanced policing, and despite the contrary claims of the sensationalist press, London was becoming a much safer city, violent crime had diminished, most wrongdoing was on a small and petty scale and, like prostitution, it was generally confined to the working classes.[54] Hence Holmes's constant lament that, despite his best hopes and intentions, there was *nothing for him to do*. 'There are,' he repeatedly complained, 'no crimes and no criminals in these days'; 'man, or at least criminal man, has lost all enterprise and originality'; 'audacity and romance seems to have passed for ever from the criminal world.' Crime was 'commonplace' (a key word), which meant existence was commonplace, and instead of interesting and challenging cases, there was merely 'some bungling villainy with a motive so transparent that even a Scotland Yard official can see through it'.[55]

This meant that for Holmes, the default mode of London living was languid depression and Wildean ennui, for all too often, he was a detective with nothing worthwhile to detect. Only on those relatively rare occasions when he was confronted by an 'interesting little problem' was his attention engaged, as the lethargic Bohemian was suddenly aroused into the (super) man of action. But a relatively small proportion of these cases involved murder or grievous bodily harm, some were 'entirely free' from any form of 'legal crime', and they tended to be domestic and conspiratorial, and professional and white-collar, rather than public, violent and working class. As a result, much of Holmes's

Left: A STREET SELLER OF SHERBERT AND WATER, CHEAPSIDE, 1893, PAUL MARTIN

work was involved with the complications and consequences of secrecy, exposing individual duplicity and concealment, or fraud and embezzlement; or, alternatively, concerned with the 'hushing up' of 'scandal' (another key word) that would result in shame and disgrace among the high-born, and with the recovery of sensitive government documents that had gone missing.[56] In 'A Case of Identity' and 'The Man with the Twisted Lip', the two wrongdoers, although they broke no laws, were perpetrators of cruel deceptions. In 'The Norwood Builder', Holmes foiled an attempt by the eponymous contractor to 'swindle his creditors', and in 'Black Peter', the plot hinged on the theft of securities from a disgraced banker. In 'A Scandal in Bohemia', Holmes (vainly) tried to recover compromising love letters from the Bohemian king to his former lover, Irene Adler; 'The Priory School' revolved around the existence and concealment of the illegitimate son of a duke; and in 'Charles Augustus Milverton', Holmes took on 'the king of all blackmailers'. His services to the British government were similar. In 'The Naval Treaty', he successfully recovered a confidential agreement between Britain and Italy; in 'The Second Stain', an intemperate and indiscreet 'letter from a foreign potentate' had gone missing, which, if published, would involve 'this country in a great war'; and in 'The Bruce-Partington Plans', the designs of a new submarine, 'the most jealously guarded of all government secrets', had 'gone – stolen, vanished'.[57]

Many of Holmes's London cases were concerned with unmasking wrongdoings that individuals sought to keep secret, or with recovering documents that governments wished to keep confidential. This in turn meant that despite his oft-repeated claim that it was the interest of the problem rather than the stature of the client that appealed to him, in practice few of those who sought his assistance came from the lower echelons of society; and as the example of 'The Priory School' makes plain, his clients were often of similar status when Holmes investigated outside the capital. There, too, the cases were frequently concerned with fraud, deception, blackmail or secrecy, most famously in *The Hound of the Baskervilles*, but also in 'The Boscombe Valley Mystery', 'Silver Blaze' and 'Shoscombe Old Place'. Even when Holmes investigated outside the great metropolis, the parts of the United Kingdom to which he ventured were generally extensions of the city, for the centre of gravity of the out-of-town stories was emphatically the Home Counties of Sussex, Surrey, Berkshire and Kent. Wales did not feature at all. The closest Holmes ever got to it was Herefordshire. Nor, despite Conan Doyle's own upbringing, did his hero ever visit Scotland on a case, and Scottish figures rarely appeared in the stories. As for Ireland, it was the land of Conan Doyle's forebears, but he rejected its Catholicism and (for most of his life) he also deplored Irish nationalism. So it is no surprise that Holmes never crossed the Irish Sea, and that the few Irish figures in the stories tended to be villains – the murderous American gang called the 'Scowrers', based on the 'Molly Maguires', that features in *The Valley of Fear*; Professor Moriarty, whose name was taken from an Irish school contemporary of Conan Doyle's, in 'The Final Problem'; and Holmes himself, when impersonating an Irish-American with strong anti-British and pro-German feelings in 'His Last Bow'.[58]

In a domestic context, then, the Holmes and Watson stories were preoccupied with the great metropolis, or the London-dominated south-east, while the rest of England and the remainder of the United Kingdom scarcely counted. As this compact and connected geography suggests, they often focused on the interlinked worlds of monarchy and government, aristocracy and plutocracy, financiers and rentiers, diplomats and military men, that were spreading across much of the city itself and out into the moneyed and mansioned Home Counties – worlds that were also being vividly depicted (and deplored) by J.A. Hobson in his book *Imperialism: A Study*, which he first published in 1902, the same year that Conan Doyle produced *The Hound of the Baskervilles*, and also resolved to bring his discarded hero more permanently back to life.[59] This, in turn, suggests a more convincing justification for Holmes's need to live and work in London than that

REGENT'S QUADRANT, REGENT'S STREET, 1886, LONDON STEREOSCOPIC AND PHOTOGRAPHIC COMPANY LIMITED

which he habitually, but somewhat implausibly, advanced. What really attracted the great detective to the great metropolis was that it was the epicentre of that large and growing nexus of national and imperial 'gentlemanly capitalists' that Hobson so perceptively identified in his powerful anti-imperial polemic. Thus understood, Holmes was not so much concerned with 'interesting problems', whatever they might be, regardless of the social standing of the client. Instead, he acted as the resident troubleshooter for those generally privileged but sometimes unfortunate people, living in the south-east of England, who were the agents and beneficiaries – or the victims – of Britain's late-nineteenth-century imperial pre-eminence and financial supremacy. And the kings and princes, popes and presidents, monarchs and bankers who constituted Holmes's more extended continental clientele belonged to a similar world, and they turned to him with similar problems.[60]

Sherlock Holmes's London was not only the financial capital of the United Kingdom and the European continent, but also of trans-Atlantic Anglo-America, a concept and a construct that was becoming closer yet also more competitive during the 1880s and 1890s. On the one hand, this was a growing era of international rapprochement and cultural inter-connectedness, as the two Anglo-Saxon nations increasingly began to appreciate the things they had in common; but it was also a time when the United States was beginning to challenge the United Kingdom as the world's industrial and financial leader, and to acquire its own imperial and maritime ambitions. 'We've got to go into partnership with them, or be overshadowed by them,' Conan Doyle perceptively concluded after his first visit, when he sensed American hostility to Britain even as he relished American friendship. Earlier, he had dedicated his (non-Sherlockian) book *The White Company* 'To the hope of the future, the reunion of the English-speaking races'. These Anglo-American ambivalences were well caught in the Holmes and Watson stories. The great detective derived his surname from Oliver Wendell Holmes, the American writer and doctor who was one of Conan Doyle's lifelong heroes; and in 'The Noble Bachelor', he expressed his creator's views when he declared, 'It is always a joy to meet an American . . . for I am one of those who believe that the folly of a monarch and the blundering of a minister in far-gone years will not prevent our children from being someday citizens of the same world-wide country under a flag which shall be a quartering of the Union Jack with the Stars and Stripes.'[61] But elsewhere, the view of America conveyed in the stories was distinctly less appreciative. The Mormons were roundly criticised in *A Study in Scarlet*; the Ku Klux Klan was denounced in 'The Five Orange Pips'; the 'Scowrers' received similar treatment in *The Valley of Fear*; in 'The Dancing Men' and 'The Three Garridebs', the villains

were both Americans 'of sinister and murderous reputation'; and the central character in 'The Problem of Thor Bridge' was the American 'Gold King', Neil Gibson, who was also singularly unattractive.[62]

The British Empire, of which London was even more the capital than it was of Anglo-America, was also treated by Conan Doyle with a certain degree of equivocation. In one guise, London was the place to which Britons returned after imperial service overseas, most famously in the case of Dr Watson himself, recovering from the wound received while on active service in Afghanistan. Some of them, having amassed their fortune in the Empire by honourable means, went home hoping to live in peace and prosperity in the mother country. In *The Hound of the Baskervilles*, Sir Charles Baskerville returned to Britain, 'having made large sums of money in South African speculation', with the aim of improving his house and estate in the West Country; in 'The Boscombe Valley Mystery', John Turner 'made his money in Australia and returned some years ago to the old country'; and in 'A Case of Identity', Miss Mary Sutherland enjoyed an income left to her by her Uncle Ned, which was derived from 'New Zealand stock, paying 4.5 per cent'.[63] In another guise, the British Empire was the destination where those who had erred in Britain might venture forth to seek redemption on the frontier. In 'The Devil's Foot', the 'great lion-hunter and explorer', Dr Leon Sterndale, was urged by Holmes to 'bury himself' in central Africa,

A CASE OF [MISTAKEN?] IDENTITY

having poisoned his enemies in a terrible (if justified) act of revenge. In
'The Priory School', the illegitimate son of the Duke of Holdernesse,
who resorted to kidnapping and condoned murder, was banished 'to seek
his fortune in Australia'. The undergraduate caught cheating in 'The
Three Students' set out for a new life in the colonies. 'I trust,' Holmes
tells him, 'that a bright future awaits you in Rhodesia. For once, you
have fallen low. Let us see, in the future, how high you can rise.' Then
there was Empire as a place, not of atonement and redemption, but
of freedom and opportunity, as in 'The Copper Beeches', in which Mr
Fowler and Miss Ruscastle escaped a wicked family by Fowler accepting
'a government appointment on the Island of Mauritius'.[64]

But there was also a 'persistent querying of Empire in the Sherlock
Holmes canon'. Conan Doyle often depicted it as a sinister place, where
desperate men did terrible things that subsequently became a source
of embarrassment or (more likely) revenge when they returned home.
The Sign of Four, which owed much to Robert Louis Stevenson and
Wilkie Collins, featured two villains who had stolen the 'Agra treasure'
in India, but had later been imprisoned there. They eventually escaped
and were determined to get the treasure back, seeking both restitution
and retribution in London, and they were accompanied by an evil and

'savage' pygmy. In 'The Disappearance of Lady Frances Carfax', the wrongdoer was 'Holy' Peters, who preyed on lonely, credulous, upper-class women. Holmes described him as 'one of the most unscrupulous rascals that Australia has ever evolved' and he added, for good measure, 'For a young country it has turned out some very finished types.'[65] Similar vengeful returnees from the antipodes and South Africa were to be found in such stories as 'The *Gloria Scott*', 'The Solitary Cyclist', 'The Creeping Man' and 'The Boscombe Valley Mystery', but they were all surpassed in 'The Speckled Band' by the violent-tempered and 'dissolute and wasteful' Dr Grimesby Roylott. As the scion of a fading gentry family, he trained as a doctor and went out to India where he 'beat his native butler to death … narrowly escaped a capital sentence', and went to prison for a long time. He also acquired 'a passion for Indian animals' and returned to Britain, 'morose and disappointed', accompanied by a cheetah and a baboon, which roamed the grounds of his country house; and he murdered one stepdaughter, and nearly eliminated the second, by setting on them both 'a swamp adder . . . the deadliest snake in India'.[66] From this perspective, Conan Doyle's version of the Empire came close to aligning with Hobson's – it was a place inhabited by 'damaged characters', who had gone out from Britain but when they returned, the 'frontier narrative came home to roost'.[67]

IV

IT WAS INTO THIS FLUID and fertile late-nineteenth-century world, by turns local and metropolitan, rural and national, European and North American, imperial and global, but always seemingly focused and centred on London, that Conan Doyle intruded his detective and his doctor. That elaborate and extended context helps explain many of the contradictions and paradoxes to be found in their creator, in the stories, in their central characters and in the treatment of London; but the picture is further complicated because the time period over which Conan Doyle wrote about Holmes and Watson – and London – was considerably longer than that in which the two friends were actively working. It bears repeating that the majority of the cases were set in the period from 1881 to 1891, and from 1894 to 1903. But *A Study in Scarlet* and *The Sign of Four*, and the short story collections *The Adventures of Sherlock Holmes* and *The Memoirs of Sherlock Holmes*, which culminated in the great sleuth's 'death', were written between 1887 and 1893; *The Hound of the Baskervilles, The Return of Sherlock Holmes* (another story

'Holmes pulled out his watch'.

collection) and *The Valley of Fear* were published between 1902 and 1914; and the two final collections, *His Last Bow* and *The Case-Book of Sherlock Holmes*, came out in 1917 and 1927, the second only three years before Conan Doyle's death. By the time the author bade his final farewell to his most famous creation, it was almost a quarter of a century since Holmes had retired, and getting on for half a century since he had made his debut in *A Study in Scarlet*.[68] As Conan Doyle remarked in *The Case-Book*, 'He began his adventures in the very heart of the Victorian era, carried it through the all-too-short reign of Edward, and has managed to hold his own little niche even in these feverish days.' This meant the perspective Conan Doyle offered on the 1880s and 1890s soon ceased to be contemporary, and became increasingly distant and anachronistic; and by the 1920s, the London of the 'bright young things' was a very different place from the 'world city' of the 1880s.[69]

The first two novellas and the first two collections of short stories that Conan Doyle wrote between 1887 and 1893 were the closest to the period in which they were fictionally set, and this gave them an immediacy and a vitality that subsequent instalments never quite recaptured. Moreover, because Conan Doyle later repeated what was essentially the same formula fifty-six times across nearly forty years, it is almost impossible to appreciate the audacious originality and powerful contemporaneity of those pioneering short stories.[70] In his identity and his methods, their central character owed something to the earlier sleuths who had appeared in the works of Charles Dickens, Edgar Allan Poe and Wilkie Collins, but Conan Doyle also drew on the personality and the techniques of Dr Joseph Bell, under whom he had studied at Edinburgh. In terms of their structure and construction, the short stories benefited from Conan Doyle's earlier experience in writing logical and ordered scientific papers, and were also indebted to the example of Poe and much more to Maupassant (so it was not altogether surprising that Holmes was given one French forebear). But he was the first author to establish the detective story as a recognisable genre, creating a format that was initially highly inventive, yet soon became reassuringly familiar. To borrow and adapt one of Holmes's Shakespearian quotations: age could not wither them, nor custom stale their infinite monotony.[71] As such, they were also perfectly judged for the new, mass, popular readership that had come into being in the aftermath of Forster's Education Act of 1870, an audience that was increasingly informed and entertained by new, high-circulation, late-Victorian newspapers and periodicals, among them the *Strand Magazine*, in which the Holmes and Watson short stories initially appeared.[72] And similar transatlantic developments in publishing (and the simultaneous tightening up of the copyright law in the United States) meant that Conan Doyle was among the first generation of British authors who was able to exploit the growing outlets provided by American periodicals, in particular *Lippincott's Monthly Magazine*.[73]

There were other ways in which the early novels and short stories were both innovative and contemporary that have long since become difficult to recover. London was a – indeed, the – *modern* city. The great railway stations, the Houses of Parliament and the Royal Albert Hall were scarcely a generation old. The technological infrastructure provided by railways, telegrams and hansom cabs (but rarely horse-drawn buses or the underground, or telephones or typewriters), upon which Holmes relied, was also a recent creation. It was not until the mid-1870s that the hansom had reached its final form, and the number of cabs on the streets had grown ten-fold between the 1830s and the 1880s.[74] In the same way, Holmes was working with (and, often, against) state-of-the-art policing. The uniformed force had only recently become widely recognised and esteemed by the general public; the London CID, which employed such well-meaning but plodding figures as Inspectors Gregson and Lestrade, had been re-established on a serious footing only in 1878, less than a decade before *A Study in Scarlet* appeared; and Norman Shaw's New Scotland Yard was built between 1887 and 1890, the very years in which the first two Holmes novellas were published. Indeed, the collaboration (and, often, confusion) of the constabulary was both a new and essential

ingredient for, as Reginald Hill has observed, 'without a police force there can be no detective fiction'.[75] Three of the early stories, 'A Case of Identity', 'The Speckled Band' and 'The Copper Beeches', described the attempts by hostile (step) fathers to prevent their (step) daughters from keeping their rightful inheritances if they took a husband, in vain defiance of the Married Women's Property Act, which had been passed in 1882. These early writings also resonated with the intensifyingly conservative political culture of those years, with their support of the established order of monarchy and Empire. On the walls of 221B Baker Street were the letters VR, the royal cypher of Queen Victoria, which Holmes had 'patriotically' shot in bullets, and there was also a picture of General Gordon, who had been killed at Khartoum in 1885.[76]

Yet these first fictions were also liberal, indeed, radical, for they were often as much concerned with the promotion of social justice as with the detection of criminal acts. Hence Holmes's praise, in 'The Naval Treaty', of the board schools that had been brought into being by Forster's Education Act, one of the major reforms of Gladstone's first ministry, which had been in power from 1868 to 1874. They were, he assured Watson, 'Light-houses! Beacons of the future!', which would help create a 'wiser, better England'. This ringing support for improved opportunities for those low down the social scale was accompanied by sympathy for mixed-race marriages (in 'The Yellow Face') and by a sustained criticism of the misdemeanours of those at the top.[77] Both 'A Scandal in Bohemia', centring on sexual licence, and 'The Beryl Coronet', dealing with serious private indebtedness, were concerned with the misdoings and delinquencies of royalty, and as such they were a thinly veiled criticism of the wayward behaviour of the Prince of Wales and his eldest son, Prince Eddy (the Tranby Croft affair took place in 1890 and the Cleveland Street Scandal erupted two years later). In 'The Red-Headed League', the villain, John Clay, described as a 'murderer, thief, smasher and forger', was descended from a royal duke. Although Conan Doyle often wrote of aristocrats and landowners in hushed and obsequious tones, as possessing the greatest names and most venerable lineages in the land, he did not treat them well in these early stories. Sir George Burnwell was a wicked baronet straight out of melodrama, and the snobbish Lord Robert St Simon, son of the impoverished Duke of Balmoral (another hit at royalty?), sought to repair the family fortunes by unscrupulously marrying an American heiress for her money.[78] Equally in Conan Doyle's sights in these early stories was official incompetence. As he initially depicted them, Inspectors Gregson and Lestrade were both arrogant and incapable, and on several occasions, their reputations were only saved by Holmes's superior brilliance and self-effacing magnanimity.

Left: THE BOARD SCHOOL ON CATHERINE STREET (NOW CRANWOOD STREET) IN HACKNEY, 1887

For almost a decade after 1893, Conan Doyle wrote no Sherlock Holmes stories, but in 1902, he brought Holmes back in *The Hound of the Baskervilles*, which was supposedly an overlooked adventure set more than a decade earlier, before his 'death'; and he then resurrected him for real in 'The Empty House', where it was revealed that Holmes had survived his encounter with Moriarty. That story was first published towards the end of 1903, and inaugurated a second phase of authorial activity that would last up to 1914. *The Valley of Fear* and all but the final story in *His Last Bow* were completed just before the First World War began. But 'The Empty House' was set in 1894, which meant the gap was gradually widening between the date of the stories and the date of their composition, and it would grow wider in the future, because Conan Doyle decided to retire Holmes late in 1903, the very time he had brought him back (and a year after Holmes refused a knighthood in fiction, whereas Conan Doyle accepted one in fact[79]). Yet while Holmes remained a late-Victorian figure, living in late-Victorian London, Conan Doyle was increasingly writing about him from an Edwardian perspective, and with Edwardian preoccupations. In 'The Abbey Grange' and 'The Devil's Foot', he intruded his contemporary concerns about the need to reform the divorce law. Although set in the 1890s, both 'The Second Stain' and 'The Bruce-Partington Plans' reflected the heightened international tensions of the 1900s – 'the whole of Europe' was 'an armed camp'. In the same way, 'The Six Napoleons', 'The Golden Pince-Nez', 'Wisteria Lodge' and 'The Red Circle' explored fears about foreign nihilists, anarchists and revolutionaries, which were Edwardian rather than late-Victorian concerns (and were being simultaneously treated by Joseph Conrad, who published *The Secret Agent* in 1907). In 'The Devil's Foot', which was set in 1897, Holmes was on the brink of a total nervous collapse, necessitating convalescence in the West Country; but his broken-down condition may also have been a reflection of the growing sense of crisis that engulfed the ruling classes in Britain between 1910 and 1914.[80]

At the same time, the Edwardian metropolis suddenly became a very different place from the London of the 1880s and 1890s, as it underwent a new and unprecedented phase of expansion and transformation. Most of the new roads and buildings associated with 'imperial London' were constructed during the decade between Holmes's retirement to the Sussex Downs and the outbreak of the First World War. Among the new thoroughfares driven through the very centre of the city were Millbank, which extended the Thames embankment east from the Palace of Westminster; Kingsway and the Aldwych, which were pushed through areas of slums and squalid housing south of Bloomsbury; and the Mall, which linked together the recently constructed ceremonial ensemble of

Admiralty Arch, the Victoria Monument and the refashioned frontage to Buckingham Palace. This grand processional route meant London could now compete with Vienna and Paris, Berlin and St Petersburg, as a setting for royal and state spectaculars. Elsewhere across the central area of the city, many new buildings were constructed in the style of 'high Edwardian Baroque', including the War Office and Treasury in Whitehall; the Old Bailey and the headquarters of the Port of London Authority; luxurious department stores, such as Harrods, Selfridges and Burberry; opulent hotels including the Ritz, the Piccadilly and the Waldorf; the London Coliseum and the theatres of Shaftesbury Avenue; the Methodist Central Hall and the Royal Automobile Club; and a start was made on County Hall, to accommodate the LCC, south of the Thames.[81] As G.M. Young rightly noted, these changes fundamentally transformed the public face of the metropolis in the years immediately after Queen Victoria died and Holmes retired. Indeed, they were so great that when Holmes and Watson set out, after their final encounter at the end of 'His Last Bow', to journey from Harwich to London in 1914, they would have found much of the place unrecognisable after their ten years away.

Even as they approached the outskirts of London, Holmes and Watson would have noticed many bewildering changes. They would have journeyed through a section of the whole new ring of suburbs that had sprung up, among them Acton, Barnes, Chingford, Golders Green, Merton and Morden. If they had paid a sentimental visit to their old haunts in Baker Street, they would have seen the vast modern blocks of mansion flats spreading across Marylebone and the area surrounding Marble Arch, offering a wholly new style of metropolitan living from that which Mrs Hudson had provided at 221B. If they had gone to Scotland Yard, they would have discovered major innovations in methods of detection, among them the use of fingerprints and photography.[82] They would also have noticed that London transport had been revolutionised, in part because of the advent of electric trams and the extension of the underground to the new, outlying suburbs. Even more significant was the virtual disappearance of the horse from the streets of London. In 1903, there were 3,623 horse-drawn buses and a mere 13 motor buses, but by 1913, just 142 horse-drawn buses remained to face 3,522 motor buses. In the cab business, there had been over 11,000 hansoms and hackneys in 1903 and one motor taxicab, while in 1913 there were more than 8,000 motor taxicabs and less than 2,000 horse-drawn vehicles left.[83] All this made Edwardian London a very different city from the late-Victorian metropolis. It was grander, bigger and more technologically advanced. Indeed, it has been suggestively argued that it would have been impossible for Holmes to have operated in such a different urban environment, where gaslamps and hansoms had been superseded by electricity and motors, which was why Conan Doyle retired his detective in 1903, and continued setting his stories in the 1880s and 1890s and at the turn of the century. And Holmes's creator increasingly found Edwardian London too much changed for his own liking. In *The Poison Belt*, a science-fiction story published in 1913, he came close to killing off the entire population of the 'dreadful, silent city', as the earth passed through clouds of apparently lethal gas.[84]

For Conan Doyle and his generation, the First World War destroyed much of late-nineteenth-century Britain. He lost a son and a brother as a result of the conflict, and he publically embraced Spiritualism, to which he had long been privately attracted. The promotion of that cause took up most of his time and energy thereafter, and it also exposed him to considerable public ridicule. Most of his writing was devoted to justifying his paranormal views, and he produced just a trickle of Holmes and Watson stories, which were collected – and concluded – in *The Case-Book of Sherlock Holmes*.[85] Yet despite his author's faith and credulity, the great detective remained convinced that this was the only world there was, and that reason and skepticism were the only sure guides to human behavior, and in these valedictory pieces he denounced human cravings for the artificial prolongation of life, as well as rejecting suicide. These later stories were also characterized by explicit references to bodily mutilation, and they addressed sexual issues more candidly than he had done before, ranging from the 'lust diary' of Baron Gruner in 'The Illustrious Client' to Holmes's declaration of 'loyalty and love' for Watson in 'The Three Garridebs.'[86] These final fictions were also shorter than the earlier narratives, often offering 'flashing glimpses of human distress and deformity', and they were further diminished by the recognition that Holmes was no longer the superman he had once been, and that it had become impossible to sustain world order and safeguard national security by the heroic efforts on a single individual, however brilliant. Hence, in these last tales, there is an all-pervasive sense of resignation and melancholy. 'Is not all life,' Holmes asked Watson at the beginning of 'The Retired Colourman', 'pathetic and futile?'[87] This was a very different sort of disenchantment from the languid, Wildean ennui of the 1880s and 1890s, a dazed bewilderment in the face of a postwar world more bleak than brave. When Holmes feared that 'our poor world' was in danger of becoming 'a cesspool', he may have echoed Watson's original description of London in *A Study in Scarlet*, but this time he offered no redemptive alternative to it.[88]

This resigned sense of disorientation may have been further intensified by the realisation that much of Sherlock Holmes's world city of the 1880s and 1890s had been transformed beyond recognition, as large parts of central London were redeveloped and the population of Greater London rose by another million between 1911 and 1931. On Piccadilly and Park Lane, many of the old aristocratic palaces were demolished to make way for flats, offices and shops. John Nash's Regent Street was pulled down and rebuilt to the designs of Sir Reginald Bloomfield. New London headquarters were established for the dominions of Canada, Australia, New Zealand and South Africa, and also for India; and the protracted construction of County Hall was finally completed. Work on Bush House was begun in 1925, and on Broadcasting House three years later – new buildings for the new medium of the wireless and, eventually, television, which would transform both the practice and the depiction of detection.[89] Horse-

AUSTRALIA HOUSE AND THE ALDWYCH FROM THE EAST, C.1930, GEORGE DAVIDSON REID

drawn cabs completely disappeared from the streets of London, replaced by motorised taxis, while the further extension of the underground led to the creation of an expanded suburban 'Metroland', encompassing Ealing, Wembley, Hendon, Finchley, Purley, Coulsdon and Dagenham; and the making of the new Great West Road not only resulted in the similar expansion of Heston and Hounslow, but also in the building of the 'Golden Mile' at Brentford where, from 1925, a succession of iconic Art Deco factories were constructed.[90] Surveying these changes, in a work that appeared in the same year as *The Case-Book of Sherlock Holmes*, Harold Clunn concluded that London remained 'the largest city and the capital of the greatest Empire the world has ever seen'; yet he was obliged to recognise that, in terms of numbers, it might soon

COVER OF THE PROGRAMME FOR THE BRITISH PREMIERE OF THE FILM *METROPOLIS* AT THE PAVILION CINEMA, MARBLE ARCH, 1927

SHERLOCK HOLMES

be overtaken by New York. But by then, it had, in fact, already been surpassed, which meant the London of the 1920s was no longer the undisputed world city it had been in its late-Victorian heyday, and it had ceased to be the place where the future – both bad and good – was already happening in the present.[91]

As early as 1914, when Conan Doyle had re-visited America, he had been amazed at the changes that had taken place on Manhattan since he had first set foot there twenty years before. 'It seems,' he observed, having made it to the top of the fifty-nine storey Woolworth Building, 'as though someone had gone over the city with a watering pot, and these stupendous buildings had grown up overnight as a result … New York,' he concluded, 'is a wonderful city, as America is a wonderful country, with a big future.'[92] In 1927, Erich Pommer and Fritz Lang made the same point even more emphatically in their epic science-fiction film *Metropolis*, which was allegedly set one hundred years hence in a vast, high-rise city, but which, in fact, was based on contemporary Manhattan, which was roaring and soaring upwards during the booming 'twenties, and offering a wholly original version of a 'jazz-age', new-world city. Even following the Wall Street Crash, which occurred just a year before

New York skyline, with the Empire State Building on the right, c.1930

Conan Doyle died, New York continued to rise and reach for the stars, with the completion of the Chrysler Building and the Empire State Building, the world's tallest skyscrapers, and the construction of the Rockefeller Center, that great monument to philanthropic endeavour and Art Deco design. In 1938, Jerry Siegel and Joe Schuster created their own, comic-book version of Nietzsche's Superman, who operated in a city called Metropolis, which owed much to the Lang and Pommer film; and in the following year, Bob Kane and Bill Finger responded with Batman, who was based in the fictional Gotham City, which was another scarcely disguised version of New York, albeit more at night than in the daytime.[93] Superman and Batman would become the iconic crusaders and knight errants of the twentieth century. They preferred tights and modern gadgets to deerstalkers and hansom cabs, they were much more credible in Manhattan than they would ever have been in Marylebone, and Batman even appropriated the accolade first bestowed on Conan Doyle's creation: for just as New York had surpassed London as the greatest world city, so Batman had superseded Sherlock Holmes as 'the World's Greatest Detective'.

V

OR HAD HE? The considered answer to that question must surely be no. Batman had not, and has not, done any such thing, and nor has Superman. For while comic books and blockbuster movies, bringing Gotham City and Metropolis vividly to life, have endowed these high-tech crusaders with a certain amount of glitzy, global glamour, they have scarcely begun to compete with Sherlock Holmes's extraordinary and enduring appeal and his still-expanding, multi-media longevity. During the last hundred years, the novels and short stories have been translated into virtually every major language, and they have never been out of print in English. In Conan Doyle's lifetime, some stories were transferred from the page to the stage, beginning in 1899 with the American actor William Gillette, who re-created Holmes as a theatrical figure and played the part for many years on both sides of the Atlantic. The first silent film, entitled 'Sherlock Holmes Baffled', appeared as early as 1900, and forty-five shorts and two feature-length movies were produced by Stoll Pictures between 1921 and 1923. The first sound film to feature Sherlock Holmes was made in 1929, and Basil Rathbone and Nigel Bruce made fourteen American Holmes and Watson talkies between 1939 and 1946.[94] Since then, Holmes has gone on to the

JEREMY BRETT TOOK ON THE ROLE OF SHERLOCK HOLMES IN THE GRANADA TV SERIES BETWEEN 1984 AND 1994.

wireless, including a complete adaption of every novel and story on BBC Radio 4, broadcast between 1989 and 1998, and there have been many television versions, among them those starring Douglas Wilmer, then Peter Cushing, between 1964 and 1968, and Jeremy Brett from 1984 to 1994. Many 'new' Sherlock Holmes stories have been written, broadcast and filmed, and statues have been unveiled to him in London, Edinburgh and Moscow.[95] In 1934, the Sherlock Holmes Society was founded in London, and the Baker Street Irregulars in New York, the first of many world-wide groups extending as far as Australia, India and Japan, and they in turn have spawned a strange, obsessive-compulsive world of 'Sherlockian' pseudo-scholarship.[96] The result is that Conan Doyle's creation has remained, in P.D. James's words, 'the unchallenged Great Detective', and he has become the most famous fictional figure in the English language and the most portrayed movie character, with more than seventy actors playing the part in over two hundred films.[97]

All this means that Sherlock Holmes has long since left behind the time and the place in which he was originally created, and has taken on a life (indeed, many lives) of his own, far beyond the particular confines of late-nineteenth-century London in which he first appeared. Indeed,

Basil Rathbone played
Sherlock Holmes in
fourteen feature films
between 1939 and 1946.

BASIL RATHBONE as Sherlock Holmes
Nigel BRUCE as Doctor Watson in
SHERLOCK HOLMES AND THE VOICE of TERROR
Based on the Story "His Last Bow" by
SIR ARTHUR CONAN DOYLE
with
EVELYN ANKERS   REGINALD DENNY
THOMAS GOMEZ   MONTAGU LOVE
HENRY DANIELL

that process had already begun while Conan Doyle was still alive and writing new stories in the 1920s, as Holmes and Watson, and the late-Victorian city they inhabited, were already being looked back on with a kind of wistful longing for what seemed to have been a happier place in an earlier time. At the end of that decade, T.S. Eliot noted that 'in the Sherlock Holmes stories, the late nineteenth century is always romantic, always nostalgic', and that 'the pleasant externals' of the city were an essential part of that nostalgia and romance. For Eliot, as for a growing number of his interwar generation, Conan Doyle's stories had become a welcome fantasy escape from the 'waste land' of modernity embodied in the damp-pavement (and still fog-bound) dinginess of contemporary London. Indeed, Eliot went further, and predicted that the nostalgia and romance would increase and intensify among those future Holmes and Watson devotees who would have had no first-hand recollection of the nineteenth century.[98] And posterity has abundantly vindicated that prediction, as countless readers, listeners and viewers the world over remain beguiled by what they imagine to have been London in 1895, with its sinister and omnipresent fogs, and with Holmes sporting his deerstalker hat, his curved Calabash pipe and his Inverness cape. But it bears repeating that London fog in the 1880s and 1890s was more widespread in the city than it was in the pages of Conan Doyle's stories, and that only after the passing of the Clean Air Act in 1953 could such life-threatening environmental pollutants become an object of nostalgia; while Holmes's hat, pipe and cape owed more to the illustrations of Sidney Paget and the films starring Basil Rathbone than they did to Conan Doyle's original texts (and they were less in evidence in the television series starring Jeremy Brett, which sought to be more true to the original stories). [99]

Yet such fuzzy, romantic, gaslit nostalgia conveniently disregards the many 'unpleasant externals' of late-nineteenth-century London – the filth and the stench, the noise and the congestion, the squalor and the poverty.[100] It shows no awareness of the limitations, inadequacies and idiosyncrasies of Conan Doyle's vision of the world city, or of the alternative inspirations for it, which owed at least as much to Edinburgh as to the great metropolis itself. It fails to appreciate the time-bound specificity and uniqueness of Sherlock Holmes, and also of his creator, who in their contradictory personalities resonated so powerfully with the 1880s and 1890s, two decades in which anxiety and hope, poverty and progress, decadence and daring were so challengingly co-mingled. It also ignores the way in which works that were initially innovative and contemporary became, even during the author's later lifetime, increasingly formulaic and anachronistic, and since then have become ever more disconnected from their historic time and place of origin. Thus understood, Holmes's posthumous career, in the decades since Conan Doyle's death, is itself a subject worthy of serious attention as a classic instance, like Gilbert and Sullivan's operettas, and P.G. Wodehouse's Jeeves and Wooster stories, of an original literary genre long and successfully outliving the circumstances in which it was first created.[101] But Holmes's own life in his own time in his own city is more fascinating still, for he was a fictional character who both embodied, yet also bridged, the gap between the two very different identities of late-nineteenth-century London – as a place where the squalid reality of urban despair co-existed with the romantic possibilities of metropolitan redemption. The essays that follow bring the great city and the great investigator vividly alive in what is, fittingly and appropriately, a major exercise in detection and discovery. Enough of the 'pleasant externals' of foggy and gaslit nostalgia, and of the deerstalker Holmes rarely wore and the Calabash pipe he never smoked. Here, instead, is historical inquiry, abundant evidence and careful reconstruction, bringing us *fin de siècle* London and late-Victorian Sherlock Holmes as they have not been seen or apprehended since they first appeared. This is no longer a case of mistaken identity. Here, in the following pages, the game is very seriously afoot.

CHAPTER ONE

The 'Bohemian Habits' of Sherlock Holmes

JOHN STOKES

FOR HOLMESIANS THE WORD 'Bohemian' is inevitably associated with the story published in the *Strand Magazine* in July 1891, but set in 1888, entitled 'A Scandal in Bohemia'. A perennial favourite, this concerns an adventuress, a beautiful opera singer named Irene Adler, and the danger that she might blackmail the hereditary King of Bohemia, thereby wrecking his plans to marry into Scandinavian royalty. Visiting Baker Street in disguise, the King tells Holmes that Adler possesses a compromising photograph taken of them in the course of a romantic liaison. In the event, the risk of blackmail is not borne out − not as a result of Holmes's attempts to regain the incriminating evidence, which don't really succeed, but because of the singer's sense of honour and her professional admiration for the detective's theatrical approach. It would seem, then, that the 'Bohemia' of the title must refer to the Eastern European territory that was part of the Austro-Hungarian Empire in the nineteenth century, known after 1918 as Czechoslovakia − unless, that is, we consider the real scandal to be not an international embarrassment, narrowly averted, so much as the fact that Holmes, an austere male mastermind, is outflanked by a glamorous female actress to whom he is uniquely, but unquestionably, attracted. Curiously enough, Conan Doyle does indeed introduce, if only glancingly, that other possibility by reminding us at the start that Holmes, solitary and frequently misogynistic, normally loathed 'every form of society with his whole Bohemian soul' ('A Scandal in Bohemia'). This is a different application of 'Bohemian' and it evokes unconventional personal characteristics rather than a single nationality. The two identifications are, however, linked by remoteness (geographical in one case, sociological in the other), and by the fascination that either might possess for Holmes's respectable English readers.

It sometimes seems that, historically speaking, there were as many Bohemias as there were Bohemians. This is because Bohemianism is invariably a way of life, a caste of mind, a time of day even, before it

becomes associated with a place. As the preface to a volume of short
stories entitled *In and About Bohemia*, published in 1892, would have it,
the fabled land of freedom could be 'anywhere, everywhere, nowhere.
It exists in the hearts of its denizens, in the lives of those who love it.'[1]
Nonetheless, the geographical label 'Bohemia' has often become tied to
specific locations where unusual options might flourish and indulgent
habits take root. Initially and most famously, it was applied to the Left
Bank of the Seine and to Montmartre in Paris, and later on to, among
several other urban locations, the Schwabing area of Munich, New
York's Greenwich Village and San Francisco's Haight-Ashbury district.
In the late nineteenth and early twentieth centuries 'Bohemia' indicated,
though imprecisely, particular areas of London.

These radiated out from the Strand – to the south, down to the
Embankment; to the north, up through Covent Garden to Soho; to the

east, down to the lower reaches of Fleet Street; to the west, gaining considerably in social status, to the Haymarket, St James, Piccadilly and 'Clubland'. 'Bohemia' took in many theatres, including the Lyceum, the Gaiety, the Adelphi, the Olympic and the Strand, as well as the offices of many newspapers and periodicals. Intermixed with these were the off-duty spaces and places where professionals who were engaged in what we might today call 'cultural industries' could indulge in 'Bohemian' recreation.[2]

The Strand, though, remained the main artery – as Holmes and Watson are well aware. When the pair travel from Baker Street to the Lyceum Theatre in *The Sign of Four*, they necessarily pass down an extremely busy highway:

Down the Strand the lamps were but misty splotches of diffused light which threw a feeble circular glimmer upon the slimy pavement. The yellow glare from the shop-windows streamed out into the steamy, vaporous air and threw a murky, shifting radiance across the crowded thoroughfare. There was, to my mind, something eerie and ghostlike in the endless procession of faces which flitted across these narrow bars of light – sad faces and glad, haggard and merry. Like all humankind, they flitted from the gloom into the light and so back into the gloom once more . . . Holmes alone could rise superior to petty influences. He held his open notebook upon his knee, and from time to time he jotted down figures and memoranda in the light of his pocket-lantern. (*The Sign of Four*)

While Holmes remains seemingly oblivious to what surrounds him, his companion peers out at a strange and threatening world; even though they must have passed through the Strand many times before, he is clearly not at home here. And Watson's reaction may be justified, especially at that time of evening. After all, as a prolific, but now forgotten, journalist, playwright and poet – and self-proclaimed Bohemian – named Shafto Justin Adair Fitzgerald recorded in 1890:

In no thoroughfare in the world does so much talent and genius and mediocrity pass and meet and rub shoulders daily as in the Strand. In no thoroughfare are there so many brilliant hopes and aspirations fostered and fed; in no thoroughfare is desperate Despair seen to creep along and attempt to hide its head as in the gay, the volatile, the classic Strand.[3]

Of course, nothing lasts forever in any city, least of all in London, and wholesale demolition, followed by architectural 'improvements', was a fairly continuous process. This was particularly true of the eastern end of the Strand with proposals dating back to the 1830s to abolish the notorious Holywell Street area. These proposals eventually resulted in Kingsway and the Aldwych conglomeration, which opened in 1905.[4] In his memoir, entitled *My Bohemian Days*, illustrator Harry Furniss recalls this locale as he knew it in the 1870s:

When I first made its acquaintance London's Bohemia consisted of a ramshackle, picturesque, and historically interesting jumble of famous old streets, narrow passages, 'inns', square taverns, and publishing shops. In this interesting quarter jostled together vice and virtue, intellect and ignorance, poverty and opulence.

In this Alsatia dwelt 'characters' both eccentric and clever, and, if not inspiring, they were at least artistic. The very pavements reeked with tobacco from the calumets of semi-savages, combined

with the onions accompanying the chops and steaks which were carried from the cook-shop to the office of the wealthy banker or the establishment of the well-to-do tradesman.[5]

BOOKSELLERS' ROW, HOLYWELL STREET, LOOKING WEST AND EAST, C.1895, ERNEST DUDLEY HEATH

The district around Holywell Street was not only the centre of the second-hand – and frequently pornographic – book trade. As the cultural historian Lynda Nead has described it, 'the site between St Clement Danes and St Mary le Strand was a particularly bad traffic bottleneck. At this point, the Strand contracted so that traffic had to be channelled through the nearby narrow old lanes to the north.'[6] The result was the unhealthy but (for the curious) intriguing labyrinth evoked by Furniss.

The concepts – and to some extent the realities – of Bohemia that were circulating in London in the late nineteenth century were derived in part from earlier myths. The English heritage goes back to eighteenth-century Grub Street although the first fictional representation of

SHERLOCK HOLMES

- The World the Flesh and the Devil:

London Bohemia, characterised by youthful indulgence in oysters, alcohol and billiards, is said to have been offered by Thackeray in his novel *The Adventures of Philip* of 1862.[7] Other myths came from slightly further away. Paris supplied lifestyle legends, widely disseminated through *Scènes de la vie de Bohème* (1848) by Henri Murger (1822–61), a popular work of fiction that inspired George du Maurier's *Trilby* (1895) and eventually led to Puccini's 1898 opera *La Bohème*. Murger's original introduction, as translated for an English edition published in 1888, is ambiguous. On the one hand, Bohemians 'have existed in all climes and ages, and can claim an illustrious descent'; on the other, 'Bohemia only exists and is only possible in Paris.'[8]

EDMUND YATES, ARTHUR SKETCHLEY, HENRY LABOUCHERE VIEWED BY THE ACTOR AND PLAYWRIGHT H. J. BYRON, HARRY FURNISS.

Left: THE STRAND AND CHARING CROSS, C.1895, LONDON STEREOSCOPIC AND PHOTOGRAPHIC COMPANY LIMITED

Conan Doyle converts this kind of uncertainty into a joke when he has Watson 'skipping over the pages of Henri Murger's *Vie de Bohème*' (*A Study in Scarlet*). English attitudes to the French precedent were always mixed. Irish writer and politician Justin McCarthy insisted that 'the London Bohemian swaggers through

A Hansom Cab Stand,
c.1890, P. Stahl

literature more roysteringly and more noisily than his *confrère* of Paris,'[9] while a fellow critic, George Saintsbury, set about attacking vulgarised, Anglicised versions of 'Bohemian':

> Sometimes it seems to be assumed that anybody who has [any] sort of connection with literature or art is a Bohemian . . . Sometimes, and more often, the assumption is made that Bohemianism consists in more or less senseless and vulgar dissipation, extravagance and display. Indeed it would appear from certain writers that the differentia of the Bohemian man consists in smoking cheroots while he is drinking claret, and that the differentia of the Bohemian woman consists in wearing blue satin and diamonds when ladies would content themselves with ordinary apparel.[10]

Within every cultural and historical period there are 'Bohemians', who are full-time members of a recognised social group, and there is 'Bohemianism', the generic tendencies that almost anyone can draw upon if and when inclination and opportunity coincide. Recreational Bohemianism flourished among most professions and classes, an indication of its often paradoxically conventional origins. Examples might be the Prince of Wales (the future Edward VII) or, more directly relevant to Holmes, Henry Irving (Conan Doyle's favourite actor from Edinburgh days) or even Conan Doyle himself – all men of high visibility and public status who were known to have their Bohemian side. A contemporary account of dinner at the Carlton Hotel in 1899 included apparently 'the mixed cream of all the societies from St James's to the pleasant land of refined Bohemia, in dress-clothes, silk, lace and diamonds'.[11] This seems close to Saintsbury's appalled vision of a vulgarly affluent English version.

Clearly, the preferences and predilections of the Bohemian were shared among people, both fictional and real, who might otherwise be far from casual in the ways in which they conducted their more public lives. It was possible even to disguise oneself as a Bohemian. Arthur Ransome, whose *Bohemia in London* first appeared in 1907, mentions a man who worked in a bank during the day but adopted a false beard at night, thereby turning himself from an anonymous clerk into a would-be member of a coterie.[12] Part-time or weekend Bohemians have always earned contempt from those who purport to be the real thing but are a perennial feature of urban life nevertheless. This further explains why the Bohemian could simultaneously be both mythic and actual, the myth relating to the complete human personality, the actuality being a range of behavioural tendencies. It may also explain why Holmes and Watson are sporadically 'Bohemian', their activities determined by an author who wanted his readers to pick up on idiosyncrasies with which they were already familiar, either in life or through other literature, including the slew of popular fiction with 'Bohemian' somewhere in its title, but who also wanted to remain free to create his own uniquely distinctive characters.

The model Bohemian life remained that of an artist, a designation that could be applied to almost any occupation that eschewed simple profit-making and had goals beyond mere productivity.[13] In its purest form, Holmes's profession matches these criteria exactly, 'working as he did rather for the love of his art than for the acquirement of wealth' ('The Speckled Band'). 'To the man who loves art for its own sake,' remarks Holmes, echoing a first principle of Aestheticism, 'it is frequently in its least important and lowliest manifestations that the keenest pleasure is to be derived' ('The Copper Beeches'). Bohemia is less interested in uniformity than individualism and follows its own path. A musician who delights in visual effects, Holmes pursues his personal moral objectives with an almost missionary delight.

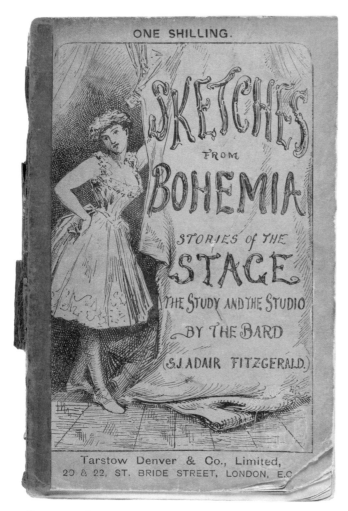

COVER OF *SKETCHES FROM BOHEMIA*, 1890, S J ADAIR FITZGERALD

In fact, probably the best-known application of the term throughout the nineteenth century was to a female, although ostensibly she had little to do with contemporary London. *The Bohemian Girl*, an immensely popular opera involving a band of gypsies, the orphaned daughter of an Austrian count and an aristocratic Polish soldier, was first performed in London in 1843, much revived on tour, and notably burlesqued.[14] Although the public idea of Bohemia tended to be overwhelmingly male – with men-only clubs and men-frequented pubs – women undoubtedly did participate in Bohemian activities, and not only to serve the sexual demands of the men. The problem for the modern historian, as Jacky Bratton has argued about a slightly earlier period, is that 'British Bohemian life, as described by the writers themselves, was a site for these conflicts of manliness, sexuality and domesticity, [and] as such it needs to be represented as homosocial.'[15] However important the contribution of women may have been to all manner of cultural activities, they tend to be excluded from both contemporary accounts and retrospective male autobiographies. By the 1880s and 1890s, although the male façades of the entertainment and communications industries were still firmly in place, as countless memoirs testify, they were more visibly permeated by 'Bohemian' women, who could flaunt their sexual independence, even from the more earnest members of their own gender. In *A Bohemian Girl* (1898) by 'P.M. McGinnis' (pseudonym of the socialist journalist Robert Blatchford) 'Daisy Spanker', a singer, objects to progressive 'New Women' whom she views as 'martyrs' and makes it clear that she likes men.[16] 'McGinnis' invents a musical play entitled, significantly enough, *The Bohemian Boy*. We probably need to remind ourselves, however, that Daisy is a fictional character created by a male author.

Wandering

OHEMIANS ARE TRAVELLERS, their adoptive name
derived from the country where, or so it was
commonly believed by the French, gypsies originated.
Recalling his own youth much later in life, Conan Doyle
admitted 'my wanderings had left me rather too
Bohemian and careless upon points of etiquette' and 'a bachelor,
especially one who had been a wanderer like myself, drifts easily into
Bohemian habits.'[17] He was referring to a whaling trip undertaken in
1880, a characteristically bold and unconventional venture. The journalist
and theatrical manager Major Fitzroy Gardner found it necessary to
explain the titles of his two books of memoirs, *Days and Ways of an Old
Bohemian*[18] and *More Reminiscences of an Old Bohemian*, like this:

> 'Bohemian' in the title of my other book may have suggested
> that my reminiscences relate only to Bohemia, in the common
> acceptation of the term, whereas the word is used in its general
> sense, that of a man who has led a wandering life and therefore
> had a variety of experiences.[19]

Much the same claim is made by Gustave Ludwig Strauss, the founder
of the proudly Bohemian and highly selective Savage Club, who in his
memoirs, entitled *Reminiscences of an Old Bohemian*[20] and *Stories of an
Old Bohemian*,[21] stresses his early *Wanderjahre* in Germany, France and
elsewhere.

Among those possessed of the Bohemian spirit a compulsion to
wander persisted, even within relatively confined areas. Commonly

THE *STRAND* MAGAZINE
COVER, DECEMBER 1903

compared to tramps and vagabonds, Bohemians roam the streets at all hours and in this respect Holmes and Watson are no different from many others. So, for instance, in 'The Resident Patient': 'For three hours we strolled about together, watching the ever-changing kaleidoscope of life as it ebbs and flows through Fleet Street and the Strand.' The nocturnal trajectory of Bohemians frequently took them among the crooked alleys and pathways of the city. The 'decadent' poet and critic Arthur Symons admitted (or boasted) to a woman friend, 'I don't know whether you have heard of our wanderings by night, our studies of the ins and outs of London … Do you know, I have no interest in what is proper, regular, conventionally virtuous. I am attracted by everything that is unusual, Bohemian, eccentric: I like to go [to] queer places, to know strange people. And I like contrast, variety.'[22] Henry Irving was said, on his arrival in London, to have soon learned 'to love the great mysterious city, and find out its strange holes and corners, its sideshows, its cheap theatres, and its infinite variety. In those days he indulged in athletic exercises, was an expert swimmer, fond of back streets and slums, as he is now, a prowler in queer places.'[23]

Whether such nocturnal wanderings around the 'queer places' of London were a sensible option for female Bohemians is perhaps more doubtful. Foreign adventures, however, had real possibilities. When, in 1884, Lady Florence Dixie, who became a notable and pioneering explorer, published poems she had written in the 1870s while travelling, she entitled them *Waifs and Strays or The Pilgrimage of a Bohemian Abroad*.[24] Two decades later travel was even more firmly established as a way of broadening the female mind. The title story of Elizabeth P. Ramsay-Laye's *The Adventures of a Respectable Bohemian* (1907) takes the form of a memoir by a widow who holidays with a lady companion (sister of a vicar) who decides to marry an Italian hotelier. The marriage is a success and the narrator learns to accept that, in the wider European context, Bohemianism is by no means 'proof of the tendency, which some historians assert exists in the human race, to recede from civilisation into barbarism'.[25] She becomes, as it were, an honorary continental Bohemian herself.

Timing

EDUCATIVE WANDERING depends on available free time.
In a classic essay on the effect of industrialisation on
the experience of time, the historian E.P. Thompson
noted that '[one] recurrent form of revolt within
Western industrial capitalism, whether bohemian
or beatnik, has often taken the form of flouting the urgency of
respectable time-keeping.' From the late seventeenth century onwards,
says Thompson, time is 'currency; it is not passed but spent'; there

John Lawrence Toole,
Sir Henry Irving and
John Sims Reeves, c.1880,
Alfred Bryan

develops a clear demarcation between 'work' and 'life' – though Thompson does also concede that the emergence of 'leisure', with its concomitant industries, introduces an element of regularisation, even purposiveness, into what the culture offers as free time.[26]

Bohemians, by comparison with more conventional workers, have their own body clock, preferring to rise and retire when they please. Holmes, we are told, 'was usually very late in the mornings, save upon those not infrequent occasions when he stayed up all night' (*The Hound of the Baskervilles*). Sometimes Watson can hear him 'marching about in the night' (*The Sign of Four*). Whenever Holmes goes out alone, Watson can never be sure when he will return ('The Beryl Coronet'). Even Watson himself admits to getting up 'at all sorts of ungodly hours' and to being 'extremely lazy' (*A Study in Scarlet*); in *The Sign of Four* he sleeps until late afternoon. Holmes works when he has to, responding to the demands of each case. By contrast, many denizens of Bohemia worked for local industries that had particularly strict hours – theatre and journalism. The curtain had to go up; the newspaper had to appear. The solution was to change the conventional order of the day so that night became day and day became night. With its own regularised customs, Bohemianism actually mirrored – put in reverse – that to which it was apparently opposed, a characteristic tendency.

Among prototypical Bohemian journalists were, by general agreement, George August Sala (1828–1895), 'a real Bohemian, a bon viveur',[27] and Edmund Yates (1831–1894), both flamboyant personalities, all-round book and newspapermen, with a taste for gossip and nocturnal pleasures. Among their theatrical equivalents, but with more discretion, Irving was pre-eminent. Although he eventually became the figurehead of his profession, he was typical when it came to the duality of his daily life. As his most recent biographer admits:

> While preaching the virtues of domesticity, marital fidelity and family life, he lived a classic Bohemian bachelor existence of late nights, convivial clubland dinners, cigars, wine and masculine conversation.[28]

Lodging

T was clearly a good deal easier to live the Bohemian life fully if you were a bachelor, free not only of regular hours but also of familial responsibility and the demands of respectability. By sharing your lodging with someone rather similar to you – if only because they were of the same sex – basic needs might be more easily agreed upon. Holmes and Watson are in one mind about such essentials as food, tobacco and the right to breakfast in one's dressing gown while reading the newspapers, even if they disagree about hard drugs and occasionally bicker about professional procedure. Bachelors are free to eat when they

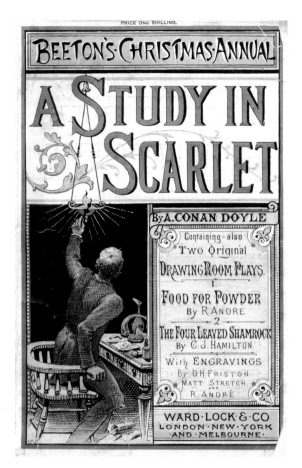

"'YOU MAY DO WHAT YOU LIKE, DOCTOR.'"

Above: COVER OF *BEETON'S*
CHRISTMAS ANNUAL,
A STUDY IN SCARLET, 1887

Above right: 'YOU MAY DO
WHAT YOU LIKE, DOCTOR',
SHERLOCK HOLMES AND
DR WATSON, *A STUDY IN*
SCARLET, 1891, GEORGE
HUTCHINSON

need or want to, or not even eat at all if preoccupied with other more important issues. In 'The Five Orange Pips' Holmes forgets to eat all day, finally 'tearing a piece from a loaf' and 'washing it down with a long draught of water'. On the other hand, when the job is done, food can be welcome, both men being prepared to act in the role of housekeeper. In *The Sign of Four*, Holmes summons up 'oysters and a brace of grouse, with something a little choice in white wines', while in *The Valley of Fear* (part I chapter 6 'A Dawning Light'), a long meeting leaves him ravenous for the high tea that Watson has ordered up for him.

Watson notes with some irritation that Holmes carries out his 'malodorous' chemical experiments inside the flat (*The Sign of Four*), and that he is obliged to make recompense for the careless scraping of his violin practice by playing some of the doctor's favourite airs (*A Study in Scarlet*). Yet Watson confesses his own failings, too: 'The rough-and-tumble work in Afghanistan, coming on top of a natural Bohemianism of disposition, has made me rather more lax than befits a medical man' ('The Musgrave Ritual'). When he finally gets married, Watson is able occasionally to persuade Holmes to 'forgo his Bohemian habits so far as to come and visit us' ('The Engineer's Thumb'). The bachelor ideal, founded upon mutually respected independence, is evidently still in place. As Holmes remarks, bachelors are good at keeping secrets: 'We may expect that more from a man who is alone than from one who lives in the bosom of his family' ('The Engineer's Thumb').

Among the writers of the *fin de siècle* who lived on their own or in pairs in closeted rooms and benefited from this kind of masculine tolerance were Arthur Symons, George Moore and Havelock Ellis, all of whom had rooms in the Middle Temple at one time or another. On his arrival in London, Oscar Wilde shared accommodation with the painter Frank Miles, first in Salisbury Street, close to the Strand, and later in Tite Street, Chelsea. W.B. Yeats had rooms at Fountains Court, then chambers in Woburn Walk. The poet Lionel Johnson (who, according to Yeats, breakfasted at seven o'clock in the evening) shifted from Charlotte Street to Gray's Inn to Lincoln's Inn Fields.[29] A man could live on his own if he had sufficient means in, for instance, Albany, the secluded all-male apartments off Piccadilly. These were 'altogether cloisteral'[30] but congenial for someone such as George Ives, a secretive but real-life gay writer whose rooms in Albany are occupied by the fictional Ernest Worthing in Wilde's *The Importance of Being Earnest*.[31]

Bachelor quarters were typically a haven that could be viewed, like 221B Baker Street, as an island of security, an anchored vessel, amid the turbulence outside. They were secure, comfortable and shared just this side of full intimacy: 'Holmes and I sat, upon a raw and foggy night, on either side of a blazing fire in our sitting-room' (*The Hound of the Baskervilles*). The familiar, comforting image has persisted. And when it came to interior decoration, Bohemians tended to prefer the reassuringly old to the new, and to value the domestic ease that is demonstrated by the careless distribution of objects. Priorities lie elsewhere. That's the Bohemian way and it's usually offered as quintessentially male. Yet the sharing of rooms by independently-minded young women, although probably less frequently represented in fiction, was to become more commonplace with the growth of a female population made up of, for instance, shop-girls and trainee teachers.[32]

By contrast with this gender-based seclusion, the world of theatre had long allowed the phenomenon of what Jacky Bratton has called the

'Is there any other point that I can make clear?', 'The Naval Treaty', The *Strand* Magazine, November 1893, Sidney Paget

'HOLMES OPENED IT AND
SMELLED THE SINGLE CIGAR
WHICH IT CONTAINED', 'THE
RESIDENT PATIENT', THE
STRAND MAGAZINE, AUGUST
1893, SIDNEY PAGET

'Bohemian family'. In fiction, the most famous example is the Crummles ménage in Dickens's *Nicholas Nickleby* (1838–39) – a model for Pinero's play *Trelawny of the Wells* (1898). Another instance is this typical vignette from a story by Adair Fitzgerald:

> They had one enormously large room though, which served as the general dining, sitting, smoking and universally useful apartment. A long dining-table stood in the centre, half littered with pay books, play bills, operas, songs, and shilling shockers. The mantel-shelf was covered with letters, tobacco pipes, boxes of matches, and photographs, with here and there an odd vase or ornament in a semi state of revolt or demolition, [on] which an old marble clock, always two hours and seventeen minutes fast, stood with broken columns, half rakishly in the middle . . .[33]

As Bratton describes it, late in life the dramatic critic Clement Scott, when recalling his upbringing in the 1860s, 'felt the Bohemian combination of domesticity and professionalism generated theatrical art' so that 'a talented circle, with its unquestioning if often tacit inclusion of women as equal partners provides him with an ideal'.[34] It's true that actresses found it easier to adopt a Bohemian lifestyle – or perhaps they had it forced upon them – than many other women, professional or otherwise. Lily Langtry and Mrs Patrick Campbell became famous examples of 'Society Bohemians' and, in Holmes's case, there's Adler, a cross-dressed performer who some critics have associated with Sarah Bernhardt.

For Holmes and Watson domesticity is, unashamedly underpinned by Mrs Hudson, who, for the most part, keeps her place. Women are rarely entertained for any length of time or found to be particularly entertaining in themselves, in which respect Holmes resembles his creator. Conan Doyle seems to have preferred his social gatherings to be exclusively male on the grounds that 'it is notorious that though ladies greatly improve the appearance of a feast they usually detract from the quality of the talk. Few men are absolutely natural when there are women in the room.'[35] Among the places where it might be more 'natural' for an informed female voice to be heard were the spacious studios of prominent artists. Whistler's studio was an élite meeting place; Louise Jopling, friend of both Whistler and Wilde, and a painter in her own right, held regular 'at homes' in hers. Studios could combine a work place with living quarters as well as providing ample space for entertaining. More privately, the studios gave off an aura of the erotic. The sexual potential that lay in the relation between a male painter and his possibly unclothed model – who might also serve as cook and even nurse – was obvious. In Henry Curwen's romantic novel *Within*

Bohemia; or Love in London (1876) the artist hero occupies an untidy
room in Newman Street, off Oxford Street, and the signs – the clues –
of a female presence are unmistakable:

> Very bare, very desolate, and still very untidy. A bed, a crippled
> table, rather on crutches than on legs, a desk, two chairs, one of
> which is partly serviceable, more ruined furniture, an easel, a
> lay figure, a guitar and music, a pile of unfinished canvases and
> sketches, three pet rose trees in pots, a lady's shawl, some hair pins,
> and the remains of a chignon.[36]

Eating and drinking

ALE ENGLISH BOHEMIANS can be said to divide into two: the solitary and the sociable. Those who loved to relax in company had their preferred haunts, more or less respectable. The most celebrated gentleman's clubs were the Beefsteak (Irving's favourite), the Savile, the Arundel, the Albemarle and the Traveller's. The Garrick and the Savage were actually attended on special occasions by Gladstone and the Prince of Wales (who was a member of both). Watson has a club, while Holmes's brother Mycroft belongs to a kind of anti-club, The Diogenes Club, founded on the perverse principle of remaining unsociable (and said to be based on the Athenaeum).

Holmes, unsurprisingly, appears to belong to no club at all and nor does he haunt public houses. Among those thought to offer a Bohemian ambience were the Crown, off Leicester Square, and the Cheshire Cheese in Fleet Street. The former was close to the great music halls, such as the Empire and the Alhambra, the latter conveniently situated near newspaper offices, not far from the Strand theatres. It was romantically antiquated. A 'homely house, with its sanded floor and old-fashioned

LADYSMITH DINNER AT THE HOTEL CECIL, 1906

SHERLOCK HOLMES

arrangements and appointments',[37] the pub is celebrated by Adair
Fitzgerald in one of his Ballads of a Bohemian:

> Bohemia is my nation –
>   My nature's that way, too!
> And so for recordation,
> I'll take a glass with you!
> What though the years are speeding!
> We'll take a fresher lease,
> While fellowship is breeding,
> With the 'Cheshire Cheese.' [38]

It was here in the 1890s that the Rhymers' Club poets, who included
Yeats, and very occasionally Wilde, met to read their work. If the
'Cheese' was for poets, whatever their quality, the Gaiety Bar, attached
to the theatre at the far end of the Strand, was the hang-out for actors,
especially in the afternoons, and particularly for 'those who happened
to be out of an engagement and to retain an expensive thirst'.[39] The
Gaiety was, according to one frequenter 'the most patronised of
all cosy drinking and chatting divans, where so many clever people
foregathered'.[40] Time of day could convert a respectable meeting
place into something rather more louche. Major restaurants in or near
Piccadilly ('a perpetual eddy of many waters')[41] that could take on a
different atmosphere late at night, when the actors were free, were the
Criterion – in the bar of which Watson first hears of Holmes (*A Study
in Scarlet*) – the Trocadero, the Café Royal, Gatti's, Frascati's and the

St James Restaurant. Theatricals also favoured Stone's Chop House in Panton Street. Holmes and Watson, we know, go to Simpson's-in-the-Strand ('The Dying Detective') and send out to Verrey's in Regent Street. Holmes's idea of a rare night out is an opera by Meyerbeer and a meal at Marcini's, which is quite possibly fictional (*The Hound of the Baskervilles*).[42] This reflects a degree of prosperity and many of their fellow nightbirds must have fared less well. Yet, although the aspirant author in George Eyre-Todd's *Bohemian Papers* (1898) is desperately broke, he manages to make the best of things: 'There was a shop near the head of Whitehall where it was possible to get a large cup of cocoa and a sandwich-roll for the modest sum of sixpence and there for a time, still within the pale of respectability, we made this slight refection stand for dinner.'[43]

BARNARD BURLESQUING IRVING.

Acting

IN THEIR DAILY LIFE, Bohemians liked to play with identity, much as actors do professionally. An assumed identity lends the freedom to move around, to experiment. It's a talent, too, that criminals share with those who would hunt them down. Balzac's Vautrin is obviously a major prototype here. In *The Hound of the Baskervilles* a criminal actually pretends to be the detective, proving that he has 'a foil as sharp' as Holmes's own.

Holmes's many disguises range from 'an aged man, clad in seafaring garb … His back was bowed, his knees were shaky, and his breathing was painfully asthmatic' (*The Sign of Four*) to 'a rakish young workman with a goatee beard and a swagger' ('Charles Augustus Milverton'). Old men predominate, however, and it's significant that the one actor with whom Holmes is specifically compared is John Hare ('A Scandal in Bohemia') who was famous for more venerable parts. Holmes is professional. He knows how to apply and remove make-up, as when he reveals the true identity of the ex-actor who poses as a beggar in 'The Man with the Twisted Lip', and how to make himself look desperately ill with vaseline and rouge ('The Dying Detective'). Irene Adler remarks on this

LONDON MUSIC HALLS – WEST END (PROBABLY THE EMPIRE), C.1895, DUDLEY HARDY

LONDON MUSIC HALLS—WEST END.

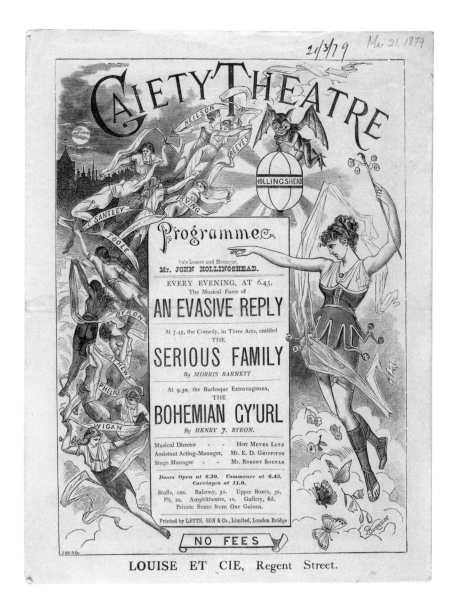

when she identifies Holmes as a fellow performer, although, as a skilled actress, she is able to surprise him herself ('A Scandal in Bohemia').

Acting is quintessentially 'Bohemian' in that the actor escapes, at least for the duration of the performance, the social constraints that normally determine personality. The question hanging over the role-play is always: What does it feel like to be that other person? This was a particularly widespread preoccupation in the late nineteenth century and actors were subject to intense questioning, as in William Archer's 1888 book *Masks or Faces*. Holmes is a master of disguise but never takes on the feelings of those he impersonates. Does he even have any feelings of his own to lose? 'The best way of successfully acting a part is to be it,' says Holmes – without, we should note, any mention of

the emotion involved ('The Dying Detective'). He's even capable of mimicking complete nervous collapse, as in 'The Reigate Puzzle', while remaining intellectually alert.

By the early twentieth century, the 'old Bohemian character of the professions' was said to be 'almost a thing of the past. The popular actor is no longer content to dine and sup at a chop-house in or near Covent Garden, but wears dress clothes in an ultra-fashionable West End restaurant.'[44] In his memoirs, published in 1921, Herbert Beerbohm Tree's long-time manager, Major Fitzroy Gardner, also notes a change in the social habits of actors:

I can remember when, with isolated exceptions, the profession lived in a little world of their own, and aspired to nothing more. Then came the so-called 'Society Actor' and others who, if not of 'Society' proper, emanated from a source which knew nothing of Bohemia – sometimes from the Army, universities and public schools; and they were followed, but not so frequently, by actresses of the same genre.[45]

Although some members of the profession were to claim a hard-won respectability, old habits died hard – as in the instance of Henry Irving – and, in any case, pillars of society were often happy to bend down and mingle with the former reprobates.

The lineal descendant of the rumbustious theatre of the early nineteenth century – and very much on the rise around the turn of the century – was the music hall, but it's very rarely (perhaps significantly for that reason) mentioned in the Holmes stories. Reporting on the scene at the Royal Command Performance in 1912, which featured nearly all the big stars, Conan Doyle described George V approvingly as a 'lover of true Bohemianism'. His remark not only recognises the origins of an extraordinarily popular entertainment, but exemplifies the claim that Bohemian styles could cross class boundaries without actually dislodging them.[46] It is also, perhaps, a sign of the clear gap, at least in this instance, between an author and his most famous creation.

SHERLOCK HOLMES

Lounging, loafing, loitering – and idling

All the afternoon he sat in the stalls wrapped in the most perfect happiness, gently waving his long thin fingers in time to the music, while his gently smiling face and his languid, dreamy eyes were as unlike Holmes the sleuth-hound, Holmes the relentless, keen-witted, ready-handed criminal agent, as it was possible to conceive . . . ('The Red-Headed League').

 HEN HOLMES LISTENS TO MUSIC he is taken to another world. The use of body language to indicate mental state is typical of Conan Doyle's character creation and Holmes frequently moves between 'extreme languor' (as here) to 'devouring energy' ('The Red-Headed League'). At home he is accustomed to 'lounging'. A typical pose might be 'lounging about his sitting-room in his dressing-gown, reading the agony column of *The Times*, and smoking his before-breakfast pipe . . .' ('The Engineer's Thumb').

On the other hand, it is impossible to imagine Holmes behaving like the lounging and lecherous speaker in a poem from Adair Fitzgerald's Ballads of a Bohemian who's in pursuit of a dancing girl:

> And so I lounge in Leicester Square,
>   Applauding my dear Sally
> Who nods and winks quite debonnaire,
>   The pride of all the ballet.[47]

London may be as Watson describes it, 'that great cesspool into which all the loungers and idlers of the Empire are irresistibly drained' but when Holmes 'lounges' he communes only with himself – and with his pipe – although far from being a mere 'armchair lounger' (*A Study in Scarlet*).

While Bohemians may often 'lounge' or show signs of 'languor', they rarely 'loiter', nor do they regularly 'loaf'. Loitering is suspicious in itself – 'I "was looking out for loiterers in the street . . ."' (*The Hound of the Baskervilles*). Holmes and Watson are themselves turned away on the grounds that 'we don't want any loiterers about here' ('Silver Blaze'). In order to appear as a 'common loafer' Holmes has to disguise himself very carefully – 'with his collar turned up, his shiny seedy coat, his red cravat, and his worn boots, he was a perfect sample of the class' ('The Beryl Coronet').

'I FOUND SHERLOCK HALF ASLEEP', 'A CASE OF IDENTITY', SEPTEMBER 1891, THE *STRAND* MAGAZINE, SIDNEY PAGET

"I FOUND SHERLOCK HOLMES HALF ASLEEP.

"I FELL INTO A BROWN STUDY."

'I FELL INTO A BROWN STUDY', 'THE CARDBOARD BOX', JANUARY 1893, THE *STRAND* MAGAZINE, SIDNEY PAGET

When he describes himself as having 'the makings of a very fine loafer', he intends the term ironically and juxtaposes it with being a 'pretty spry sort of figure' (*The Sign of Four*).

These distinctions are to do with creativity and purpose. For the true Bohemian, time is never wasted. Although a moment may be fallow in terms of action, it may well constitute an investment in thought. In this respect, Holmes is a pre-eminent example of the advantages of the Bohemian attitude to time. By contrast, the working-class loafer merely has time on his hands. The word was indelibly associated with disreputable gypsies and the suspiciously unemployed. Loafers were an urban spectacle. In one of his Fleet Street Eclogues the poet John Davidson writes of a 'loafer-burnished wall'.[48] A 'small knot of loafers' can be expected to hang around any crime scene, as for example in 'The Lauriston Gardens Mystery', (part I chapter 3, *A Study in Scarlet*).

'Idling' deliberately straddled both modes of behaviour – 'lounging' and 'loafing'. In the 1890s the humourist Jerome K. Jerome edited a literary magazine entitled *The Idler* in which Conan Doyle's *The Stark Munro Letters* appeared. Prominent figures, such as Henry Irving and Conan Doyle himself, were interviewed in *The Idler* in a suitably relaxed manner. The idea was to represent reading as a provocatively leisured pursuit – hardly a new notion, although the title made it up-to-date and invited the reader to join in a class fantasy. In 1892 Conan Doyle actually joined a real-life Idlers Club, situated in Arundel Street off the Strand, and the name does sound like an anticipation of P.G. Wodehouse's fictional Drones Club.[49] As Holmes remarks, in more or less Wildean mode, 'I never remember feeling tired by work, though idleness exhausts me completely (*The Sign of Four*, chapter 8, 'The Baker Street Irregulars'). Boredom is the price the Bohemian, the dandyish intellectual, pays for his freedom from an ordered working life and, paradoxically, it's a mark of superiority.

This was another comparatively modern idea. 'Boredom' writes Peter Toohey in his history of the subject, 'can sometimes make a person stand apart from other people, from the world and, odd as it is to say, even stand apart from themselves. Boredom intensifies self-perception.'[50] Feeling bored is akin, perhaps, to the pleasurable sense of being marked out from the rest that often accompanies the material deprivation of the Bohemian. Some critics make a distinction between mere boredom and Baudelairean ennui, claiming that while boredom is 'a response to the immediate', ennui is 'a judgment of the universe'.[51] There are times, though, when Sherlock Holmes, like his contemporaries the English decadent poets, seems to be experiencing both simultaneously: 'Crime is commonplace, existence is commonplace, and no qualities save those which are commonplace have any function on earth' (*The Sign of Four*).

Holmes is indeed bored with the 'commonplace' – a favourite word of impatience – if only because, paradoxically, most people can't see how remarkable and 'bizarre' – another favourite word ('The Red-Headed League', 'The Blue Carbuncle') – the quotidian can actually be. What's good enough for everybody else – what they have 'in common' – simply isn't good enough for Holmes. It's as a direct consequence of his propensity for a brand of superior boredom that Holmes needs frequent stimulus. Sometimes this takes the form of an intellectual problem or 'case', but when these are in short supply, he resorts to artificial means, like Baudelaire, the supreme French Bohemian, reaching for the cocaine bottle (*The Sign of Four*, chapter 12 'The Strange Story of Jonathan Small').[52]

'Sherlaw Kombs' in 'Detective Stories Gone Wrong', 1892, *The Idler* Magazine, Luke Sharp

Sherlock Holmes—Act II

Holmes and his "hypodermic" with Dr. Watson—Act II

SHERLOCK HOLMES, PLAYED BY WILLIAM GILLETTE, AND HIS 'HYPODERMIC' WITH DR WATSON, 1900

WILLIAM GILLETTE

aſ

SHERLOCK

HOLMES

NEW YORK
R.H.RUSSELL
PUBLISHER

Moving on

VEN IN BOHEMIA success counts and failure hurts:

> Bohemia's the land to which I refer,
> The College of Genius and Art,
> Where so many brave men rise and fall by the pen
> In Literature's grim thankless Mart;
> But with all its sad care 'tis the world's greatest fair,
> Where we learn with Life's battles to cope,
> The Sweet Land that teems with Elysian dreams,
> The Nursery of Fame's Golden Hope.[53]

Arthur Ransome tells of a visit to a would-be novelist who lived in dingy rooms with wife and baby:

> We drank out of a couple of glasses my great man brought from a box in the corner. Then he talked of literature, and so well that the untidy bed, the unclean room, the wife and baby were as if they had never been. In spite of his unwashen hands, in spite of the dressing gown he won his way back into greatness. He lifted the tumbler magnificently to watch the ruby of the wine, while he talked of Edgar Allan Poe, and of his methods … From Poe we came to detective and mystery tales, Gaboriau, Sherlock Holmes, and the analytical attitude, and so to the relations between criticism and art.[54]

According to Ransome, this particular novelist eventually achieved some success and gave up his extreme Bohemian lifestyle. In his case, sacrifice and devotion obviously paid off, although we might speculate that perhaps, now and then, he might have returned to old haunts. After all, as Ransome also says, 'of all bondages vagabondage is the one from which it is most difficult to escape'.[55] In the end, though, most Bohemians, real or fictional, did change their ways by settling down to retirement, as Holmes does, or by simply disappearing for a while, as Holmes also does.

In romantic novels of the period, with their predominantly female protagonists, Bohemia may be a temptation, a trap or simply a rite of passage, but it's invariably temporary. Capri, heroine of J. Fitzgerald Molloy's *It Is No Wonder. A Story of Bohemian Life*, is an artists' model (a forerunner of du Maurier's *Trilby*) who, starting off poor and carefree, knows that she must soon leave her life behind. 'I often wish,' she tells her painter boyfriend, Marc, 'I was not such a Bohemian as I am. It is all very well and pleasant when you are young, but here in London one must grow respectable and rich when one leaves one's teens, especially

'AFTER THE SUPPER', 1884, WITH FROM LEFT TO RIGHT HENRY IRVING, J L TOOLE AND SQUIRE BANCROFT, PHOTOGRAPH OF A DRAWING BY PHIL MAY

Left: WILLIAM GILLETTE AS SHERLOCK HOLMES, J OTTMANN LITHOGRAPHY COMPANY, R H RUSSELL PUBLISHER, 1900

women.'[56] Berenice, the ingénue heroine of Fanny Aikin-Kortright's *A Bohemian's Love Story*, spends time with the man she thinks of as her uncle, a struggling author resigned to failure. 'I was full of great aspirations two years ago, when I came up to London,' he tells her, 'but now all that is over.' He would prefer 'a comfortable arm-chair, in a cosy study, with a good Havana between my teeth, sending forth a column of graceful smoke, while I dream or read another man's thoughts, grave or gay, without the trouble of concocting ideas myself.'[57] Aikin-Kortright was a devout Christian and girls' school teacher who held to the doctrine of 'separate spheres'; her heroine will learn some of life's lessons from her observation of male malaise. In a later addition to this sub-genre, Florence Warden's *The Bohemian Girls* (1899), we are told early on that the heroines 'were not Bohemians by birth – not one of them. A handsome house in the outer suburbs of London, and a charming flat in Paris; these were the surroundings of Dinah and Mildred Wilde as they grew up from childhood to bright young womanhood.'[58] When the Wilde family suffers financial collapse, the girls get work in the theatre, are obliged to live in digs and are pursued by men, but eventually settle down into marriage.

Although Bohemia survived in new modernist forms, most accounts of late-Victorian Bohemia are written after the event and are invariably infused with nostalgia. Following the First World War, it became clear how much the world was changing; London had come to look very different. Composing his memoirs in 1919, Harry Furniss paid ambiguous tribute to what had been lost in the preceding years:

> All these odiferous rookeries have been razed to the ground, and upon their site have arisen stately and imposing edifices in which are to be found the offices of the Marconi Company, colonial agencies, banks, etc., together with palatial newspaper and other offices. In such an environment it is impossible that Bohemianism could ever exist. It would be gross anachronism, as a matter of fact the death of Bohemianism is really due more to the genius of the architect than to any vagaries of fashion or fortune.[59]

Similarly, writing in 1917, journalist and playwright George R. Sims saw an altogether different scene around him from the one he remembered. In his *Sixty Years' Recollections of Bohemian London* he wanders the streets alone:

> I find myself at night in the Strand and Leicester Square and Shaftesbury Avenue, where Theatreland has spread from its old boundaries, and I see in front of the Temples of Thespis only a ghostly blue light that suggests the entrance to a police station.

There were no blazing electric lights in Theatreland fifty years ago but the gas flared gaily . . .[60]

'LONDON BY NIGHT' CHARING CROSS STATION, c.1910

We may be inclined to dismiss that invocation of nineteenth-century gaslight as a lingering London cliché, by this time an over-determined metaphor for the transformative workings of memory itself. Inevitably perhaps, we're going to be aware of the extent to which its special effects contributed to the environmental atmosphere of the Holmes stories, working like a theatrical technique, like an encircling spot or a gauze curtain, to conceal outlines and add mystery, transforming mere men into urban myths. Some say that Bohemia must always be viewed in this way, as a prospect or in retrospect, as a kind of cultural illusion.[61] Yet testimonies such as these have more than just poetic authenticity. When the lamps finally went out, the experiences of a whole generation of Bohemians went with them.

Sherlock Holmes

Sherlock Holmes's Central London in Photographs and Postcards

PORTLAND PLACE, 1906, ALVIN LANGDON COBURN

These photographs and postcards capture the detail and complexity of central London, not far from Sherlock Holmes's consulting rooms at 221B Baker Street. There are two contrasting images of London. In Coburn's photograph, a solitary Hansom cab occupies the centre of the muddy road with fog hanging in the air while in the view of Regent Circus, the pavements are shown filled with pedestrians and the thoroughfare with Hansom cabs, omnibuses and carts. Crossing the road must have been a hazardous occupation. The river is revealed as no less crowded, thronged with tugs, steamships, barges and lighters. Large hotels, a new element of the city, feature prominently in the Sherlock Holmes stories as do the mainline railway stations.

Left: REGENT CIRCUS, OXFORD STREET, c.1890

Sherlock Holmes

Trafalgar Square (detail), c.1880, Francis Frith

'Have your fare ready, and the instant that your cab stops, dash through the Arcade, timing yourself to reach the other side at a quarter-past nine. You will find a small brougham waiting close to the curb, driven by a fellow with a heavy black cloak tipped at the collar with red. Into this you will step, and you will reach Victoria in time for the Continental express.'   *The Final Problem*

Left: High Holborn, near Chancery Lane, 1902

Mainline station postcards, c.1908
by H Fleury, Mische & co.
Top: Victoria, The Dover Boat Train
Middle: Charing Cross, The Paris Boat Train and
Bottom: Waterloo, The Southampton Boat Train

Right: Victoria Station, c.1905, Christina Broom

SHERLOCK HOLMES

VICTORIA STATION.

THE UPPER POOL OF LONDON, c.1890

Right: LONDON BRIDGE, c.1890

'At that moment, however, as our evil fate would have it, a tug with three barges in tow blundered in between us. It was only by putting our helm hard down that we avoided a collision, and before we could round them and recover our way the Aurora had gained a good two hundred yards. She was still, however, well in view, and the murky uncertain twilight was setting into a clear starlit night. Our boilers were strained to their utmost, and the frail shell vibrated and creaked with the fierce energy which was driving us along. We had shot through the Pool, past the West India Docks, down the long Deptford Reach, and up again after rounding the Isle of Dogs.'   *The Sign of Four*

'He telegraphed to me from London that he had arrived all safe, and directed me to come down at once, giving the Langham Hotel as his address. His message, as I remember, was full of kindness and love. On reaching London I drove to the Langham, and was informed that Captain Morstan was staying there, but that he had gone out the night before and had not yet returned. I waited all day without news of him.'

The Sign of Four

HÔTEL RUSSELL, LONDON.

HOTEL CECIL, LONDON.
FROM RIVER THAMES.

HYDE PARK HOTEL,
LONDON
from the Serpentine

Langham Hotel, c.1890,
George Washington Wilson

Hotel Postcards:
Top: Hotel Russell, c.1912
Middle: Hotel Cecil, c.1908
Bottom: Hyde Park Hotel from
the Serpentine, c.1908

CHAPTER TWO

Sherlock Holmes, Sidney Paget and the *Strand* Magazine

ALEX WERNER

To Sherlock Holmes she is always the woman. I have seldom
heard him mention her under any other name. In his eyes she
eclipses and predominates the whole of her sex. It was not that
he felt any emotion akin to love for Irene Adler. All emotions,
and that one particularly, were abhorrent to his cold, precise
but admirably balanced mind. He was, I take it, the most perfect
reasoning and observing machine that the world has seen, but as
a lover he would have placed himself in a false position. He never
spoke of the softer passions, save with a gibe and a sneer.

'A Scandal in Bohemia'

THE BRITISH AND AMERICAN PUBLIC really woke up
to the captivating and unusual character of Sherlock
Holmes during the second half of 1891. 'A Scandal
in Bohemia', published in the July issue of the *Strand*
Magazine, was followed month after month by fresh
instalments of his adventures. Conan Doyle's two short novels featuring
Holmes, the first *A Study in Scarlet*, which appeared in *Beeton's Christmas
Annual* of 1887, and the second, *The Sign of Four* in *Lippincott's
Magazine* in February 1890, had met with some limited appreciation
on publication but had failed to make a major impact.[1] Nevertheless,
they were very important for what was to follow, because Conan Doyle
had worked out all the basic ingredients of Sherlock Holmes's world.
In particular, the detective's remarkable mental and observational
powers had been set out, as well as a number of his other unusual,
distinctive traits and habits. Conan Doyle created an authorial frame to
the stories by employing Dr Watson as a personable and fairly ordinary
narrator through whom readers viewed Sherlock Holmes's actions
and amazing deductions. The geographical locality of the detective's
consulting rooms at 221B Baker Street was fully formed and set against

Left: YORK PLACE,
BAKER STREET, LOOKING
NORTH, C.1900

Arthur Conan Doyle, c.1890

the backdrop of the late nineteenth-century Imperial capital. However, Sherlock Holmes's character did develop between the first and second story.[2]

At the beginning of *A Study in Scarlet*, Conan Doyle makes his detective aloof and at times little more than a cold 'calculating machine'. Dr Watson notes that Holmes had no knowledge of literature or philosophy. It is his scientific expertise that is stressed above all, particularly in chemistry. The first time the world meets Sherlock Holmes, he is engrossed in a laboratory at St Bartholomew's Hospital, trying to establish a test to identify bloodstains. The second story undoubtedly shifts and extends Holmes's character in a number of directions, making him seem more human, something that emerges especially in his Bohemian attributes. The graphic description of him injecting himself with a seven per cent solution of cocaine, at the start of the story, reveals a scientific precision in his formulation of the exact strength of the drug. However, there is also a worrying recklessness in his attempt to escape from the boredom of life through such stimulation. Watson is also 'irritated' by his egotism and sees 'a small vanity that underlay' his 'quiet and didactic manner'. Slightly later on, Holmes fails to recognise that uncovering 'unhappy' traits about Watson's departed brother just from a close examination of his watch would upset his friend in such a dramatic way. Quickly, he makes good in a measured and heartfelt apology, claiming that he had 'forgotten how personal and painful a thing' the memory might have been. And in turn, Watson also regrets his outburst when he discovers that Holmes's reasoning had been made just from examining the watch rather than prying into his brother's affairs.

With his knowledge of literature and philosophy set at 'nil' by Watson in *A Study in Scarlet*, shown particularly in his claim not to have even heard of Thomas Carlyle, in *The Sign of Four*, surprisingly, Holmes refers to the writer Jean-Paul Richter, as well as implying that he had read but thought little of the work of Carlyle. His development as a man of action is much more pronounced in the second tale as he climbs up on to the roof of Pondicherry Lodge at Norwood and 'like an enormous glow-worm' crawls along its ridge. Later, he criss-crosses south London on foot with Dr Watson and the mongrel Toby, tracking the scent of creosote found at the murder scene, before finally, in the dramatic river chase, while urging the captain of the police steam launch to go faster and faster, ducking 'one of the murderous darts' delivered by Tonga, the 'little Andaman Islander'.

The *Strand* Magazine

A number of monthly magazines were coming out at that time, notable among which was 'The Strand', then as now under the editorship of Greenhough Smith. Considering these various with their disconnected stories it had struck me that a single character running through a series, if it only engaged the attention of the reader, would bind that reader to that particular magazine. On the other hand, it had long seemed to me that ordinary serial might be an impediment rather than a help to a magazine, since, sooner or later, one missed one number and afterwards it had lost all interest.
Memories and Adventures, Sir Arthur Conan Doyle, 1924

HE SHERLOCK HOLMES STORIES that Conan Doyle submitted to the *Strand* Magazine, via his new literary agent, A.P. Watt, were something quite new and unusual. He proposed to write a series of 'adventures', as he called them. 'The ideal compromise was a character which carried through, and yet instalments which were each complete in themselves, so that the purchaser was always sure that he could relish the whole contents of the magazine.'[3] This serial approach allowed readers to develop a familiarity with the main characters and the locale in which they lived and operated. Conan Doyle claimed that he was 'the first to realise this'. His skill as a storyteller seemed to fit this format perfectly, allowing him to create short and beautifully formed stories around particular challenges of detection. Readers warmed to the way that Sherlock Holmes showed off his extraordinary feats of reasoning as the run of the stories unfolded. He did not rely on chance happenings but on his own special observational skills. The public delighted in the way that each story came to a satisfying conclusion as Holmes solved the case, usually with an unexpected twist at the end. Furthermore, they found that the self-contained stories could be read in any order.

If the *Strand* Magazine had floundered at its outset in the first few months of 1891, which was unlikely given its strong financial backing, then it is possible that Conan Doyle might never have written any more Sherlock Holmes stories.[4] The format and style of the magazine was new to Britain. George Newnes, a successful publisher, had made his fortune from *Tit-Bits*, a weekly penny magazine that he launched in 1881. He had a knack of sensing what would engage and attract the general public. *Tit-Bits* was targeted at the urban lower-middle classes, who delighted in its miscellany of small snippets of information and instruction, backed by jokes and humorous comment. Readers were encouraged to send in short pieces of their own for inclusion and

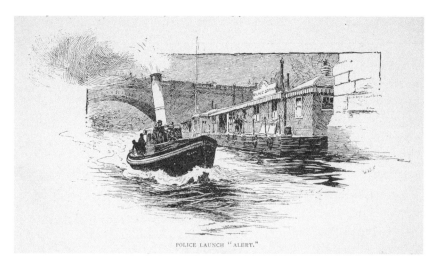

POLICE LAUNCH 'ALERT',
FEBRUARY 1891, THE *STRAND*
MAGAZINE

their attention was captured by a constant stream of competitions and promotions. One of its most famous marketing ploys was the '*Tit-Bits* insurance scheme': The magazine offered to pay £100 to the heirs of a reader killed in a railway accident while carrying the magazine.[5]

Ten years later, Newnes decided to add a new title to his publishing business and move up-market by producing a monthly title aimed at a broadly middle class, urban readership. He was inspired by American magazines that carried popular stories and factual pieces illustrated with engravings and photographs. 'A night with the Thames Police', which appeared in the second issue of the *Strand* Magazine, was the first of a number of essays about contemporary London written in a light journalistic style that mixed reportage with general history, and it focused on an aspect of the metropolitan city that relates to the world of the Sherlock Holmes stories. A news feature with an almost identical approach that appeared in *Harper's New Monthly Magazine* of March 1887 examined crime fighting by the New York police. The illustration of the police launch 'Alert' in the *Strand* is reminiscent of the vessel used in the chase down the Thames in *The Sign of Four*. *Harper's New Monthly Magazine*'s illustrations, however, present much more dramatic scenes, such as the arrest of a thief at the Grand Central Depot, and river and harbour police brandishing pistols as they tackle criminals from a small rowing boat.

RIVER AND HARBOUR POLICE,
MARCH 1887, *HARPER'S NEW*
MONTHLY MAGAZINE

Two further pieces in the early issues of the *Strand* focused on the East End of London – 'A Day with an East End Photographer' and 'A Night in an Opium Den'. The first essay is unattributed but the second one is credited as having been written by the author of 'A Dead Man's Diary'. This is Coulson Kernahan, who had caused a great stir in 1890 with an account of his own near-death experience and visions. A similar type of account in the *Strand* described the effects of opium on the human mind and body. This opium-den setting followed a tradition established in fiction by Charles Dickens, as well as in factual essays by authors such as James Greenwood, who had described actual opium-smoking scenes in the East End. The illustrations by J.L. Wimbush in the *Strand* evoke the dark and seedy backstreet entrance with 'its villainous staircase' off Ratcliff Highway. This is followed by an interior view of the den itself with two Chinese men lying on a bed. One has succumbed to the drug, still clutching the pipe, while the other is still puffing away with, probably the proprietor, Mr Chang, on the left, blowing out a candle. The opium den features in the Sherlock Holmes adventure, 'The Man with the Twisted Lip'. This essay and Conan Doyle's story were probably the two most sensational pieces to be published in the first year of the magazine's production, at some remove from the respectability of a purely family title reflected in stories for children, such as George Sand's 'Fairy Dust' and Daniel Dare's 'The Blue Cat'.

IN THE DEN, JUNE 1891, THE *STRAND* MAGAZINE, J.L. WIMBUSH

From the start, the *Strand* featured a considerable number of translated works by famous foreign authors. French writers made up the largest compliment, including Alphonse Daudet, Prosper Merimée, Alfred de Musset, Honoré de Balzac and Guy de Maupassant, but there were also stories from Russians, Hungarians, Germans and Spaniards. This international flavour was supplemented by fictional pieces with North American or Australian settings. Only a small amount of the fictional content had a specifically British locale or context. One of these, Conan Doyle's 'The Voice of Science', was published in the March 1891 issue and was his first contribution to the magazine.

Set in the fictional city of 'Birchespool' (probably Liverpool), a modern technological device – a phonograph – plays a crucial role in the storyline. This is not dissimilar to the gramophone that is used in 'The Mazarin Stone', set in around 1903, to trick the criminals, Count Negretto Silvius and Sam Merton, into thinking that Sherlock Holmes is playing the violin in the adjoining bedroom. The *Strand* published regular features on discoveries and inventions, engaging readers' burgeoning scientific interest in the modern world, and the Sherlock Holmes stories supported this especially well with forensic evidence gathering and the employment of the electric telegraph to send messages and gather data quickly.

The overall content and balance of the *Strand*'s literary matter was under the control of Herbert Greenhough Smith, who had come up with the original idea of translated short stories by foreign authors. The number and range of works in translation presented in a literary magazine was unusual at this period and perhaps carried an element of risk since it could have alienated readers. However, it was offset by other lighter sections, such as 'Portraits of Celebrities at Different Times of Their Lives'. These were probably sanctioned by Newnes, the overall editor and owner, with engravings, usually copied from photographs, filling the pages of the magazine. Members of the royal family and leading aristocrats appeared alongside politicians, artists, actors and explorers. Another feature, 'Types of English Beauty', focused largely on young, attractive, society women, actresses and opera singers. In the same month as the publication of 'A Scandal in Bohemia', a new section of 'Illustrated Interviews' was launched, in which famous people were interviewed in their own domestic surroundings by a young and chatty journalist, Harry How. Celebrity interviews had been pioneered by Edmund Yates in the 1870s, but within the context of the rest of the *Strand*'s content and through the use of specially commissioned photographs by Elliot & Fry, the pieces must have felt very novel and made for compulsive reading, revealing for the first time the daily lives of famous people. Conan Doyle himself was interviewed in 1892. The magazine, with no Sherlock Holmes stories ready for publication, filled the gap with a feature that aimed to satisfy the public's curiosity and clamour for more information about the creator of the extraordinary fictional detective. How's interview, 'A Day with Conan Doyle', did not form part of the main interview series, probably because Conan Doyle's fame was seen as 'of the moment' in contrast to others who had a much more established profile, such as Henry Irving, ' the leading actor in the land', and Sir Frederick Leighton, the 'President of the Royal Academy'. Appropriately, the piece begins by stating that Conan Doyle had given the world 'detectivism up to date'.[6]

The detective story was all the rage by the 1880s. Conan Doyle was clearly influenced by Edgar Allan Poe's fictional amateur detective C. Auguste Dupin and Emile Gaboriau's Monsieur Lecoq. Both feature in a number of stories and have a special ability to solve crimes and mysteries. The British public's interest in such a genre was spurred by newspaper reports of real detectives at work investigating crimes, hunting down criminals and bringing them to justice. The fact that detectives wore plain clothes and went 'undercover' was especially exciting. Gentlemen of the popular press were avid reporters of real crimes, especially murders. Authors and publishers quickly realised that there was a market for fictional works that focused on criminal detection.

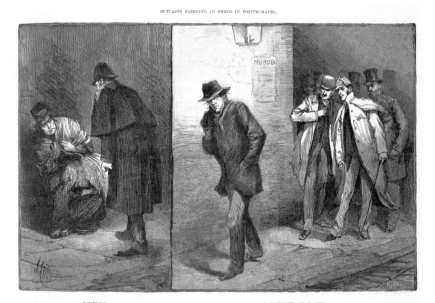

MURDER

HOMELESS.   A SUSPICIOUS CHARACTER.

WITH THE VIGILANCE COMMITTEE IN THE EAST-END.

'WITH THE VIGILANCE
COMMITTEE IN THE EAST-
END', AT THE TIME OF THE
JACK THE RIPPER MURDERS,
ILLUSTRATED LONDON NEWS,
13 OCTOBER 1888

The Jack the Ripper murders of 1888 threw a spotlight on the police force and particularly the detectives who appeared incapable of apprehending the killer.

Conan Doyle was just one of many authors who grasped the opportunity to write popular detective stories. Fergus Hume's *The Mystery of a Hansom Cab* was a bestseller in the late 1880s. Set in Melbourne, it begins with 'an extraordinary murder' in the back of a cab by 'an unknown assassin' and Mr Gorby from the city's detective office leading the investigation. However, in many fictional stories of the period, private or amateur detectives solve crimes with greater success than the professional police force. One author, G.R. Sims (1847–1922), known especially for his reporting and fictional depiction of the low life of the metropolis, wrote a number of detective stories that were published in newspapers in the late 1880s.[7] In one of them, entitled 'The Bloomsbury Murder', a solicitor sets out to prove the innocence of his friend, who is implicated in the murder of his own wife. Another story, 'A Private Inquiry', features John Ellerton, 'late Inspector of the Criminal Investigation Department of Scotland Yard', who leaves the police service through frustration at the limited monetary allowances given to officers in the pursuit of criminals. He sets up as a 'Private Enquiry and Detective Agency' in 'a couple of rooms on the second floor of a little house in a side street running off the Strand'. Sims' collection of stories was published under the title of *Tales of To-Day*. The Sherlock Holmes stories published between 1891 and 1893 usually look back to a few years earlier although they are intrinsically contemporary in character. Their setting is the modern city with Sherlock Holmes and Dr Watson waiting in the consulting rooms at 221B Baker Street for the next client to arrive. From their first-floor windows, they look down on a typical metropolitan thoroughfare, a familiar setting to many late nineteenth-century urban dwellers. Readers wrote in, addressing their letters to Sherlock Holmes, thinking that he was a real-life detective, which implies that the realism of the stories had a very powerful impact.

Newnes' concept for the magazine was to have an illustration on as many pages as possible. The magazine's art editor, W.H. Boot, played an influential role in selecting and commissioning many of the best graphic artists of the day. Their names were acknowledged on the index page at the start of each month's issue. Although not unknown – some magazines, such as *London Society*, had championed their illustrators in the 1860s – this approach signals the particular character of the *Strand* from its inception as 'an illustrated magazine' that uses 'eminent artists'.[8] The cover design of the magazine, printed in a distinctive blue colour, is noteworthy also. The artist George Charles Haité (1855–1924) depicts a view of the Strand, one of London's busiest central thoroughfares, looking east from the corner of Burleigh Street where the publisher's offices were located. In the foreground, pedestrians, including a policeman, throng the pavement under overhanging shop awnings. A *Tit-Bits* magazine-boy stands on the corner of Burleigh Street. For the published cover, in the middle distance, another newspaper boy

A London Street by Night, 1893, Joseph Pennell

is seen hurtling across the street. A hansom cab, coming towards the viewer (on the wrong side of the road for London), slants slightly to the left, along with the horse, contributing to the feeling of movement and bustle. It had probably cut across from the right-hand side and was about to deposit or pick up a passenger. A large globe gaslight hangs over the corner of No. 359 the Strand with a smaller pear-shaped lantern beyond. The distant skyline is punctuated by two church towers, St Mary le Strand and St Clement Danes with, in the far distance, the clock tower of the Royal Courts of Justice, which had been completed in 1882. The letters of the title of the magazine are centred above. For the final printed cover, the letters of the title have been hung on what appear to be electric wires, suggesting that they could be lit up at night. This is no doubt a reference to the way that Newnes had erected a giant illuminated sign for Tit-Bits on the roof of his publishing house. In the first essay in the magazine, appropriately on the history of the Strand itself, illustrated by Haité, an engraving shows the street with the prominent Tit-Bits sign.

Conan Doyle uses the Strand as a location in a number of the Sherlock Holmes stories, most prominently in a famous passage in 'The Resident Patient', when Sherlock Holmes and Dr Watson take an evening walk through the central part of the city:

> For three hours we strolled about together, watching the ever-changing kaleidoscope of life as it ebbs and flows through Fleet Street and the Strand. His characteristic talk, with its keen observance of detail and subtle power of inference held me amused and enthralled. It was ten o'clock before we reached Baker Street again.

Here, the attributes of the modern city are set out and provide the backdrop of Sherlock Holmes's world. The phrases 'ever-changing kaleidoscope' and 'ebbs and flows' work in counterpoint. The movement of the city is seen on the one hand to be tidal in nature as it comes and goes, but it does possess some pattern or structure and repeats itself on a daily basis, while on the other hand the detailed prismatic view has much more complexity as it constantly shifts and varies and its pattern fragments. This passage engages with the way that Holmes's 'keen observation' is able to make sense of city life through detailed observation, while Watson only surveys the scene. Sidney Paget's illustration to this passage has Holmes and Watson walking arm-in-arm, something that Conan Doyle had not specified in the text. Interestingly, in Edgar Allan Poe's 'The Murders in the Rue Morgue', Dupin and his friend go arm-in-arm through the streets of Paris, like Holmes and Watson, 'seeking, amid the wild lights and shadows of the populous city, that infinity of mental excitement which quiet observation can afford'.[9] Paget has Watson all wrapped up against the cold with his gaze fixed straight ahead while Holmes seems more relaxed with the surroundings and turns his head to converse with his friend.

Sidney Paget's Sherlock Holmes

His very person and appearance was such to strike the attention
of the most casual observer. In height, he was rather over six feet,
and so excessively lean that he seemed to be considerably taller.
His eyes were sharp and piercing, save during those intervals of
torpor to which I have alluded; and his thin, hawk-like nose gave
his whole expression an air of alertness and decision. His chin,
too, had the prominence and squareness which marks the man of
determination.

A Study in Scarlet

 KEY ELEMENT IN THE PUBLIC'S APPRECIATION of the
Sherlock Holmes stories was their accompanying
illustrations. Great credit must be given to Sidney
Paget (1860–1908), as through his illustrations the
great detective's appearance became visually memorable
for the first time. Holmes's angular face contrasts with Watson's more
rounded head and distinctive moustache. Each character can therefore
be easily distinguished whether at 221B Baker Street (most commonly)
or out on one of their 'adventures' in London or farther afield. Sidney
Paget had been commissioned by the *Strand* to illustrate a number of
stories and essays in the first six months of 1891, before the Sherlock
Holmes adventures appeared. There was a military focus to his output
as he supplied two drawings for a piece on 'Stories of the Victoria Cross,
told by those who have won it' and another four for Prosper Merimée's
'How the Redoubt was taken'. A mix-up occurred in the Sherlock
Holmes commission. The letter was intended for Walter Paget, Sidney's
brother, who was also a skilled illustrator, but it was addressed just to
'Mr Paget' and opened by Sidney, something that was to prove very
fortuitous. Sidney Paget was born in 1860 and trained as a painter at
Heatherley's Art School and then at Royal Academy Schools from 1881
where he won a number of prizes. He began to work as a graphic artist
at this period and produced illustrations for a number of magazines. His
work for the *Strand* Magazine was to bring him international fame.

Sidney Paget's inaugaral illustration for the first Sherlock Holmes
story sets up the two principal characters. Holmes stands with his back
to the fire, looking at a seated Watson.[10] Paget captures the posture of
Holmes perfectly as the detective warms his back and hands in front
of the fire (the drawing caption is 'Then he stood before the fire') while
turning to observe Dr Watson 'in his singular introspective fashion'.
Paget had only a limited number of specific details to base his realisation
on in this story. How much time he had spent researching the characters,

SIDNEY PAGET, C.1890,
ELLIOTT & FRY

by reading the first two Sherlock Holmes books, is unclear. Perhaps, like Conan Doyle, who had already fully formed the characters and their environment, Paget had absorbed their world and nature to a much greater extent than normally would have been the case for a standard commission to supply illustrations for a story.

Conan Doyle explained later that he had based his detective on Dr Joseph Bell, one of his tutors at Edinburgh University Medical School. Bell's analytical skills and his physical appearance match those of Sherlock Holmes. Early depictions of Holmes by D.H. Friston and Charles Doyle fail to portray anything remarkable or memorable about the detective, except perhaps his oddity. George Hutchinson, a capable and experienced graphic artist, made another attempt in 1891 when he illustrated a new edition of *A Study in Scarlet*. Hutchinson tried to match details that Conan Doyle had set out in his description of the two characters. However, comparing them with Paget's illustrations, his portrayals seem flat and lumbering. When Hutchinson tackled Sherlock Holmes again the following year – in a spoof piece written by Luke Sharp (the pseudonym of Robert Barr) entitled 'Detective Stories gone Wrong. The Adventures of Sherlaw Kombs' published in *The Idler* magazine – his Holmes had been informed by Paget's realisation.[11] There is a naturalness and confidence in Paget's interpretation of the two characters, which captures something of their essence and spirit. Perhaps these portrayals were not what Conan Doyle had intended but readers instantly warmed to them. Sherlock Holmes had become distinctive. Paget retained his 'hawk-like nose' but made him more appealing through his fuller body shape and confident posture. Conan Doyle claimed that the illustrator had based Holmes's appearance on his younger brother, Arthur Paget.[12] Dr Watson, with his moustache, was even more well-groomed than Holmes, perhaps a reflection of 'the fair sex' being 'his department'.

The first illustration also reveals Paget's ability to select an appropriate

SHERLOCK HOLMES

scene to represent and a confidence in striking out on his own with details that Conan Doyle had not specified. The author mentions just a few objects – an armchair, a fire, a case of cigars, a spirit flask and a gasogene (a type of soda siphon). Even with these few items, Paget is selective and ignores everything except the fire and the armchair, but he adds extra details of his own, including a dresser in the background, two elaborate oil lamps alongside a clock and a vase on the mantelpiece, as well as the grate of the fire and fire surround and fire tongs. These tongs make another appearance in 'The Copper Beeches' when Holmes lights his 'long cherry-wood pipe' with a 'glowing cinder' from the fire. Paget uses a number of regular props, especially chairs and sofas, associated with 221B Baker Street. Over the course of the stories, readers learn more about discrete areas of the consulting room but they are rarely joined up, so that the entirety and size of the space remains obscure. Paget's approach is to focus on the poses of the characters and delineate just a few objects that are in close proximity. The background remains sketchy and often non-existent.

"'I'VE FOUND IT! I'VE FOUND IT!' HE SHOUTED.'
9

"'I'VE FOUND IT! I'VE FOUND IT!' HE SHOUTED.' *A STUDY IN SCARLET*, 1892, GEORGE HUTCHINSON

The *Strand* Magazine used a number of different graphic mediums in the 1890s, the majority engravings, in the traditional sense of the word, where the shading and forms are made up of a mass of fine lines and hatchings. Engravers employed by the magazine worked up the drawings supplied by illustrators. Paget was particularly skilled in a freer type of illustrative technique, with washes of tonal greys and blacks. An examination of surviving Paget drawings shows that some of their subtlety is fashioned by using a white wash especially to pick out areas of light and accentuate points of contrast. This can be seen clearly in the famous full page 'The Hound of the Baskervilles' illustration, where the ghostly, frightening nature of the hound has been evocatively realised by the addition of white around the outline of its muzzle and head. In this instance, on the back of the drawing, Paget has added a note for the engraver, requesting that he '[k]eep background of fog as <u>flat</u> as possible' so implying that he wants nothing to detract from the glowing hound in the foreground.

These full-page drawings placed at the start of each issue of the magazine gave the illustrator an opportunity to make a dramatic visual statement. The first Sherlock Holmes story to have one is 'The Final Problem'. This illustration captures the drama of the moment when Moriarty and Holmes fight it out at the Reichenbach Falls. Entitled

'I FOUND HIM PLAYING THE VIOLIN,' 1892, GEORGE HUTCHINSON

'the Death of Sherlock Holmes', it gives readers a clear idea of the ending of the story, something Conan Doyle found problematic since it took away the element of surprise from the story's dramatic conclusion. Sherlock Holmes and Dr Watson appear very clearly defined in another of these full-page illustrations, which introduces 'The Second Stain'. Holmes's dramatic discovery of a secret compartment in the floor while Dr Watson looks on, still wearing his bowler hat, is set against an almost luminous floor. The original illustration shows the skilful way in which Paget has used watercolour washes to create the reflections in the floor as well as picking out, in the background, vases in a display cabinet and a flower bowl on a table.

The manner in which Paget's drawings were treated by the

photographic engraver varied. For all but one of the 104 illustrations in the first twelve stories that make up *The Adventures of Sherlock Holmes*, Paget's fluid, sketch-like brushwork was reproduced directly by using a halftone photomechanical engraving process,[13] which allowed the subtle detail of the drawings to be retained and reproduced accurately. The printed illustrations are made up of very small dots, which can be seen when magnified. These dots were created by using a screen between the lens and photographic plate when making a photographic copy of the drawing. The specialist photographic engravers would have worked further on the plate. Their task was to retain the quality of Paget's original drawing while accentuating details that could be lost or become unclear in the printing process. A number of engraving firms, including Swain, Waterlow & Sons Ltd and Hare, are identified by their initials or names along with Paget's much more prominent 'S P' signature. In the earliest-known surviving drawing, 'All afternoon he sat in the stalls', published in August 1891, which depicts Sherlock Holmes enjoying a concert at St James's Hall, all the different elements of Paget's original drawing have been retained.[14] The engraver, (probably working for Waterlow & Sons Ltd, although there is no identification on the printed illustration in the *Strand*), has increased the highlight of Holmes's hair and accentuated the stripes of his trousers. The drawing has been reduced considerably to fit the page of the magazine, and the intention at the outset must have been for it to sit in the midst of the two-column text layout. This drawing, like many others, successfully captures a moment in the narrative of the story, picking up on Conan Doyle's description and transferring it into visual form. The important phrases that Paget has concentrated on for Sherlock Holmes's face and pose are 'wrapped in the most perfect happiness', 'his gently smiling face' and his 'long thin fingers', which seem as if they are ready to wave 'in time to the music'.

The solitary drawing that conforms to a more standard engraving type with the treatment of lines and hatchings is signed by Paul Naumann, a skilled German-born engraver who had recently settled in London. It is a dramatic illustration of Holmes in disguise as the 'simple-minded Non-conformist clergyman', where he attempts to protect Irene Adler from the fight that he has choreographed as she steps down from her carriage. It is unclear why there was a shift to Naumann as the sole engraver for all the following stories that make up *The Memoirs of Sherlock Holmes*. It is possible that there had been issues about the variable quality of the reproduction of some of the illustrations. A few have a smeared and blotchy appearance, suggesting that the halftone photomechanical engraving process was at fault in some way or that the ink was adhering badly at the printing stage. With

Naumann's engraving process there was less chance of this happening, resulting in a sharper and more detailed image. It is likely that Naumann used some photographic processes in his engraving method. In the best of his work, he succeeds in retaining Paget's fluidity and flow while increasing the clarity of the illustrations on the printed page. This can be seen when comparing the three early illustrations set in railway

"WE HAD THE CARRIAGE TO OURSELVES."

"THE VIEW WAS SORDID ENOUGH."

Above: 'WE HAD THE CARRIAGE TO OURSELVES', 'THE BOSCOMBE VALLEY MYSTERY', THE *STRAND* MAGAZINE, OCTOBER 1891, SIDNEY PAGET

Above right: 'THE VIEW WAS SORDID ENOUGH', 'THE NAVAL TREATY', THE *STRAND* MAGAZINE, OCTOBER 1893, SIDNEY PAGET

Right: 'HOLMES GAVE ME A SKETCH OF THE EVENTS', 'SILVER BLAZE', THE *STRAND* MAGAZINE, DECEMBER 1892, SIDNEY PAGET

"HOLMES GAVE ME A SKETCH OF THE EVENTS."

carriages. Swain's engraving in 'The Boscombe Valley Mystery' from October 1891 retains a sketchy aspect while Naumann's two versions, the first in 'The Silver Blaze' from December 1892 and the second in 'The Naval Treaty' from October 1893, have more detail and are better defined. All three drawings capture the scene successfully but in their own different ways. Credit here lies also, of course, with Paget himself who has composed the scenes to perfection with the two characters facing each other in the carriage. 'The Silver Blaze' one illustrates the more capacious space of a first-class carriage, something that Conan Doyle's text specifies, while in 'The Naval Treaty' Holmes and Watson have less leg room, suggesting that they occupy a second-class railway carriage.

These drawings are also interesting from the point of view of the clothing worn by the two characters. 'The Boscombe Valley Mystery' illustration has Holmes wearing a deerstalker hat for the first time. Conan Doyle describes him wearing a 'long grey travelling cloak, and a close-fitting cap'. It is Paget who interprets this as a deerstalker and adds a tweed coat to match. This is appropriate clothing for a detective who has left the metropolis for the country in order to embark on a case and where he will track and hunt down evidence. In the illustrations he is shown examining a pair of boots closely and then lying on the ground, minutely studying footprints. The clothing is used in a representational way to reveal a different sort of Sherlock Holmes, who has cast aside his normal urban attire for that of a hunter:

> Sherlock Holmes was transformed when he was hot upon such a scent as this. Men who had only known the quiet thinker and logician of Baker Street would have failed to recognise him. His face flushed and darkened. His brows were drawn into two hard black lines, while his eyes shone out from beneath them with a steely glitter. His face was bent downward, his shoulders bowed, his lips compressed, and the veins stood out like whipcord in his long, sinewy neck. His nostrils seemed to dilate with a purely animal lust for the chase, and his mind was so absolutely concentrated upon the matter before him that a question or remark fell unheeded upon his ears, or, at the most, only provoked a quick, impatient snarl in reply.

Conan Doyle sometimes specifies the clothes worn by Sherlock Holmes and Dr Watson as well as those worn by other characters in the stories. However, it is Paget who fills out the detail of their style of dress. He always has Holmes wearing a flat bow-tie and a turn-down collar and Watson an upright collar and more elaborate neckties. This aspect, along with their facial appearance and proportions, allows readers to tell them apart instantly when they are portrayed alongside each other.

'What a lovely thing a rose is', 'The Naval Treaty', The Strand Magazine, October 1893, Sidney Paget

'The Pipe was still between his lips', 'The Man with the Twisted Lip', The Strand Magazine, December 1891, Sidney Paget

This distinction was probably something that late nineteenth-century readers had no trouble deciphering, but for a twenty-first-century audience it is less clear what it says about the two men. The way that Sherlock Holmes wears his tie and collar would have been viewed as more casual and less fashionable than Watson's. However, when wearing their morning dress and overcoats, they are representatives of a class of respectable and well-dressed gentlemen who would have been seen out and about in the West End and the financial and mercantile districts of the metropolis.

When it comes to casual dress, Sherlock Holmes often removes his coat and waistcoat indoors and wears a dressing gown with pockets. The dressing gown becomes associated with two opposing sides of his character. It suggests, on the one hand, a relaxed and comfortable mode that allows his analytical brain to function at its peak. The dressing gown becomes a sort of smoking apparel for the detective. As he turns over different lines of inquiry in his mind, he uses tobacco as a powerful stimulant but also to block out distractions, enabling him to concentrate in a focused way:

"To smoke," he answered. "It is quite a three pipe problem, and I beg that you won't speak to me for fifty minutes." He curled himself up in his chair, with his thin knees drawn up to his hawk-like nose, and there he sat with his eyes closed and his black clay pipe thrusting out like the bill of some strange bird. I had come to the conclusion that he had dropped asleep, and indeed was nodding myself, when he suddenly sprang out of his chair with the gesture of a man who has made up his mind and put his pipe down upon the mantelpiece.

The dressing gown, on the other hand, also represents his Bohemian character and is associated with disorder, lethargy and lounging around. It is an apparel that he wears when carrying out his scientific experiments and almost certainly when 'scraping upon his violin'. Paget captures Sherlock Holmes in a number of these distinctive poses, which were taken up in later stage and film interpretations.

Another form of distinctive dress found in the illustrations is Holmes's disguises. In the first *Strand* story, Paget sketches him as a 'drunken-looking groom' as well as a 'simple-minded clergyman'. In 'The Man with the Twisted Lip', Holmes is shown wearing a wig and crouching by a brazier in the opium den. Perhaps the most refined illustration of all appears in 'The Final Problem', where Dr Watson is surprised by Holmes disguised as an 'aged ecclesiastic'. Watson assists him on the platform at Victoria Station and is incapable of communicating with

SP

'My decrepit Italian friend', 'The Final Problem', The *Strand* Magazine, December 1893, Sidney Paget

'My decrepit Italian friend', pen, ink and wash drawing for 'The Final Problem', 1893, Sidney Paget

the 'venerable Italian priest' as he occupies a place opposite him in his reserved railway carriage. Dr Watson is completely taken in by Holmes's disguise. It is Paget who has interpreted the detail of the dress and particularly the pose of Holmes. Conan Doyle describes how, as the train departs, Holmes removes his disguise of 'the black cassock and hat' and packs them away in a 'hand-bag'. As can be seen, especially in Paget's original wash drawing for the illustration, Holmes's hands are wrapped around the head of the stick, implying that he is still in role, playing the aged cleric. His intensity of concentration and stillness, all the same, reminds readers of the great detective's analytical mind at work. The upholstery, curtaining and partitioning of the carriage are finely executed as well as the detail of the 'hand-bag' placed on the seat alongside Holmes. The background fluidity of the drawing is apparent in contrast to the care and attention focused on Holmes's face.

Below: 'WE FOUND OURSELVES IN THE INNER ROOM', 'THE STOCK-BROKER'S CLERK', THE *STRAND* MAGAZINE, MARCH 1893, SIDNEY PAGET

Below right: 'IT'S NO USE, JOHN CLAY', 'THE RED-HEADED LEAGUE', THE *STRAND* MAGAZINE, AUGUST 189, SIDNEY PAGET

The *Strand's* Sherlock Holmes illustrations fall into two distinct types – scenes set indoors at Baker Street or at Dr Watson's lodgings, and those that depict places where the adventures take place. Some of the latter accompany descriptions of events related to Holmes and Watson by a client or police detective at Baker Street, which had taken place at a distant location. The most memorable illustrations are those

that depict Sherlock Holmes and Dr Watson together. Paget was astute in the way that he selected the best scenes and moments from the stories to illustrate. As they sit, stand, stretch out, converse or study some curious object or letter, read a newspaper, or fall asleep, Paget succeeds in building a sense of familiarity between the two men while giving them their own characteristics and mannerisms. He stands apart from many other illustrators of the period in his skill in conveying natural posture, which is believable and distinct. Holmes as a man of action appears in a number of the drawings. One thinks of the detective 'springing' out to apprehend John Clay in 'The Red-Headed League', lashing 'furiously' at 'the swamp adder' in 'The Speckled Band' or clapping a pistol to the head of Sir George Burnwell in 'The Beryl Coronet'.

Left: 'Trevor used to come in to inquire after me', 'The Gloria Scott', The Strand Magazine, April 1893, Sidney Paget

Above: '"Nothing could be better", said Holmes', 'The Stockbroker's Clerk', The Strand Magazine, March 1893, Sidney Paget

For over seven years, from December 1893 through to August 1901, there were no new Sherlock Holmes stories. Paget continued to be employed by the *Strand*, illustrating the work of other authors, including Arthur Morrison's 'Martin Hewitt, Investigator' stories, which the magazine hoped would help to fill the gap left by Sherlock Holmes. However, Paget did not illustrate Conan Doyle's Brigadier Gerard stories, which were published in the *Strand* Magazine in 1894 and 1895, but he did provide the drawings for his novels *Rodney Stone* in 1896 and *The Tragedy of the Korosko* in 1897, as well as other short stories by him in 1898 and 1899, all of which were published in the *Strand*. In 1897, Conan Doyle commissioned Paget to paint his portrait, a mark of trust in his friend's ability to capture his appearance and character faithfully.[15]

Conan Doyle had no intention of resurrecting the detective after killing him off in 1893. Nevertheless, five years later he prepared a Sherlock Holmes stage play, based on an amalgamation of sections from a few of the stories, in the belief that it would make him money, despite harbouring concerns that it would undermine his standing as a serious writer. His play came to nothing but in the same year, actor William

CHARACTER SKETCH OF SHERLOCK HOLMES—ACT II

Above: WILLIAM GILLETTE IN TWEED AND DEER STALKER, 1900

Above right: 'CHARACTER SKETCH OF SHERLOCK HOLMES – ACT II', WILLIAM GILLETTE, C.1900

Gillette, with Conan Doyle's approval, adapted Sherlock Holmes for the stage. Gillette's interpretation of the detective was novel. He gave him an allure and charm that is not present in Conan Doyle's text and only hinted at in Sidney Paget's illustrations. Holmes was personified in a new and unforgettable way and one prop – a curved pipe – became synonymous with him from then on. In costume terms, he was very smartly attired; even his dressing gown was stylish. In 1901, just at the time that Gillette was performing the part at the Lyceum Theatre in Drury Lane to great public acclaim, even if the critics were not so enamoured by the performance or the play, Conan Doyle was writing a new Sherlock Holmes short novel, *The Hound of the Baskervilles*. He renewed his partnership with Paget seamlessly as if no time had passed since the last appearance of Holmes. The novel was published in the *Strand* Magazine over nine issues, and Paget's sixty illustrations wonderfully capture the excitement and mystery of the story, at the same time portraying Sherlock Holmes in many of his familiar poses as he contemplates, looks for clues and finally, as a man of action, empties

'five barrels of his revolver into the creature's flank'. *The Hound of the Baskervilles* proved to be their greatest, most successful collaboration as writer and illustrator to date.

A series of Holmes stories followed in 1903 and 1904 with Paget providing ninety-five illustrations that make a worthy accompaniment to Conan Doyle's texts. It is difficult to judge the impact of the stories but a number of reports confirm that they were eagerly consumed by the public. Film director Michael Powell remembered being told by his uncle and grandfather how every commuter waiting at Forest Hill Station in south London had 'his head in the *Strand* Magazine, devouring the latest [Sherlock Holmes] Adventure'. Powell believed

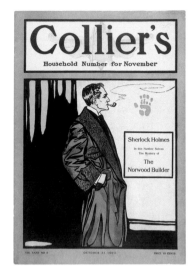

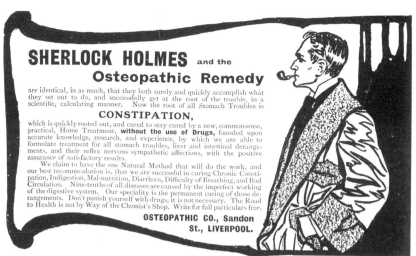

SHERLOCK HOLMES **and the**
Osteopathic Remedy

are identical, in as much, that they both surely and quickly accomplish what they set out to do, and successfully get at the root of the trouble, in a scientific, calculating manner. Now the root of all Stomach Troubles is

CONSTIPATION,

which is quickly rooted out, and cured to stay cured by a new, commonsense, practical, Home Treatment, **without the use of Drugs,** founded upon accurate knowledge, research, and experience, by which we are able to formulate treatment for all stomach troubles, liver and intestinal derangements, and their reflex nervous sympathetic affections, with the positive assurance of satisfactory results.

We claim to have the one Natural Method that will do the work, and our best recommendation is, that we are successful in curing Chronic Constipation, Indigestion, Mal-nutrition, Diarrhœa, Difficulty of Breathing, and Bad Circulation. Nine-tenths of all diseases are caused by the imperfect working of the digestive system. Our speciality is the permanent curing of those derangements. Don't punish yourself with drugs, it is not necessary. The Road to Health is not by Way of the Chemist's Shop. Write for full particulars free.

OSTEOPATHIC CO., Sandon St., LIVERPOOL.

Above: COLLIER'S MAGAZINE COVER FOR 'THE NORWOOD BUILDER', OCTOBER 1903, FREDERIC DORR STEELE

Above right: OSTEOPATHIC REMEDY ADVERT, THE *STRAND* MAGAZINE, DECEMBER 1903

Right: 'A LITTLE WIZENED MAN DARTED OUT', 'THE NORWOOD BUILDER', THE *STRAND* MAGAZINE, DECEMBER 1903, SIDNEY PAGET

Following pages: 'A DAY WITH CONAN DOYLE', *STRAND* MAGAZINE, AUGUST 1892

that Paget's illustrations as 'much as the text, created the immortal folk figure'.[16]

At this time, the depiction of Sherlock Holmes in popular culture becomes more complex. Frederic Dorr Steele was commissioned by American magazine *Collier's* to illustrate the same set of stories, and he based his interpretation of the detective on William Gillette's portrayal on the stage. In a series of marvellous colour covers and many black and white illustrations, he drew a number of definitive profiles and poses, which set up a different rendering of the detective. Now there were two key, competing representations of Sherlock Holmes. They were seen together, possibly for the first time, in the 1903 December edition of the *Strand* Magazine. Paget's Sherlock Holmes appeared in the 'The Dancing Men' whereas Steele's profile of the detective featured in an advert promoting an osteopathic home-treatment cure. Right through to today, film and TV adaptations have made use of both these visual interpretations. Sidney Paget died in 1908 at the relatively young age of forty-seven but subsequent illustrations in the *Strand* Magazine remained true to his concept of the appearance of the detective. Paget was the first illustrator to fix the look of Sherlock Holmes and he played a defining role in the creation of one of the world's most iconic popular figures.

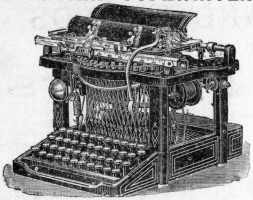

A Day with Dr. Conan Doyle.

By Harry How.

From a Photo, by]   DR. CONAN DOYLE AND MRS. CONAN DOYLE.   [Elliott & Fry.

 ETECTIVISM up to date—that is what Dr. Conan Doyle has given us. We were fast becoming weary of the representative of the old school; he was, at his best, a very ordinary mortal, and, with the palpable clues placed in his path, the average individual could have easily cornered the "wanted" one without calling in the police or the private inquiry agent. Sher-

lock Holmes entered the criminal arena. He started on the track. A clever fellow; a cool, calculating fellow, this Holmes. He could see the clue to a murder in a ball of worsted, and certain conviction in a saucer of milk. The little things we regarded as nothings were all and everything to Holmes. He was an artful fellow, too; and though he knew "all about it" from the first, he ingeniously contrived to hold his secret until we got to the very last line in the story. There never was a man who propounded a criminal conundrum and gave us so many guesses until we "gave it up" as Sherlock Holmes.

I thought of all this as I was on my way to a prettily-built and modest - looking red-brick residence in the neighbourhood of South Norwood. Here lives Dr. Conan Doyle. I found him totally different from the man I expected to see ; but that is always the case. There was nothing lynx-eyed, nothing "detective" about him —not even the regulation walk

DR. CONAN DOYLE'S HOUSE.
From a Photo. by Elliott & Fry.

I, accompanied by his wife, a most charming woman, went through the rooms as a preliminary. The study is a quiet corner, and has on its walls many remarkable pictures by Dr. Doyle's father. Dr. Doyle comes of a family of artists. His grandfather, John Doyle, was the celebrated "H. B.," whose pictorial political skits came out for a period of over thirty years without the secret of his identity leaking out. A few of these, which the Government purchased for £1,000, are in the British Museum. A bust of the artist is in the entrance hall. John Doyle's sons were all artists. "Dicky Doyle," as he was known to his familiars, designed the cover of *Punch*. His signature "D.," with a little bird on top, is in the corner. On the mantelpiece of the study, near to an autograph portrait of J. M. Barrie, is a remarkably interesting sketch, reproduced in these pages. It was done by John Doyle, and represented the

of our modern solver of mysteries. He is just a happy, genial, homely man ; tall, broad-shouldered, with a hand that grips you heartily, and, in its sincerity of welcome, hurts. He is brown and bronzed, for he enters liberally into all outdoor sports— football, tennis, bowls, and cricket. His average with the bat this season is twenty. He is a capital amateur photographer, too. But in exercise he most leans towards tricycling. He is never happier than when on his tandem with his wife, and starting on a thirty-mile spin ; never merrier than when he perches his little three - year - old Mary on the wheels, and runs her round the green lawn of his garden.

Dr. Doyle and

From a Photo, by]   THE STUDY.   *[Elliott & Fry,*

From a Sketch]   QUEEN VICTORIA AT THE AGE OF SIX.   *[by John Doyle.*

Queen at the age of six driving in Hyde Park. The story is told how the little princess caught sight of old John Doyle trying to get a sketch of her, and graciously commanded her chaise to stop, so that it might be done.

The dining-room contains some good oil paintings by Mrs. Doyle's brother. On the top of a large book-case are a number of Arctic trophies, brought by the owner of the house from a region where the climate is even chillier than our own. The drawing-room is a pretty little apartment. The chairs are cosy, the afternoon tea refreshing, and the thin bread and butter delicious. You may notice a portrait of the English team of cricketers who

went out to Holland last year. Dr. Doyle is among them. Here are many more pictures by his father.

"That plaque in the corner?" said Dr. Doyle, taking down a large blue-and-white plate. "It was one of the late Khedive's dinner plates. When I was leaving Portsmouth, an old patient came to bid me

From a Photo, by]   THE DRAWING-ROOM.   *[Elliott & Fry.*

THE KHEDIVE'S PLATE.
From a Photo. by Elliott & Fry.

wrote the poetry. He remained here seven years, when he went to Germany. There were a few English boys at this particular school, and a second magazine made its appearance. But its opinions were too outspoken ; its motto was, "Fear not, and put it in print." As a matter of fact, a small leading article appeared on the injustice of reading the boys' letters before they were given into their hands. The words used were very strong, and a court-martial was held on the proprietors of the organ, and its further publication prohibited. At seventeen Dr. Doyle went to Edinburgh, and began to study medicine. At nineteen he sent his first real attempt—a story entitled, "The Mystery of the Sassassa Valley," to *Chambers's Journal*, for which he received three guineas.

"I remained a student until one-and-twenty," said Dr. Doyle, "medicine in the day, sometimes a little writing at night. Just at this time an opportunity occurred

good-bye. She brought this as a little something to remember her by. Her son was a young able-bodied seaman on the *Inflexible* at the bombardment of Alexandria. A shot made a hole in the Khedive's palace, and when the lad landed he found it out, and crawled through. He found himself in the Khedive's kitchen ! With an eye to loot, he seized this plate, and crawled out again. It was the most treasured thing the old lady possessed, she said, and she begged me to take it. I thought much of the action."

We lighted our cigars, and settled down again in the study.

Dr. Doyle was born in Edinburgh in 1859. He went to Stonyhurst in Lancashire at nine, and there had a school magazine which he edited, and in which he

From a Photo. by]   MRS. CONAN DOYLE AND DAUGHTER.   *[Dr. Conan Doyle.*

for me to go to the Arctic Seas in a whaler. I determined to go, putting off passing my exams. for a year. What a climate it is in those regions ! We don't understand it here. I don't mean its coldness—I refer to its sanitary properties. I believe, in years to come, it will be the world's sanatorium. Here, thousands of miles from the smoke, where the air is the finest in the world, the invalid and weakly ones will go when all other places have failed to give them the air they want, and revive and live again under the marvellous invigorating properties of the Arctic atmosphere.

"What with whaling, shooting, and boxing—for I took a couple of pairs of gloves with me, and used to box with the steward in the stokehole at night—we had a good time. On my return, I went back to medicine in Edinburgh again. There I met the man who suggested Sherlock Holmes to me—here is a portrait of him as he was in those days, and he is strong and hearty, and still in Edinburgh now."

I looked at the portrait. It represented the features of Mr. Joseph Bell, M.D., whose name I had heard mentioned whilst with Professor Blackie a few months ago in the Scotch capital.

"I was clerk in Mr. Bell's ward," continued Dr. Doyle. "A clerk's duties are to note down all the patients to be seen, and muster them together. Often I would have seventy or eighty. When everything was ready, I would show them in to Mr. Bell, who would have the students gathered round him. His intuitive powers were simply marvellous. Case No. 1 would step up.

"'I see,' said Mr. Bell, 'you're suffering from drink. You even carry a flask in the inside breast pocket of your coat.'

"Another case would come forward.

"'Cobbler, I see.' Then he would turn to the students, and point out to them that the inside of the knee of the man's trousers was worn. That was where the man had rested the lapstone—a peculiarity only found in cobblers.

"All this impressed me very much. He was continually before me—his sharp, piercing grey eyes, eagle nose, and striking features. There he would sit in his chair with fingers together—he was very dexterous with his hands—and just look at the man or woman before him. He was most kind and painstaking with the students—a real good friend—and when I took my degree and went to Africa the remarkable individuality and discriminating tact of my old master made a deep and lasting impression on me, though I had not the faintest idea that it would one day lead me to forsake medicine for story writing."

It was in 1882 that Dr. Doyle started practising in Southsea, where he continued for eight years. By degrees literature took his attention from the preparation of prescriptions. In his spare time he wrote some fifty or sixty stories for many of the best magazines, during these eight years before his name became really known. A small selection of these tales has been published since, under the title of "The Captain of the Polestar," and has passed through some four editions. He was by no means forgetting the opportunities offered to such a truly inventive mind as his in novel writing. Once again the memory of his old master came back to him. He wrote "A Study in Scarlet," which was refused by many, but eventually sold outright by its author for £25. Then came "Micah Clarke"—a story dealing with the Monmouth Rebellion. This was remarkably successful. "The Sign of Four" came next, and the publication of this enhanced the reputation of its author very considerably. Sherlock Holmes was making his problems distinctly

From a Photo. by]   DR. CONAN DOYLE.   *[Elliott & Fry.*

agreeable to the public, which soon began to evince an intense interest in them, and expectantly watched and waited for every new mystery which the famous detective undertook to solve. But Holmes—so to speak—was put back for a time.

"I determined," said Dr. Doyle, "to test my own powers to the utmost. You must remember that I was still following medicine. Novel writing was in a great measure a congenial pastime, a pastime that I felt would inevitably become converted into a profession. I devoted two years to the study of fourteenth-century life in England—Edward III.'s reign - when the country was at its height. The period has hardly been treated in fiction at all, and I had to go back to early authorities for everything. I set myself to reconstruct the archer, who has always seemed to me to be the most striking figure in English history. Of course, Scott has done him finely and inimitably in his outlaw aspect. But it was not as an outlaw that he was famous. He was primarily a soldier, one of the finest that the world has ever seen—rough, hard-drinking, hard-swearing, but full of pluck and animal spirits. The archers must have been extraordinary fellows. The French, who have always been gallant soldiers, gave up trying to fight them at last, and used to allow English armies to wander unchecked through the country. It was the same in Spain and in Scotland. Then the knights, I think, were much more human-kind of people than they have usually been depicted. Strength had little to do with their knightly qualities. Some of the most famous of them were very weak men, physically. Chandos was looked upon as the first knight in Europe when he was over eighty. My study of the period ended in my writing, 'The White Company,' which has, I believe, gone through a fair number of editions already.

"I made up my mind to abandon my practice at Southsea, come to London, and start as an eye specialist—a branch of the profession of which I was peculiarly fond. I studied at Paris and Vienna, and, whilst in the latter city, wrote 'The Doings of Raffle Haws.' On my return to London I took rooms in Wimpole-street, had a brass plate put on the door, and started. But orders for stories began to come in, and at the expiration of three months I forsook medicine altogether, came to Norwood, and started writing for THE STRAND MAGAZINE."

I learnt a number of interesting facts regarding "The Adventures of Sherlock Holmes." Dr. Doyle invariably conceives the end of his story first, and writes up to it. He gets the climax, and his art lies in the ingenious way in which he conceals it from his readers. A story—similar to those which have appeared in these pages—occupies about a week in writing, and the ideas have come at all manner of times—when out walking, cricketing, tricycling, or playing tennis. He works between the hours of breakfast and lunch, and again in the evening from five to eight, writing some three thousand words a day. He receives many suggestions from the public. On the morning of my visit the particulars of a poisoning case

As to my companion neither the country nor the sea presented the slightest attraction to him. He loved to lie in the very centre of five millions of people with his filaments stretching out and running through them, responsive to every little rumour or suspicion of unsolved crime.

had been sent to him from New Zealand, and the previous day a great packet of documents relating to a disputed will had been received from Bristol. But the suggestions are seldom practicable. Other letters come from people who have been reading the latest of his stories, saying whether they guessed the mystery or not. His reason for refraining from writing any more stories for a while is a candid one. He is fearful of spoiling a character of which he is particularly fond, but he declares that already he has enough material to carry him through another series, and merrily assures me that he thought the opening story of the next series of " Sherlock Holmes," to be published in this magazine, was of such an unsolvable character, that he had positively bet his wife a shilling that she would not guess the true solution of it until she got to the end of the chapter !

After my visit to Dr. Doyle, I communicated with Mr. Joseph Bell, in Edinburgh —the gentleman whose ingenious personality suggested Sherlock Holmes to his old pupil. The letter he sent in reply is of such interest that it is appended in its entirety :—

2, Melville-crescent,
Edinburgh, June 16, 1892.

Dear Sir,—You ask me about the kind of teaching to which Dr. Conan Doyle has so kindly referred, when speaking of his ideal character, "Sherlock Holmes." Dr. Conan Doyle has, by his imaginative genius, made a great deal out of very little, and his warm remembrance of one of his old teachers has coloured the picture. In teaching the treatment of disease and accident, all careful teachers have first to show the student how to recognise accurately the case. The recognition depends in great measure on the accurate and rapid appreciation of

small points in which the diseased differs from the healthy state. In fact, the student must be taught to observe. To interest him in this kind of work we teachers find it useful to show the student how much a trained use of the observation can discover in ordinary matters such as the previous history, nationality, and occupation of a patient.

The patient, too, is likely to be impressed by your ability to cure him in the future if he sees you, at a glance, know much of his past. And the whole trick is much easier than it appears at first.

For instance, physiognomy helps you to nationality, accent to district, and, to an educated ear, almost to county. Nearly every handicraft writes its sign manual on the hands. The scars of the miner differ from those of the quarryman. The carpenter's callosities are not those of the mason. The shoemaker and the tailor are quite different.

The soldier and the sailor differ in gait, though last month I had to tell a man who said he was a soldier that he had been a sailor in his boyhood. The subject is endless : the tattoo marks on hand or arm will tell their own tale as to voyages ; the ornaments on the watch chain of the successful settler will tell you where he made his money. A New Zealand squatter will not wear a gold mohur, nor an engineer on an Indian railway a Maori stone. Carry the same idea of using one's senses accurately and constantly, and you will see that many a surgical case will bring his past history, national, social, and medical, into the consulting-room as he walks in. Dr. Conan Doyle's genius and intense imagination has on this slender basis made his detective stories a distinctly new departure, but he owes much less than he thinks to yours truly JOSEPH BELL.

MR. JOSEPH BELL.
From a Photo. by A. Swan Watson, Edinburgh.

CHAPTER THREE

The Art of Sherlock Holmes: 'The air of London is the sweeter for my presence'

PAT HARDY

 ONDON IS AT THE HEART of the Sherlock Holmes stories. London streets, hotels and train stations are all knowledgeably and indeed lovingly referenced, repeated and recited. As soon as London is mentioned in the same breath as Sherlock Holmes, a certain image of the city comes effortlessly to mind – a smoke-ridden, congested metropolis, populated by exotic figures, the heart of a global Empire in which iconic landmarks, such as the Houses of Parliament, have come to represent its essence and flavour. The stories move seamlessly from actual locations, including the Strand, the Langham Hotel and Waterloo Station, to fictional places in the form of 221B Baker Street, Hotel Cosmopolitan and the Diogenes Club. This blurring of boundaries has resulted in the creation of a mythic London, which has become a dominant image affecting not only how we view late nineteenth-century London at the time when the stories were set but also has indirectly influenced contemporary adaptations.

One reason for the persistence and strength of this image lies in art produced at the end of the nineteenth century, featuring London as its subject. The most famous 'modern' capital in the world was the key location for artists who wanted to represent the modern. They found striking forms in the new buildings that were being constructed in London and in the density of crowds and cabs thronging the streets. For artists to 'know' the city meant, on the one hand, having a panoptical gaze, encompassing the whole of the city, in which all is visible and immediately comprehensible, as shown in John Crowther's *Panoramic View from the top of Monument*, c.1890; and, on the other, focusing on the unfolding vista of the pedestrian at ground level, an immersion in street life.[1] The tension between ordered design and untidy contingency was key to the translation of the modern to the urban aesthetic and it meant a new way of viewing the city. In the

Left: PANORAMIC VIEW FROM THE TOP OF THE MONUMENT (DETAIL), c.1890, WATERCOLOUR, JOHN CROWTHER

same way as artists developed ideas and techniques to depict this phenomenon of the Imperial capital, so did Sherlock Holmes stories develop to take in this dual aspect of the city. The stories are mapped out by Conan Doyle in great specificity in terms of character, location and plot, but they are immersed in a Gothic, atmospheric coating in which the weather and light play an active role in guiding the reader towards particular emotions. This interaction between the detailed referencing of a great, sprawling, bewildering city and the natural elemental forces of the weather (both tamed, at least for the duration of the short story, by the deductive ability of Sherlock Holmes) was the guiding force of Sherlock Holmes fiction and the art that was produced at the end of the nineteenth century. 'Picturing' the city at this time meant the artists had a desire to distance ugliness through an aesthetising fog while still referencing key locations. Conan Doyle seems to have used a similar approach in his deployment of location and atmosphere against the backdrop of London.

This dual way of viewing a city – a lofty, distanced overview combined with a desire to be on the streets among the crowds – could also be found in other modern cities, in writings and paintings, Paris for instance. Arguably, what compelled artists to visit and linger in London was the weather, namely the industrial levels of fog and its effects on light. Artists and photographers from abroad, including Claude Monet (1840–1926), James McNeill Whistler (1834–1903), Joseph Pennell (1857–1926) and Alvin Langdon Coburn (1882–1966), all wanted to find ways to depict these fleeting effects, to note perceptions rather than to document the city topographically. Their vision was atmospheric and timeless, not read in any particular order and showed a series of subjective responses to a real place at apparently very particular times. But this aspect of London, in which a city of timeless beauty was created, has perhaps been emphasised to the detriment of the views of the city created by British artists such as John O'Connor (1830–1889) and John Atkinson Grimshaw (1836–1893) who combined this aestheticisation with authentic, realistic detail that was very much of its time. These are the artists who can be said to represent the London of Sherlock Holmes and whose works can be explored in relation to this.

As early as the 1900 *Exposition Universelle* in Paris where Great Britain exhibited 276 paintings, British art of this period was felt to be underwhelming, an awkward interlude between Pre-Raphaelitism and Modernism. Commentators at the British section of the *Exposition Universelle* reported that the art was uneven and this view has continued to date. Despite the naturalism of John Lavery, William Quiller Orchardson, Stanhope Forbes and George Clausen, it was agreed among visitors that the predominance of Millais, Burne-Jones, Leighton and Alma-Tadema had produced 'something insipid, old-fashioned, verging on the puerile at times . . . if England wants to remain worthy of its old glory, it must leave its museums, studios and pundits and look outside!'[2]

Artists of this period did engage with depicting the excitements of the modern city, in particular London, although they were, like Monet, mostly absent from the *Exposition Universelle*. Many artists were endlessly experimenting with 'looking outside' at the motifs of the city as well as testing new techniques for so doing. How to paint London was frequently discussed. One of the most famous articles was written by Tristram J. Ellis in the *Art Journal* 1884, in which he lamented the fact that the only modern buildings worthy of depiction in London, in his view, were the Houses of Parliament and the Law Courts on the Strand. He did recognise, however, that these landmarks attracted huge attention as famous iconic buildings.[3] It is certainly the case that the Houses of Parliament were endlessly depicted, not least for the tourist trade, one of the first visualisations being the stupendous evening view by John

Anderson, *Westminster, The Houses of Parliament and Westminster Bridge seen from the river*, 1872. The subject reached an apotheosis in Claude Monet's view *Houses of Parliament, Trouée de soleil dans le brouillard*, 1904. This repetition of the same celebrated landmarks, usually located on the Thames, in paintings and graphic and photographic material was harnessed to the artistic desire to capture new light effects created by the industrial city. It embedded in the visual imagination a very definite aesthetic, which became intimately associated with the vision of London in the Sherlock Holmes stories themselves.

The predominant aspect of the London of Sherlock Holmes, and usually the first to be described, is the atmospheric fog and mist, which seem to envelop the city. These were certainly unique to London at the close of the nineteenth century, and the frequency of the dense industrial fogs reached a peak between 1886 and 1890. They were caused by coal fires and enhanced by smoke from factories, gasworks and railway engines, and steam from the tugs and steamers of the River Thames.[4] Tar from low-temperature coal combustion gave morning fogs a yellow hue, which assumed a darker hue as the day progressed.[5] Newcomers to London were immediately struck by the thick fog, which changed not only from day to day but within each day, and it attracted many artists. Claude Monet, for instance, visited three times between 1899 and 1902 to attempt to capture its effects on the London landscape. A key notion for him was to anticipate the unpredictable in the city and to insist on the

spontaneity and the 'impression' in the painting. Monet described how, like other Impressionists, he had to be ready to act with great speed to whatever landscape effect presented itself, which meant he had to have a flexible technique in expectation of any number of weather effects. He developed the notion of sequentiality by producing numerous canvases with the same motif to capture fleeting weather effects. But various problems presented themselves, such as the sun remaining behind a cloud but with its effects still being glimpsed on water, or the solid, iron immobile bridge which also vibrated under the rhythm and pace of the bustling traffic, or the weightlessness of smoke which appeared to cut through buildings. So, to resolve these dichotomies, Monet also developed a structural cohesion through colour and the application of paint, a repetition of the same motif and a composition that kept in balance the opposing vertical and horizontal competing lines.

Consumed by painting the temporal immediacy of visual experience, Monet produced a seminal set of London views, comprising ninety-five paintings, while he was staying in the Savoy Hotel, off the Strand. This location was vital for Monet to be able to paint the Thames and was recognised as such at the time. In *Homes of the Passing Show*, an account of London landmarks, published in 1900, the Savoy Hotel was

The Savoy Hotel from Victoria Gardens, c.1890, albumen print, George Washington Wilson

advertised as looking on to smoky and vaporous views of the Thames. It housed, the book boasted, the most renowned and fashionable restaurant in the world, which overlooked, by day, the most beautiful garden and river view in Europe and, by night, a fairy scene. Monet stayed on the sixth floor during his visit in 1899 and the following February in 1900, and later, in 1901, in rooms 541 and 542 where the angle of elevation was less steep. From both floors, he painted Charing Cross and Waterloo Bridges. He also had permission to paint in St Thomas's Hospital on the other side of the river to capture the view looking towards the Houses of Parliament. Monet's routine was to work in the Savoy in the morning, focusing on Waterloo Bridge in the early morning, then moving to the Charing Cross Bridge paintings at midday, have lunch in the Savoy Grill, then walk across to St Thomas's Hospital in the afternoon to capture the late afternoon sun on the Houses of Parliament. By the end of March 1900, Monet had eighty canvases on which he was working.

By staying on the fifth and sixth floors and using the elevation so provided, Monet solved the problem of how to paint the crowds without being immersed in them at street level. He could look down on this view and show the hustle and bustle on the streets and bridges, all of which were suffused in the ever-shifting configuration of wind and fog. *Pont de Londres (Charing Cross Bridge, London)* 1902 is one such painting, and was one of about thirty-seven views of Charing Cross Bridge, all of which showed variations on the morning light. This painting demonstrates the acrid yellow of the industrial fog flooding the city with the rectilinear bridge in the centre and a ghostly Houses of Parliament behind. The bridge seems to float in the composition with a succession of planes of colour establishing the sense of perspective. Monet admitted that he liked the fog most of all in London. It suffused his compositions and out of it would emerge a seductive, iconic motif, Charing Cross Bridge or the Houses of Parliament. Monet described his practice in a letter to his wife Alice on 26 February 1900: 'at daybreak there was an extraordinary mist entirely yellow; I made an impression of it, not bad I think.'[6] Art critic Octave Mirabeau wrote of these paintings, 'whether muted or bright, all the colours blend together; ethereal reflections, virtually imperceptible influences, transform objects

or even deform them into fantastic shapes.' He analysed the Charing Cross Bridge views, commenting on the massive pylons at the side of the bridge, which seemed to evaporate in the distance and, further away, 'the delicate silhouettes where one senses the crowded dwellings and the uproar of the factories'. Trains passed over the bridge: 'their undulating smoke coming from different directions mixes, fuses and vanishes into the air against the river.'[7] Awkward landmarks that even the fog couldn't disguise were omitted, such as the conspicuous monument Cleopatra's Needle, which appeared in only two early sketches of the Charing Cross Bridge series.

Monet therefore reduced buildings to near silhouettes and he found he could achieve this in the painterly effects of London's fogs. He admitted that he loved London but 'only in the winter … for without the fog London wouldn't be a beautiful city. It's the fog that gives it its magnificent breadth. Those massive regular blocks become grandiose within that mysterious cloak.'[8] By 1901, he was becoming much more confident, and wrote, 'my practised eye has found that objects change in appearance in a London fog more and quicker than in any other atmosphere and the difficulty is to get every change down on canvas.'[9]

PONT DE LONDRES (CHARING CROSS BRIDGE, LONDON), 1902, OIL ON CANVAS, CLAUDE MONET (NATIONAL TRUST)

These fogs, which in the adventures of Sherlock Holmes veiled crimes of the metropolis from all but the eye of the master detective, were for Monet a cloak, which enabled him to distance an aesthetic from society. The fog allowed Monet to concentrate on painting the surface not the actuality of the buildings and surroundings of the city. Mirabeau explained, 'Every day at the same hour, for the same number of minutes in the same light … he would come back to his motif.' Just as shapes emerge from the fog and mist in the painting, prompting memories, ebbing and flowing, so in the stories figures come in and out of focus blurring the narrative, obscuring crime and criminals, and leaving traces that only Sherlock Holmes can decipher.

But the apparent ease and spontaneity of these artistic works (and, indeed, the nonchalant brilliance of the Conan Doyle creation) belie the industrious nature of their production, heightened by the repetition of the same formula, the same set of motifs produced time and again. Many of Monet's paintings reveal layers of overpainting or retouching, showing that this apparent spontaneity was, in fact, the result of significant work, often back in the studio in Giverny. Monet was especially interested in trying to locate the position of the sun as it affected his colour palette by making the fog more or less dense. His intense desire to translate its effects was recorded by a visitor, Gustave Geffroy, in February 1900 on the balcony of the Savoy. Unlike Monet, Geffroy couldn't see the sun: 'looked in vain, we still only saw an expanse of woolly gray, some confused forms, the bridges as if suspended in the void, smoke that quickly disappeared and some swelling waves of the Thames … we applied ourselves to see better, to penetrate this mystery and indeed we ended up by distinguishing we didn't know what mysterious and distant gleam which seemed to be trying to penetrate this immobile world. Little by little things were illuminated with a gleam and it was delicious to see …'[10]

In much the same way, Sherlock Holmes appears to have an unerring way of piercing through the murk to work out the crime, to the surprise of Watson and Lestrade. Conan Doyle makes much use of a metaphorical fog as well as a climatic weather condition, in which only the acute intellect and knowledge of the consulting detective can resolve the crimes. He brings in not only foggy weather but also the smoke-laden rooms in which thick, swirling tobacco smoke induces intellectual torpor and befuddles the minds of the official police and detectives who cannot work out the answers by the rational application of knowledge to the existing situation. Lestrade from the first story in *A Study in Scarlet* is described as 'having got himself into a fog recently over a forgery case'. As the mystery is solved, Holmes reports, 'the mists in my own mind were gradually clearing away.'

For the weather in the stories is quickly recognised as playing a part in the creation of atmosphere in London, an obvious form of Gothic sublime, which through the voice of Watson invariably begins many accounts. The wind is often referenced. In 'The Golden Pince-Nez', it was 'a wild tempestuous night towards the close of November' and 'the wind howled down Baker Street while the rain beat fiercely against the windows'. A sense of the terrible immensity of London enters the work when we read, 'Ten miles of man's handiwork on every side of us to feel the iron grip of nature and be conscious that to the huge elemental forces, all London was no more than the molehills that dot the fields'; and again, 'the droning of the wind, stamping of a horse's hoof and long grind of a wheel'. In 'The Empty House', 'It was a bleak and boisterous night and the wind whistled shrilly down the long street'. In 'The Five Orange Pips', September was introduced by wind, 'equinocturnal gales set in with exceptional violence. Even in the heart of great handmade London we were forced to raise our mind for the instant from the routine of life and to recognise the presence of those great elemental forces which shriek at mankind through the bars of his civilisation like untamed beasts in a cage.'

Fog is often noted in the Sherlock Holmes stories, although not as often as in the later film adaptations. Fog is used to create a definite mood, linked to the progression of narrative, for the darkness and murk are always thickest at the beginning of the stories. In 'The Missing Three-Quarter', it is 'a gloomy February morning'; in 'The Abbey Grange', 'it was a bitterly cold and frosty morning during the winter of '97 … dimly see the occasional figure of an early workman as he passed us, blurred and indistinct in opalescent London reek'; in 'The Solitary Cyclist', Farnham, the place of the crime, was 'glowing all the more beautiful to the eyes which were weary of the duns and drabs and slate grays of London'; in 'The Dancing Men', Norfolk was described as 'far from the fogs of Baker Street'; in 'The Sussex Vampire', 'it was evening of a dull foggy November'; in 'The Copper Beeches', 'a thick fog rolled down between the lines of dun coloured houses and the opposing windows loomed like dark shapeless blurs through the heavy wreaths'; in *A Study in Scarlet*, off the Brixton Road a 'foggy cloudy morning and a dun coloured veil hung over the house-tops looking like a reflection of the mud-coloured streets beneath'. Usually, by the end of the story a more hopeful tone is set by a glimpse of sun 'shining with a subdued brightness through [the] dim veil which hangs over the great city' as described in 'The Five Orange Pips'.

The artistic effects of fog were explored not only by Monet but also by American photographer Alvin Langdon Coburn, who championed an aesthetic of brushed, textured surface and foggy, smoke-laden air,

focusing on the ceremonial core of London in photographs such as *The Houses of Parliament* and *The British Lion.* He had an Impressionist emphasis on atmospheric treatment but with a more symbolic 'essential' expression, which included radical cropping derived from Japanese prints. He reworked photographs in his studio in order to emphasise elements of a scene, and hand-worked images in the printing process to minimise the detail in favour of how atmosphere was portrayed, all of which gave the photograph a painterly quality. This was done despite his statements that the photogravures (photomechanical prints resembling aquatints or etchings) appeared as produced direct from nature, with the minimum of interference. The subtle schematised

tones of photogravures emphasised atmosphere over description, the
gravure giving control over tonal values and image resolution. The
focus of the work therefore lessened with distance, so that Waterloo
Bridge, for example, exuded the calm of the river with reflections
caused by sunlight and shadows cast by the bridge. The images sought
to emphasise connoisseurship and uniqueness, to present a counterpoint
to the replication and mass production of the age. As Coburn said, 'The
artist-photographer must be constantly on the alert for the perfect
moment when a fragment of the jumble of nature is isolated by the
conditions of light or atmosphere until it becomes a perfect expression.'[11]

The image of London was painted and photographed therefore at

many different times of day and night in an effort to capture the fleeting light effects. James McNeill Whistler painted his last views of London in cold, overcast March weather. Like Monet, he painted from a corner suite at the Savoy. In 1896, he waited in the hotel room, watching his wife, who was dying, and drawing the views he knew so well. This high panoramic viewpoint was perfect for his lithographic sketches, which depicted an angle of 180 degrees in a series of three different views; some showed the view downstream towards St Paul's with Waterloo Bridge, others upstream to Westminster with Charing Cross Bridge and still others the Thames by night with the south bank directly opposite

the hotel. He made his last view of the river, *The Thames*, working directly on to stone supplied by the printer, Thomas Way in Well Street, and by using lithotint with the image printed in reverse, he captured the effect of dark March days blanketed by coal smoke and fog. From right to left are seen Lambeth Lead works and the Lion Brewery, and the delicacy of the work conveys the impression of memories, evanescent souvenirs of a mournful river. Favouring the old and the careworn, he gives a vivid account of the Thames but it is a completely tonal one, not coloured like that of Monet. He also shows a timeless city, suspended in a dense, and nearly obliterating, atmosphere, which was described as a tourist attraction in guidebooks such as *London and its Environs: Handbook for Travellers*, 1911.

Joseph Pennell, who also followed Whistler across the Atlantic from America, brought new skills in etching to London, bolstering the recently founded Royal Society of Painter-Etchers, and many of his prints exploit techniques to convey atmospheric night scenes. In 1887, Pennell and his wife were living in North Street, Westminster

DARK DAY ON EMBANKMENT, 1909, AQUATINT, JOSEPH PENNELL (PRINTS & PHOTOGRAPHIC DIVISION, LIBRARY OF CONGRESS, WASHINGTON D.C.)

LONDON, REFLECTIONS ON THE THAMES, 1880, OIL ON CANVAS, JOHN ATKINSON GRIMSHAW (LEEDS CITY ART GALLERY)

with their landlady, Mrs Dunbar, 'a neat Scotch woman, in tiny rooms which were immaculately clean'. His studio was in Buckingham Street, off the Strand, where his windows over looked the Thames, framing views such as Waterloo Bridge or the dome of St Paul's Cathedral in the distance. Influenced by Whistler's sharp detail and unusual angles, Pennell produced numerous views of London, such as *Dark Day on Embankment*, 1909, aquatint. In a collection of etchings published in February 1894, the preface stated they were 'simply records of things seen at various times and in different parts of London … often the outcome of a ramble with a few plates in my pocket or at times only a scrap of paper. In no sense are they the result of a tour in search of the picturesque.'[12]

One British artist who has become intimately associated with depictions of modern cities is John Atkinson Grimshaw (1836–93) who came to London from Leeds to take advantage of the art market and the increasing number of buyers. He painted a large number of canvases of London, many of which were night scenes, taking a studio in Manresa Road, Chelsea between 1885 and 1887 where Whistler was his neighbour. The two artists became friends and Whistler is credited

as saying that he thought he was the inventor of nocturnes until he saw Grimshaw's moonlight pictures.[13] Grimshaw painted many scenes of the Thames with landmark buildings and bridges, presenting no radical new perspective on the city, and his *London, Reflections on the Thames, Westminster* 1880 can be directly referenced to the painting of Anderson described above. He was frequently attracted to the outer areas of the city at that time, such as Wimbledon, Chelsea and Barnes. Hampstead was a popular subject and he painted several scenes with a foregrounded solitary female figure with umbrella in an empty night-time street. In *Hampstead Looking down Heath Street*, the upper end of the street shown in the work is one of the original lanes leading into the village of Hampstead, which was lengthened in 1887–89 under the Town Improvement Scheme to link it to Fitzjohn's Avenue. This is a very different mood from that of the mid-century, fallen woman depictions in which the solitary female conveyed notions of prostitution, suicide, shame and disgrace. Here reflective melancholia and nostalgia pervade the scene. Mystery, solitude, an enclave far from the centre but still part

HAMPSTEAD HILL, LOOKING DOWN HEATH STREET, 1882, OIL ON CANVAS, JOHN ATKINSON GRIMSHAW (PRIVATE COLLECTION)

of the London conglomerate – Hampstead was an ideal location for one of Holmes's more memorable encounters with an evil villain. In 'Charles Augustus Milverton', 'on a wild and tempestuous evening when the wind screamed and rattled against the windows' Holmes and Watson caught a hansom cab to Church Row to visit Appledore Towers, the home of Milverton, to play out the drama and foil the blackmailing magnate.

Another view by a British artist drawing upon the historical artistic interest in night-time scenes is Francis Forster's *The Quadrant, Regent Street*, 1897. Central London here is depicted as at once sinister and welcoming, a place of violence, scandal and intrigue, which was immortally described in *A Study in Scarlet* as 'that great cesspool into which all the loungers and idlers of the Empire are irresistibly drained', but also the place where such crimes are solved in the reassuring rooms of 221B Baker Street. There are ever-present dangers in the street as Watson makes clear in *The Sign of Four* while he watches people move from shop window to shop window: 'there was to my mind, something eerie and ghostlike in the endless procession of faces which flitted across

these narrow bars of light – sad faces and glad, haggard and merry. Like all humankind they flitted from the gloom into the light and so back into the gloom once more.' This scene is vividly conveyed by an mezzotint by Joseph Pennell called *Rainy Night, Charing Cross Shops*. This work also captures the sense that, by the end of the nineteenth century, the city was viewed in art and in literary texts as a transitory experience. Even in aestheticised views of the city, sharp diagonals were often inserted in the composition to speed the eye through pictorial space, conveying the idea of the depicted landscape being glimpsed on the move. The suburb, in particular, was perceived as an area to be traversed as a momentary and partial experience just as the suburb itself was seen as transitional between centre and countryside.

Artists started to appreciate that the massive proportions of London with its sprawling suburbs and extensive train networks, its sheer extent and complexity, meant the city could no longer be neatly drawn and encompassed. London was far from the neat, tidy watercolours of Thomas Shotter Boys or Thomas Hosmer Shepherd of the earlier Victorian period. 'London is a very difficult city to know – a city of bewildering contrasts, often tragically monotonous in its mean ugliness … hard in its materialism, yet always genial, city without too much tenacity of purpose, easily dismissed, easily bored . . .' wrote Sidney Dark, author of several illustrated books about London in which he used Pennell's prints to demonstrate his point.[14] Maps were still an essential means of picturing the city but they were of intricate and now industrial complexity and production, as instanced in Charles Booth's *Descriptive Map of Poverty*. The response of many artists seeking to depict London was therefore to draw upon the strong topographical tradition of picturing the city through place names and landmarks while distancing its uglier aspects through aesthetising light effects; they could retain an elevated, broad-sweep overview of the landscape while recording the daily life that signified the Imperial capital.

This dual experience of the city, namely a panoptical gaze coupled with an immersion in street life, is summed up in 'The Illustrious Client' when Holmes has lunch at Simpson's-in-the-Strand, 'looking down at the rushing stream of life in the Strand', at once a part of London life, able to immerse himself in the crowd and often to disappear into it, and yet set apart by his superior knowledge and ability to get to the truth. Holmes's knowledge of the city was crucial to the authenticity of the narrative, for the realism and naturalism of the locations contributed to the reader's awareness of his great deductive abilities. He had to be perceived by readers to be someone who knew London well, who could easily navigate the city despite the blanketing fog or extreme weather conditions that enveloped it. This detective personified the earlier view of the city that it could be categorised, classified, catalogued and comprehended, and he appears as a disciple of Henry Mayhew, a social analyst who tried to characterise the city as shown in *London Labour and the London Poor* (1851), or Douglas Jerrold, another investigative journalist, who wrote *London: A Pilgrimage*, 1872. Sherlock Holmes is no flâneur of aimless wandering but is purposeful around the city, navigating the often Gothic backdrop. He has a map of London in his head, which ensures he can successfully orient himself and arrive at the precise destination. He embodies in his detective work the reassuring solidity of an earlier Victorian society far from the hazy aestheticism of *fin de siècle*.

Throughout the stories, London streets are frequently name-checked and an imaginary map of London is formed for the reader. In 'The Empty House', according to Watson, 'Holmes's knowledge of the byways of London was extraordinary . . . [He] passed rapidly and with an assured step through a network of mews and stables, the very existence of which I had never known.' In *A Study in Scarlet*, a mantra of street names is recited – Wandsworth Road, Priory Road, Larkhill Lane, Stockwell Place, Robert Street, Coldharbour Lane – so that Holmes seems to personify the multifariousness of the city in all its dark ambiguities. When driving in a closed cab, Watson tells us, 'I lost my bearings and knew nothing save that we seemed to be going a very long way. Sherlock Holmes was never at fault however and he muttered the names as the cab rattled through squares and in and out by tortuous by-streets.' In repeated references throughout the stories, Conan Doyle makes clear that being 'well up on London' is an important part of Holmes's character. How unusual it is to have a mental map is highlighted in *A Study in Scarlet* when Jefferson Hope, the central character, becomes a cab driver in order to hunt down the wrongdoers: 'The hardest job was to learn my way about for I reckon that of all the mazes that ever were contrived this city is the most confusing. I had a map beside me and when once I had spotted the principal hotels and stations I got on pretty well.'

The fact that London could be mentally mapped by Sherlock Holmes, demonstrating his extraordinary powers to observe, detect and deduce in a city that many found overwhelming, disorientating and incomprehensible, is central to the elevation of the character. The context of the city and the impossibility (for the everyday Londoner) of controlling it, therefore, contributes to readers' appreciation of Holmes's intelligence. Ironically, this knowledge was not based on actual personal experience by Conan Doyle. He did not live a long time in central London (for less than a year, in 1891) although from his previous visits to the city as mentioned in letters to his mother, Mary Doyle, we glimpse the type of things he liked to do. For instance, he describes his visit to London in spring 1878 when he went to a violin recital of Neruda, attended lectures, visited the Royal Academy, lunched at the Saville Club, had dinner at the Langham Hotel, went to see Henry Irving in *Louis XI*, which made quite an impression, attended cricket matches at Lords, visited the Westminster Aquarium and spent time at the Guards' Parade where he caught a glimpse of the Crown Prince of Germany and the Duke of Cambridge, all the while looking at the clubs and public buildings illuminated in the evenings.[15] He admits in a letter of 1878 that he was too Bohemian for his hosts for he roamed about London, soaking up the atmosphere.[16]

The writing of the first series of Holmes stories coincided with Conan Doyle's move to London, where he had lodgings around 23 Montague Place at the back of the British Museum. In the census of 5 April 1891 the occupants are listed as Mary Gould spinster (54), who was the landlady; her sister Jane, who was a teacher at an elementary school; Jane Sutherland (64); Edwin Davies (18), clerk; Frank and Percy Jefferson, licensed victuallers; Carl Falstedt, the Swedish consul in Sidney and his English wife Cecilia; two domestic servants; and Arthur Conan Doyle (31), ophthalmic surgeon, his wife Louise (33) and their baby daughter Mary. Conan Doyle had rented a front room as a consulting room and had part use of a waiting room at 2 Upper Wimpole Street, which he shared with another doctor. He also signed up to the Royal Westminster Ophthalmic Hospital, so this central part of London featured very heavily in the stories as the point from which the narrative radiated outwards.

By the close of the nineteenth century, therefore, 'picturing' the city encompassed the desire to record beauty and distance ugliness as demonstrated in the works described above, but also included a focus on the precision of location and naturalistic detail. John O'Connor's (1830–1889) *From Pentonville Road looking West: Evening* 1884 evokes the worship of business, technology and modern transport as the Gothic spires of St Pancras railway station rise above the humdrum banality of street life where the ephemera of newspapers and advertisements litter the road and abandoned crates and baskets lie on the rooftop. Populated by grey figures hurrying home and horse-drawn trams and hansom cabs, this is not a fashionable street and, although not in the suburbs, it has the air of a rundown residential area, a conduit to the greener pastures beyond, not a place to linger but to hurry past. Pasted-over notices, such as the *Daily News*, present signs of the speed of incident and experience in the capital, where newspapers and magazines are thrown away and replaced every day. Painted from a deserted rooftop, looking downhill towards the setting sun, which illuminates St Pancras, a warmth is conveyed by the colouring in the sky in contrast to the bare stark branches of the tree, making the work a combination of aesthetic beauty, engineering prowess and the ephemeral. The railway station is glowing, its Gothic spires resonant of a cathedral, whereas the railway shed is almost invisible. It is a picture wholly of its time, for the tramline was only installed in 1883, but despite its photographic realism it is carefully composed with, for instance, in the foreground, one policemen, one postman emptying a red pillar box, one white horse trudging down the hill, one tram and one female figure in black, signalling with her umbrella – and it perfectly captures the prevailing aesthetic of the city.

From Pentonville Road looking West: Evening was bought by Sir Isaac Holden MP, who had a large estate in Yorkshire. It appears that he caught the train from St Pancras to his northern home.[17] The ability to move speedily from location to location, efficiently and punctually, is key to the narrative in the Holmes stories. Catching trains to rush from London to the scene of a crime is a frequent device used to move the action to different parts of the country, and, just as importantly, to enable clients to reach Baker Street to give their accounts to Holmes. For example, in 'The Dancing Men' Holmes takes the 3.40 train from Norfolk to be back in Baker Street for dinner; in 'The Solitary Cyclist', the governess rode to Farnham station on 23 April 1895 to catch the 12.22 to Waterloo; in 'The Priory School', Holmes caught the train from Euston to the north of England; in 'The Golden Pince-Nez', they negotiate the journey to Yoxley, seven miles from Chatham, by the Charing Cross train. The train and the train station were essential motifs of the modern city, indicating technological prowess, speed of communication and the fragmentary nature of society, which could no longer be viewed as an integrated phenomenon. In the painting *From Pentonville Road looking West: Evening* this dissonance is captured perfectly by the opposing

From Pentonville Road looking West: Evening, 1884, oil on canvas, John O'Connor

registers of emotion conveyed by the ethereal sky and Gothic spire, which evoke a sense of eternal spirituality, contrasting with the drab street, the railway terminus and the pasted advertisements pointing to the materiality of everyday life.

London therefore provided the necessary subject matter for the modern in both art and literature. Conan Doyle repeatedly emphasises the importance of London to Sherlock Holmes and to the plots in the adventures. In 'The Problem of Thor Bridge', we read that Holmes 'being like all great artists (he) was easily impressed by his surroundings' and for him only London it seems could supply the necessary raw material. As he says in 'The Norwood Builder', 'To the scientific student of the higher criminal world no capital in Europe offered the advantages which London then possessed.' In 'The Empty House', Holmes was 'free to devote his life to examining those interesting little problems which the complex life of London so plentifully presents'.

London always had the machinery of justice close by, ready to be activated, as noted in 'The Copper Beeches' when there was but a step between the crime and the dock, unlike the lawless countryside where crimes would remain undetected and unsolved. Sherlock Holmes's London in each story plays an active role in the narrative, not least by setting the scene and creating atmosphere and mood. The city also subtly influences how we feel about characters in the books as we assess them by where they live, how they live and by their appearance. The traces left by the city on these characters, on their clothes and skin, become part of the plot, so the city literally seeps into these figures, and the traces are visible to Sherlock Holmes as he investigates the crimes. By the close of each story, London appears as a benign presence, just as the satisfactory resolution of the plot instils a comfortable and satisfied feeling in the reader. The face of London changes throughout the story, mirroring the narrative, so that the ominous suspense and Gothic impenetrability of the early pages become, by the close, a resolution of crime and London a place where it is possible to walk safely in the sunlight. And this transformation, in which London itself is harnessed to the successful and satisfactory resolution of each plot, is key to understanding how the London of the stories retains its iconic status in our imagination.

Conan Doyle was working in an artistic climate, in which painters from the early 1870s were producing works to show the 'modern urban', following Antoine Proust's stricture that they 'had a duty to record for posterity the subjects of their own time, however ugly'.[18] They created a new vision of the city as defining and eternal as that of Sherlock Holmes. This fictional consulting detective is a proliferating cultural icon, a literary simalcrum without origin or end. Unsuccessfully killed off in 'The Final Problem', which was anything but final, in the same way as 'The Last Bow' was anything but last, Conan Doyle brought Sherlock Holmes back ten years later as a kind of copy of himself. Having revealed himself to Watson in 'The Empty House' in the disguise of a book collector, Holmes leads Watson through London to gaze at another version of himself, a model in wax, a museum exhibit in the window of Baker Street where the collector has become a collectible. Likewise, the artistic portrayals of London produced at the end of the nineteenth century have been endlessly reproduced, collected, exhibited and replayed so that this vision of the capital has become intimately and inextricably part of the myth that is Sherlock Holmes.

158 Sᴛ. Pᴀᴜʟ's Cᴀᴛʜᴇᴅʀᴀʟ ғʀᴏᴍ Lᴜᴅɢᴀᴛᴇ Cɪʀᴄᴜs

Alvin Langdon Coburn's London

These evocative photographs of London were taken by the American photographer Alvin Langdon Coburn (1886-1966). They provide a visual portrait of the city that epitomizes the character and mood of Sherlock Holmes's London. Published in 1909 with an introduction by Hilaire Belloc, Coburn's photogravures have a painterly look and feel, capturing above all the atmosphere of the capital. Their special quality was produced through the printing process which softened outlines within the image. Belloc writes of another 'character which may be arbitrarily noted is the effect upon London of its smoke and cloud'. The famous photograph, 'St. Paul's, from Ludgate Circus', sets the distinctive form of the cathedral against the smoke of a steam train and the general polluted air of the city.

WATERLOO BRIDGE

LONDON BRIDGE

Hyde Park Corner

St Paul's Cathedral from the river

Trafalgar Square

TOWER BRIDGE

Paddington Canal

LEICESTER SQUARE

REGENT'S CANAL

Westminster Bridge

KENSINGTON GARDENS 171

THE TOWER

ON THE EMBANKMENT

SHERLOCK HOLMES

CHAPTER FOUR

Throwaway Holmes

CLARE PETTITT

RTHUR CONAN DOYLE tried repeatedly to throw Sherlock Holmes away. As early as November 1891, when Holmes had only a few 'cases' to his name, Conan Doyle was already writing to his mother: 'I think of slaying Holmes . . . and winding him up for good and all. He takes my mind from better things.'[1] From then on, throughout the rest of his career, he launched sporadic and murderous attacks on his own creation. He tried to price the detective out of the market by asking seemingly preposterous sums of money for new stories; and he famously tried to kill him off by throwing him over the Reichenbach Falls in December 1893.[2] But Holmes was not to be thrown away so easily. The detective was to return to the pages of the *Strand* Magazine in 1901 and thereafter made frequent reappearances until 1927. Taking up Holmes again after a break, Doyle wrote wearily to his editor at the *Strand* Magazine, Herbert Greenhough Smith, '[y]ou will be amused to hear that I am at work on another Sherlock Holmes story. So the old dog returns to its vomit.'[3]

Smith was probably more delighted than amused. The appearance of a Sherlock Holmes story in an issue of the *Strand* was guaranteed to push sales figures up most satisfactorily. In 1908, twenty-one years after Holmes's first appearance in print, Conan Doyle was to supply the latest crop of Sherlock Holmes stories, later collected as *His Last Bow*, in time for the Christmas numbers of the magazine, ensuring a seasonal advantage over the increasing numbers of competitors in the now crowded middlebrow magazine market. After the first stories were published in the *Strand* in 1891 and 1892, Conan Doyle commanded large fees, so his attitude to this goose that kept laying him golden eggs is odd. Sherlock Holmes was a creation who outran his author's intentions, and continued to run and run. In fact, he ran beyond

Left: 'THE DEATH OF SHERLOCK HOLMES', FROM 'THE FINAL PROBLEM', THE *STRAND* MAGAZINE, DECEMBER 1893, SIDNEY PAGET

'*Holmes pulled out his watch*'.

ILLUSTRATION OF DR WATSON AND SHERLOCK HOLMES FROM 'THE GREEK INTERPRETER', THE *STRAND* MAGAZINE, SEPTEMBER 1893, SIDNEY PAGET

CHARING CROSS STATION

Lieu d'arrivée, point de départ !

Conan Doyle's control. Holmes was spawned and sustained by a new kind of press and a new kind of public sphere that Conan Doyle helped establish even while remaining deeply ambivalent about its throwaway ephemerality and what he perceived to be its lack of cultural authority.

The *Strand* Magazine was conceived by its founder, George Newnes, as being first and foremost 'engaging.' Modelled on American monthly family magazines, such as *Scribner's* and *Harper's*, the *Strand* generously promised an illustration on every page but was priced at only 6d (2½p) rather than a shilling (5p). Its characteristic blue covers were soon to

be spotted everywhere. Conan Doyle himself remarked to Smith that, '[f]oreigners used to recognize the English by their check suits. I think they will soon learn to do it by their *Strand* Magazines. Everyone on the Channel boat, except the man at the wheel, was clutching one.'[4] The *Strand* was greeted as a new kind of magazine, which called into being a new mode of reading. W.T. Stead described it as 'light reading from cover to cover; bright, entertaining, illustrated matter admirable for passing the time, and quite safe against suggesting forbidden speculations; nor does it provoke its readers to too great exercise of thinking.'[5] Reading as a method of 'passing the time' without the 'exercise of thinking' signals a kind of readerly distraction that is, I suggest, part of the essential context and meaning of the Holmes stories themselves. For these stories, all of which insist so forcefully and repeatedly on Holmes's peculiar quality and intensity of attention, are designed to be read and forgotten by distracted and inattentive readers. The stories play upon contemporary ideas about attention and distraction, and about ephemerality and consumption.

'I am all attention,' said Sherlock Holmes in 'The Greek Interpreter' and Conan Doyle's stories are structured around the rhythms of Holmes's attention and distraction. Holmes's restless interest is often 'waning' ('The Abbey Grange') but '[t]he swing of his nature took him from extreme languor to devouring energy' ('The Red-Headed League'). And when Holmes's attention is engaged, his focus is intense: '[h]e squatted down in front of the wooden chair and examined the seat of it with the greatest attention' ('The Speckled Band'). Yet Holmes can also be distracted, as when he 'sat in the stalls . . . enwrapped in the music at St. James's Hall' ('The Red-Headed League') or at '[a] Wagner night at Covent Garden' ('The Red Circle'), and his 'languid, dreamy eyes were as unlike those of Holmes the sleuth-hound, Holmes the relentless, keen-witted, ready-handed criminal, as it was possible to conceive' ('The Red-Headed League'). The alternation between Holmes's attention and his inattention in the stories is choreographed to reflect the attention and

Left: HEADING TO THE CONTINENT FROM LONDON: CHARING CROSS STATION, 1894, MAURICE BONVOISIN

PHOTOGRAPHIC PORTRAIT OF
SIR ARTHUR CONAN DOYLE,
C.1902

Right: COMMUTERS HEAD
HOMEWARDS FROM THE CITY:
LUDGATE HILL EVENING, PEN
AND INK DRAWING, C.1887,
JOHN O'CONNOR

inattention of a new urban and fast-moving readership. This was also a wide-ranging readership that spanned the social classes. The *Strand* was soon selling 300,000 to 400,000 copies a month in Britain, which in reality probably represented around a million readers per issue as the magazines were passed around, read in libraries and coffee shops, shared between friends and re-sold secondhand. Some of the Holmes stories were reprinted in *Tit-Bits* too, where they reached a second readership. This is a newly industrialised reading public made up of people hastily grabbing a copy of the *Strand* Magazine from the bookstall as they rush to catch boats and trains and omnibuses; they are reading on the run. Consuming their reading matter fast, allowing their attention to be temporarily or partly engaged, they read in order to be distracted from the discomfort of their journeys, from the idle time spent waiting in stuffy waiting rooms or from the banality of a daily commute.

Literary critics have been thinking quite a lot recently about issues of 'attention' and the kinds of attention, and sometimes the lack of attention, that readers give to certain kinds of writing. Do different genres invite different kinds of readerly attention? Do we attend to a long multi-plot novel, for example, differently from the way we attend to a short poem? What factors might alter our attention? If we read a poem on a poster displayed in a busy carriage on the underground, is that different from reading it in a book? And have there been key points in history when reading as a practice has substantially changed? Literary critic, Nicholas Dames suggests that in the nineteenth century there was an important shift in what he calls 'cultural norms of attentiveness', and he suggests that nineteenth-century reading practices were 'a training ground for the industrialized consciousness, not a refuge from it'.[6] Readers, he argues, were being trained in sifting and skimming through ever greater amounts of printed matter and information – editorial, advertising and fiction – learning to recognise the detail, the significant fact, the useful information in what Watson describes as the 'cloud of newspapers' that 'surround[s]' everybody in this newly enveloping world of print.

The newspapers had been reorganising and repackaging information in increasingly compressed ways from the mid-century onwards. News agencies, such as Reuters, which was established in London in 1851, syndicated stories, sending them out to a slew of regional papers in concise form and, in the later part of the century, transmitting them by cable, which made this concision even more necessary. What came to be known as the 'New Journalism' reflected these technological changes by developing a characteristic style and page-layout of striking headlines, short paragraphs and abundant illustration.[7] Publications such as *Tit-Bits*, which George Newnes launched in 1881 before he

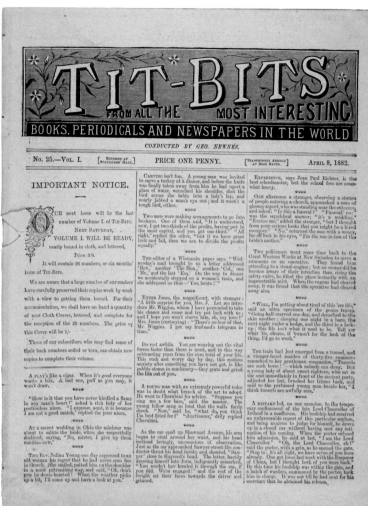

went on to create the *Strand* Magazine, were digests. They condensed text into excerpts or synopses – 'tit-bits' – for easier consumption. W.T. Stead, editor of the *Pall Mall Gazette*, launched the *Review of Reviews* in 1889, which used summary and condensation to 'sample' the plethora of British and foreign journals and present them as a series of snippets and extracts. Paradoxically, though, such brevity did not mean there was less to read, since the speed and volume of production, as Laurel Brake has shown, continued to increase, 'from quarterlies to monthlies to weeklies, to more than once a week, to dailies and to evening dailies'.[8] The digest is not a form of compression so much as a response to excess. This plethora of print demanded some new reading strategies in order to find and decode needful or useful messages from the mass of communicative possibilities.

This is where reading meets detection, as Holmes lectures Watson in 'The Reigate Puzzle': '[i]t is of the highest importance in the art of detection to be able to recognize, out of a number of facts, which are incidental and which vital. Otherwise your energy and attention must be dissipated instead of being concentrated.'

Conan Doyle resisted writing the Holmes stories as a 'serial' as such. He wrote to his editor: 'I don't suppose so far as I see that I should write a new "Sherlock Holmes" series but I see no reason why I should not do an occasional scattered story under such [a] heading a[s] "reminiscences of Mr Sherlock Holmes (Extracted from the Diaries of his friend, Dr James [*sic*] Watson)".'[9] The stories, although they exhibit all the apparatus of the serial with repeated characters and an episodic structure of 'cases', do not in fact function serially at all. Their chronology is far from a linear sequence, for a start, but rather dots about confusingly. Watson is constantly returning to old cases – 'I was looking over my old notes, and classifying some of our past results' ('The Stockbroker's Clerk') – or sometimes Holmes digs out old papers from a box, or is reminded of a distant case by perusing his voluminous collection of scrapbooks. Despite the precise dates and times we are often given – 'I find it recorded in my note-book that it was a bleak and windy day towards the end of March in the year 1892' ('Wisteria Lodge') or '[o]n referring to my notes, I see that it was upon the 14th April that I received a telegram from Lyons' ('The Reigate Puzzle') – the reader is not asked to care very much about the sequence of the cases. In Conan Doyle's autobiography he claims that the idea of 'a single character running through a series' of short stories struck him as an 'ideal compromise' between the two staples of the magazine market – the serial and the disconnected short story. 'I believe I was the first to realize this and "The Strand Magazine" the first to put it into practice,' he added.[10] This recurrent but non-serial structure seems to have allowed him to continue to think of Holmes as disposable, and it also encouraged the reader to move away from each episode after reading,

TALKING TO EUROPE: CONTINENTAL CIRCUITS CABLE ROOM, CENTRAL TELEGRAPH OFFICE, LONDON, 1891

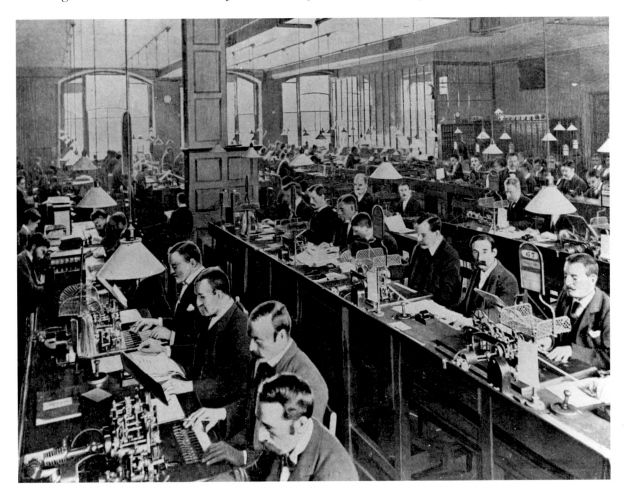

OFFICE TELEGRAPH TICKER
TAPE RECEIVER, C.1902

TELEGRAPH RECEIVER, C.1880

rather than attempt to form connections with the previous or the next episode as he or she might do, for example, in reading a serialised novel. Each Sherlock Holmes story could be quickly forgotten and left no trace. Indeed, the editor at the *Strand* was aware of this and on one occasion wrote to ask Conan Doyle, 'if you could insert a few lines at the beginning of the story, in order to make the character of Sherlock Holmes intelligible' to those who had not previously encountered the detective.[11] As Jim Mussell has noticed, this practice was, in fact, common to the *Strand* Magazine as a whole – '[e]ach number of the Strand was relatively self-contained: serial articles are scarce and rarely do narratives stretch between numbers.'[12] The reader's attention is not stretched beyond the contents of each edition, and the publication had no 'memory'. The *Strand* was deliberately commodifying itself for easy consumption and swift disposal.

The illustrated cover of the *Strand* Magazine reflected, like the Sherlock Holmes stories inside, 'the ever-changing kaleidoscope of life as it ebbs and flows through Fleet Street and the Strand' ('The Resident Patient').[13] Electric telegraph lines looped and dangled over the street and by the 1890s the central London roofline was messily entangled with the cables and wires. The telegraph as a means of sending coded messages down wires as electrical signals had developed alongside the railways in the 1830s and 1840s and by the late nineteenth century the telegraph network had spread across the globe. The cover of the *Strand* reminds its first readers that paper communications, such as letters, newspapers and journals, now coexist with a complex electrical communications network. Indeed, Holmes 'never wrote a letter when a telegram would suffice'. The Sherlock Holmes stories are insistently telegraphic in several senses. Most literally, Holmes is often seen stepping into 'the nearest telegraph office' in order to 'dispatch ... a long telegram' (*A Study in Scarlet*), and he keeps a stock of 'cable forms' ready in his study in Baker Street ('The Dancing Men'). Several stories start with a telegram, such as 'The Boscombe Valley Mystery' in which a message from Holmes interrupts Watson's breakfast with his wife, and Watson starts 'The Missing Three-Quarter' by acknowledging that '[w]e were fairly accustomed to receive weird telegrams at Baker Street'. Sometimes Holmes's telegrams are transatlantic, as in 'The Five Orange Pips' when a cable message from America provides a resolution, or in 'The Dancing Men' when Holmes cables his friend Wilson Hargreave of 'the New York Police Bureau' for information about a Chicago criminal, or in *A Study in Scarlet* when Holmes asks contacts in Cleveland to confirm his view of the case.

Holmes's messages, like all telegraphic messages, are translated into code for transmission and then decoded back into words at the

THE *STRAND* MAGAZINE
COVER DESIGNED BY GEORGE
CHARLES HAITÉ. THIS ISSUE
OF MARCH 1891 CONTAINS
ARTHUR CONAN DOYLE'S
STORY 'THE VOICE OF
SCIENCE', HIS FIRST TO BE
PUBLISHED IN THE MAGAZINE.

receiving station; and the Sherlock Holmes stories are more generally
'telegraphic' in the interest they show in speed, transmission, codes and
coding. In *A Study in Scarlet*, Jefferson Hope and John Ferrier overhear
two Mormon watchmen whispering 'Nine to seven!/Seven to five!' and
realise that '[t]heir concluding words had evidently been some form
of sign and countersign,' a realisation that will later save them their
lives, and the life of Lucy Ferrier, too. In 'The Red Circle', the Italian
word 'PERICOLO' is encoded in the flashes of a lamp. In 'The *Gloria
Scott*' Holmes produces 'a little tarnished cylinder' that contains 'a short

note scrawled upon a half-sheet of slate-grey paper: '*The supply of game for London is going steadily up. Head-keeper Hudson, we believe, has now been told to receive all orders for fly-paper and for preservation of your hen-pheasant's life.*' Holmes is able to decode this to: 'The game is up. Hudson has told all. Fly for your life.' Puzzled by the rows of pictograms of little dancing men that keep appearing at a Norfolk manor house, he explains to Watson that, 'I am fairly familiar with all forms of secret writings, and am myself the author of a trifling monograph upon the subject, in which I analyze one hundred and sixty separate ciphers.' Of course, Holmes has soon cracked the code of 'The Dancing Men' and is turning it back upon its criminal author, by trapping him with a message in his own code. The stories often graphically reproduce codes and puzzles, such as the 'facsimile' of the scribbled words on the corner of torn paper in 'The Reigate Puzzle', or the pictograms that dance and weave through the text of 'The Dancing Men', inviting the reader to choose whether to pause and attend carefully to the puzzle presented here, or to ignore it and read on for the solution.

nt me a letter then, imploring
way and saying that it would
art if any scandal should come
band. She said that she would

"See if you can read it, Wat
with a smile.
It contained no word, but t
of dancing men :—

when her husband was asleep at
morning, and speak with me
end window, if I would go away
nd leave her in peace. She

"If you use the code whic
plained," said Holmes, "you
it simply means 'Come here
was convinced that it was

As well as using the cable for point-to-point communications, Holmes also uses it as a means of quickly broadcasting a message publicly, resorting to the telegraph to place advertisements swiftly in the papers when he is out of town. These stories dramatise the close links, by the 1890s, between the 'wire' and the newsrooms and advertising offices of the London newspapers. "'I sent wires from Woking station to every evening paper in London. This advertisement will appear in each of them." He handed over a torn sheet from a notebook. On it was scribbled in pencil: £10 reward. The number of the cab which dropped a fare at or about the door of the Foreign Office in Charles Street at quarter to ten in the evening of May 23rd. *Apply 221B Baker Street*' ('The Naval Treaty'). Sometimes, though, he uses one of the rapidly proliferating 'advertising agenc[ies]' instead. In 'The Blue Carbuncle' he sends a boy to place an advertisement in the London evening papers, 'the Globe, Star, Pall Mall, St. James's, Evening News, Standard, Echo, and any others that occur to you.'

Holmes and Watson are, in fact, often to be found knee-deep in newspapers. Their messy shared rooms at 221B Baker Street are littered with discarded papers of all kinds. Holmes is 'buried in the morning papers' ('The Copper Beeches') and papers are frequently delivered to them – '[f]resh editions of every paper had been sent up by our newsagent' ('Silver Blaze') – and end up on the floor, so that Watson 'picked up the morning paper from the ground' ('A Case of Identity') and Holmes 'rummaged amidst his newspapers' ('The Blue Carbuncle'). Whenever he passes through a major railway station in London, Holmes takes the opportunity to procure a 'bundle of fresh papers' ('Silver Blaze'). Newsprint feeds Holmes so that he resorts to cocaine only when the 'papers were scanty' ('The Yellow Face') or 'the papers are sterile' ('Wisteria Lodge').

Newsprint also feeds the stories, since Conan Doyle elaborated upon

suspense.—HELENE.

C. W. F. W.—Communicate. Can have assistance. H. C. W. W.

DICKIE.—Will you meet Dick any day?—From DICK.

HONEY.—Sweetest and most wonderful of darlings, how good of you and how clever. I never expected you could have managed. How my heart goes out, and everything, to you, my precious. Fond kisses.

L. —Is "L" of the D.T. and M.P. my "L," otherwise "Europe," who went to "Am—ica"? If so "U" may trust me, otherwise "Melbourne," with an address to send a letter to.—Fondest love.—L.

MIMOSA S. and VIVIENNE, of Park-lane, would like to hear.—Write Kelly's Library, 54, Shaftesbury-avenue.

V. V. H. S.—Left P.-street, gone to Highgate. Make appointment.—V. V. H. S.

W. G.—Not to-morrow; next Friday certain. Am in the North.

ONE POUND REWARD.—LOST, on April 15, at Victoria Station, or between Baker-street and Victoria, a long, flexible GOLD BAND BRACELET.—Apply to F. H., 81, Cannon-street, E.C.

FIVE SHILLINGS REWARD.—LOST, between Belgrave-square and Mayfair, on May 18, a BUNCH of KEYS, containing one gilt and one latch key.—Apply to Bramah, 100, Bond-street.

LOST, on Tuesday morning, cream POODLE, not clipped. Answers to "Charlie." Liberal REWARD.—6, Stanhope-place, Marble Arch, W.

INSTITUTE of ACTUARIES' JUBILEE DINNER

actual news stories and found inspiration for many of Holmes's fictional cases in the personal columns of the London press. Newspapers are often pivotal to Holmes's cases, as in 'The Red-Headed League' when his client 'pulled a dirty and wrinkled newspaper from the inside pocket of his greatcoat', or when the client in 'A Case of Identity' produces the *Morning Chronicle* of 27 April, 1890, explaining that, "'I advertised for [Mr Hosmer Angel] in last Saturday's *Chronicle*," said she. "Here is the slip, and here are four letters from him."' Watson often uses the form of the newspaper article to advance the plot and summarise some of the key information in a case. In 'The Stockbrokers Clerk' he reproduces an entire article under the headline 'Crime in the City. Murder at Mawson & Williams's', which he claims is quoted from the 'early edition of the *Evening Standard*', and which provides important details for the reader. In 'The Engineer's Thumb' he plays the opposite game by telling the reader that '[t]he story has, I believe, been told more than once in the newspapers … set forth *en bloc* in a single half-column of print' but that it will be more 'striking' in his version 'when the facts gradually evolve before your own eyes and the mystery clears slowly away as each

READING ON THE MOVE:
A MAGAZINE SELLER AT
LUDGATE CIRCUS, 1893,
PAUL MARTIN

new discovery furnishes a step which leads on to the complete truth'. The newspaper maintains an indexical relationship to the Sherlock Holmes stories, and the narratives appear to recode the compressed 'half-column of print' into a complex narrative. It is a narrative that promises to do all the hard work of decoding itself, however, and the reader is not required to go to great efforts to penetrate its cryptography – the mechanism of the story is self-propelling and will carry the reader with it.

'I read nothing except the criminal news and the agony column,' announces Holmes, adding '[t]he latter is always instructive' ('The Noble Bachelor'). The political or national news rarely catches Holmes's attention. More often it is the personal advertisements that nourish him, such as 'the first announcement in the "Found" column' (*A Study in Scarlet*); or 'the advertisement sheet of the *Daily Telegraph*' ('The Copper Beeches'); or the trail that Watson traces through the newspapers in order to reconstruct the story of the marriage of 'Miss Hatty Doran,

SHERLOCK HOLMES

of San Francisco Calif.' from the personal columns of the *Morning Post*, to 'one of the society papers of the same week' and then again in the 'morning paper of yesterday' ('The Noble Bachelor'). The various editions, morning and evening, of the newspapers track a particular story through time as it unfolds. As Steven Marcus has noticed, '[w]e see Holmes reading a variety of daily newspapers, scanning them for the information that he more or less systematically files and processes'.[14] In 'The Copper Beeches', Sherlock Holmes is 'silent all the morning, dipping continuously into the advertisement columns of a succession of papers'.

With the relaxation of the advertising tax in 1853, the advertising sections of the newspapers began to expand rapidly, and *The Times* in particular became known for its second column of personal advertisements, which developed 'the moniker of the agony column for its "pathetic appeals for runaway husbands" and "plaintive cries for attention from lonely hearts".'[15] Other papers followed, and the *Leader* even re-published selections from *The Times* under the heading 'The Romance of *The Times*', explaining that '[s]ome of the strangest glimpses of the romance of reality that any place presents – not excluding the police offices – are to be found in that dusky, hieroglyphical, yet most humanly interesting, corner of the great diurnal. Tragedies, comedies, farces – love, wretchedness, despair – the outpourings of broken hearts, and the supplications of parents to their runaway children – the last struggles of desperate poverty, and the slow wiles of swindling – suggestions of strange plots, as yet in the bud.'[16] The personal columns of the London daily papers constituted a kind of broadcast medium *avant la lettre*, which Holmes himself is adept at tuning into and using. In 'The Blue Carbuncle' he first reminds us that, 'as there are some thousands of Bakers, and some hundreds of Henry Bakers in this city of ours, it is not easy to restore lost property to any one of them.' But Holmes is confident that Henry Baker will 'keep an eye on the papers' and see his advertisement offering to restore to Baker his lost hat and his goose – 'the introduction of his name will cause him to see it, for everyone who knows him will direct his attention to it.' The personal advertisements could command the focused attention of those for whom they were intended, despite being openly and publicly available to view for the 'four million human beings all jostling each other within the space of a few square miles' ('The Blue Carbuncle'). Holmes's use of advertisements as bait in the stories is very effective in representing a mass readership and an urban density of population that made it possible to lose people and things in the city, and difficult to find them again.[17] Indeed, things were constantly getting lost in the nineteenth-century city. Scotland Yard and the main London railway

Left: ELECTRONIC COMMUNICATION NETWORKS: DERRICK ABOVE HOLBORN TELEPHONE EXCHANGE, LONDON, c.1900

THE LOST PROPERTY OFFICE, METROPOLITAN POLICE DEPARTMENT, SCOTLAND-YARD.

termini all established Lost Property offices and, for an article in the *Strand* Magazine in 1895, William Fitzgerald visited all of them. He reported that the Great Eastern Railway Company Lost Property Office had accumulated among its unclaimed property: '140 handbags … five huge cases of books; 459 pairs of boots and shoes; 614 collars, cuffs and fronts; 252 caps; 505 deerstalker hats; 2000 single gloves; 230 ladies' hats and bonnets; 90 brushes and combs; 265 pipes; 110 purses; 100 tobacco-pouches; 1006 walking sticks; 300 socks and stockings; 108 towels; 172 handkerchiefs; [and] 2301 umbrellas'.[18]

In an accelerated information culture, efficient coding was becoming more and more urgently necessary. Locating and identifying individuals quickly in 'so dense a swarm of humanity' ('The Blue Carbuncle') was increasingly difficult.[19] Equally, any form of message transmission cost money and so technologies of information compression were developing fast. The newspaper advertisement columns were themselves bristling with compressed information in the form of cryptograms and codes. Alice Clay, who published a volume of anthologised personal advertisements from *The Times* in 1881, explained that, '[i]n some cases numbers have been substituted for the letters of the alphabet, and

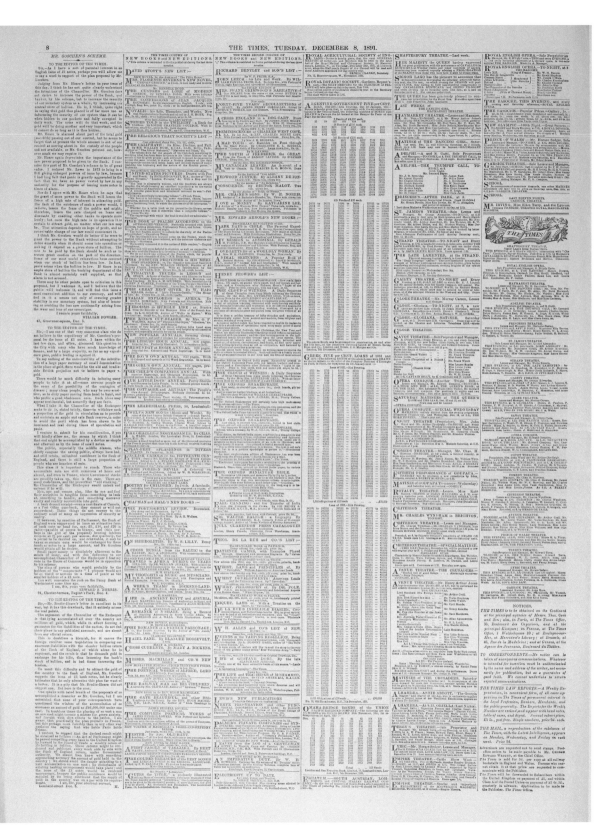

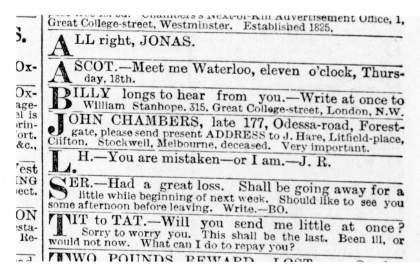

are easily deciphered,' but that, '[i]n some advertisements the alphabet is slightly altered. Instead of reading the letter B as printed, read C. Thus "head" would read "if be". An advertisement of this description is found on June 23rd, 1864 (No. 1387) – "Alexander Rochefort reported dead. I saw you yesterday. Moate vainly searched ten years."'[20] She adds, '[i]n advertisements No. 1701 and 1705 the alphabet is again altered, and this time more ingeniously. Instead of the letter written, supply the second following. Thus we read in the first, "Umbrella. Dear Fanny meet your distracted friend beneath the willow by the lake. Row under the stars. Common sea-breezes. Feather-weight. Yours, Bicycle".'[21] Alice Clay concludes that 'what looks so unintelligible at first sight may, with a little patience, be read as easily as the plainest English printed in our newspapers.'[22] Quite what 'Umbrella' and 'Bicycle' are doing here is hardly 'plain', however, and although Clay can break the codes, the meanings of many of these messages remain highly personal and utterly unfathomable.

It is the 'patience' at reading 'what is unintelligible at first sight' that Holmes supplies with his 'three pipe problem[s]' ('The Red-Headed League'), making 'minute and laborious investigations' so that his readers do not have to. But, in the new economy of attention and distraction that these stories are registering, the reader is both distracted by the 'easy-reading' middlebrow story, while simultaneously being given the pleasurable impression that she or he is being instructed in how to screen information for the significant detail. 'You did not know where to look, and so you missed all that was important,' Holmes tells Watson in 'A Case of Identity'. If Watson relates the stories as narratives of misdirection, Holmes's 'keen observance of detail and subtle power of inference' ('The Resident Patient') is rarely diverted from the details that matter. 'You know I like to work the detail of my cases out,' he says in *The Sign of Four*, yet the duration and effort of the 'patient' work involved in the cases is never fully represented, as Holmes speeds up the processes of deduction by cutting rapidly to the relevant information and assembling a solution. 'I pay a good deal of attention to matters of detail,' he says ('The Norwood Builder') but the reader rarely sees a redundant detail or a wrong turn. The effect is of almost telegraphic compression, speed and direction. None of the stories are very long, and they succeed by cutting out a lot of the 'noise' and redundancy that attends real-life communication.

Codes demand intense attention but once they are 'broken' or 'cracked', the auxiliary parts can be thrown away as merely the spent medium that has carried the important kernel of information. In the Sherlock Holmes stories, the solution of a code is analogous to, and sometimes coterminous with, the solution of the mystery itself. Like the code, detective fiction demands close attention but once the case is solved, it is easily shed and forgotten. Sherlock Holmes is often putting on his coat and consulting the railway timetable to plan his departure before Watson or the reader has quite understood how he has solved the case. Conan Doyle had struck upon a fundamentally ephemeral form that is not about development or *bildung* but is rather about processing, or consuming, the narrative until the essential information is assembled or discovered. These are narratives about deciphering information rather than about accumulating knowledge. Sherlock Holmes himself seems to consume his cases, to race through them, only to need another one: 'my mind . . . rebels at stagnation. Give me problems, give me work, give me the most abstruse cryptogram.' As distractions, his 'cryptograms' are addictive, compulsive and ultimately unsatisfactory. As commodities, the Sherlock Holmes stories command the reader's attention only enough to create a distraction and leave him or her eager for another.

If newspapers are fundamentally ephemeral, the agony columns, the 'lost and found' and the advertising sheets are surely the most ephemeral parts of the paper. They reflect the ephemerality of detective fiction as a form that constantly consumes itself, leaving nothing behind. But Conan Doyle's stories resist consigning themselves entirely to the throwaway culture. Against the ephemerality of the newspaper advertisement and the contingencies of code as a medium, there is another kind of paper in these stories. This is paper that is not thrown away, but, on the contrary, is carefully conserved and kept. While Holmes feeds on newspapers

MR. PUNCH'S PERSONALITIES.
XII.—SIR ARTHUR CONAN DOYLE.

CONAN DOYLE IMPRISONED BY HIS OWN CREATION AND UNABLE TO RID HIMSELF OF HOLMES: *PUNCH* MAGAZINE, MAY 1926, SIR BERNARD PARTRIDGE

Collier's

Household Number for October

DRAWN BY FREDERIC DORR STEELE

VOL XXXI NO 26   SEPTEMBER 26 1903   PRICE 10 CENTS

only to cast them aside, he is contradictorily and simultaneously shown with 'his gum brush' in his hand ('The Red Circle'). In his enormous collection of 'scrapbooks' he pastes 'reports from the *Daily Telegraph*, the *Standard*, the *Daily News*' (*A Study in Scarlet*). Sometimes it is Holmes and sometimes Watson who is the archivist. Watson remembers, 'I was looking over my old notes, and classifying some of our past results' ('The Stockbroker's Clerk'), and these 'ponderous commonplace books' ('The Engineer's Thumb') sit on the shelves at Baker Street alongside other reference materials, such as the *Continental Gazetteer, Lloyds's Shipping Register* and a *Guide to the Peerage*.

'[T]he great scrapbooks' ('The Red Circle') serve as Holmes's primary reference resource. 'Kindly look [Irene Adler] up in my index, Doctor,' he asks Watson in 'A Scandal in Bohemia', and Watson explains, '[f]or many years he had adopted a system of docketing all paragraphs concerning men and things, so that it was difficult to name a subject or a person on which he could not at once furnish information. In this case I found her biography sandwiched in between that of a Hebrew rabbi and that of a staff-commander who had written a monograph upon the deep-sea fishes.' This archival and encyclopedic Holmes seems the obverse of the eager consumer of the daily newspapers, racing through them only to cast them aside. An anxiety about keeping newspapers betrays, perhaps, Conan Doyle's own uneasiness with the mass culture of print that he saw around him. Holmes's scrapbooking seems often to coincide with a general 'tidying up' – 'as he had finished pasting extracts into his commonplace book, he might employ the next two hours in making our room a little more habitable' ('The Musgrave Ritual'). The will to transform the refuse and litter of old papers blowing around the streets and accumulating in the corners of 221B Baker Street into a valuable resource plays strangely against the lack of memory of the stories themselves, none of which truly remember each other, and indeed, as we have seen, in this they mirror the lack of memory in the *Strand* Magazine as a whole. Remembering, archiving, taxonomising and conserving sequence in the stories seems almost to suggest the opposite of the transmission of telegraph code and the cable. The swift and weightless electric pulses of the telegraphic signal stand contrary to the 'heavy brown volume[s]' ('Scandal in Bohemia') and 'ponderous' scrapbooks on Holmes's shelves. Speed seems to collide with slowness here, and this contrast perhaps points towards an unresolved tension in the whole of the Sherlock Holmes enterprise. Conan Doyle's anxieties about this new world of print at the end of the nineteenth century meant that Holmes was intended to be thrown away. But, in fact, of course, he was not thrown away. The *Strand* Magazine was itself bound into large volumes by libraries and by schools and also by private

PICTORIAL COVER OF AN EARLY PIRATED COPY OF ARTHUR CONAN DOYLE'S SECOND SHERLOCK HOLMES NOVEL AND THE FIRST TWO SHORT STORY COLLECTIONS, c.1900, JAMES ASKEW AND SONS, PRESTON

Left: ENDLESS HOLMES: 'THE RETURN OF SHERLOCK HOLMES', COVER OF *COLLIER'S* MAGAZINE, SEPTEMBER 1903, FREDERIC DORR STEELE

families, who often kept the volumes on their bookshelves, and returned to them time and again. The Holmes stories themselves were collected and reissued as a series of books, but even collected and bound between covers, the stories retained some of their original disposability and interchangeability.

If the stories are 'distractions' which 'take [the] mind from better things', as Conan Doyle suggested, it is this very anxiety about their ephemerality that, paradoxically, has ensured their permanence and endurance. At one level these stories ask difficult questions about how to cope with a newly-accelerated information culture. What is the best strategy – speed reading or slow reading? Can anything permanent be rescued from the ephemeralities of the newspaper? Do the detective stories of Sherlock Holmes disappear after reading? Clearly they have not, in fact, disappeared at all, as they continue to circulate so powerfully in our culture today, but that is partly because Conan Doyle, perhaps unintentionally, built into his stories this very anxiety about their repeatability. The stories operate under a logic of substitution, which is the logic of coding and cryptography, but is also the secret code that explains the eternal life of Sherlock Homes, the detective whom Edgar W. Smith, the founder of the *Baker Street Journal*, described in 1944 as an 'age-less timeless man'.[23]

If codes depend on substitution for encryption – the substitution of one letter or one word for another – substitution is also a recurring motif in the stories. In 'The Copper Beeches', one person is substituted and sits in place of another; Mr Hall Pycroft is substituted by another in 'The Insurance Clerk'; and in 'The Empty House' Holmes is himself replaced by a French 'bust in wax' puppeteered by a very obliging Mrs Hudson. The logic of substitution obtains beyond these local examples, though. Once a reader has read through a substantial number of the fifty-six short stories and the four novels that make up the phenomenon that we call 'Sherlock Holmes', it becomes very difficult to remember exactly what happened in any particular story, or to place it in any kind of sequence with any of the others. But oddly, it is precisely this disconnection between the stories that is what drives their lasting appeal. Although they are designed to be consumed, they are not a serial, so they do not develop as a sequence with a beginning or an end. Instead, Holmes is in perpetual motion, and there is no end to the times that the stories can be re-read or rearranged. One story can substitute for another because they all act out the same process of un-puzzling.[24]

The fact that there is no serial or linear chronology for Holmes's cases makes it, in fact, impossible to throw Holmes away, as Conan Doyle discovered. He is, literally, 'endless'. In his undead state, he can be remediated back into presence through any number of technologies –

print, theatre, radio, film and television. The oft-discussed 'timelessness' of Holmes, then, is perhaps not so much about reactionary nostalgia as about the peculiar and partly accidental modernity of the stories themselves. Matt Hill has argued that 'Holmes represents the benevolent bourgeoisie – with his servants, his biographer, his proletarian helpers, his payment per case – all clothed in meritocratic garb,' and, discussing Steven Moffatt and Mark Gattis's BBC hit series of 2010, *Sherlock*, he warns darkly that 'we fail to see that such reboots in fact retreat into ideologies of cultural timelessness, albeit deceptively dressed up in the sharp suits and billowing coats of fashionable transformation.'[25] I am not so sure. If we read the stories in the context of their media history as being, from their very first appearance, always in some sense 'about' the ephemeral, a pessimistic reading of them as 'reactionary' does not prove ultimately sufficient. Benedict Cumberbatch's Sherlock Holmes is not at all '*deceptively* dressed up . . . [and] . . . fashionable' because the stories were always about the moment when 'fashion' became available and affordable for more and more people, deliberately written for a mass readership in a cheap magazine with a huge circulation in a newly throwaway culture. Sherlock Holmes was very much 'in fashion' in the 1890s, and the Sherlock Holmes phenomenon continues to represent the ephemeral commodity that is always in play, always moving, always circulating, and always still pleasurable and desirable because it has never 'finished'.[26] This reading still relies on Marx's definition of the commodity as a quintessentially mobile 'thing', but resists the pessimism of the 'bourgeois' reading of Holmes, because it is too quick to discount the importance of the process of the democratisation of leisure and reading of which the Holmes stories were so much a part. The 'reactionary bourgeois' reading of the stories forecloses on some of the complex ways in which these narratives collided with a newly emerging public sphere and ephemeral print culture, and a new understanding of distraction, leisure and pleasure at the end of the nineteenth century.

It is still surely 'of the highest importance' in the twenty-first century 'to be able to recognize, out of a number of facts, which are incidental and which vital' and in our continually spawning internet-media culture ,we are perhaps ever more in danger of our 'energy and attention [being] dissipated instead of being concentrated' ('The Reigate Puzzle'). The complex ways in which the Sherlock Holmes stories continue both to command our attention and allow our distraction may still be training us to cope with the insistent rhythms and counter-rhythms of an accelerating information culture today, because we may not, in fact, have travelled as far away from the intense modernity of the late nineteenth century as we sometimes like to think.

FASHIONABLE TRANSFORMATION? BENEDICT CUMBERBATCH AS SHERLOCK HOLMES

'In rapid succession we passed through the fringe of fashionable London, hotel London, theatrical London, literary London, commercial London, and, finally, maritime London, till we came to a riverside city of a hundred thousand souls, where the tenement houses swelter and reek with the outcasts of Europe.'

The Six Napoleons

Maps of Sherlock Holmes's London

Arthur Conan Doyle had only a limited knowledge of London when wrote his first two Sherlock Holmes short novels – *A Study in Scarlet* and *The Sign of Four*. To enable him to plot the journeys that Holmes and Watson made across the city, he used a Post Office map of London. The size and complexity of the city meant that maps were needed to make sense of its geographical layout, especially the thousands of streets and alleyways as well as numerous bridges and railway stations. Maps had to be constantly updated, so rapid was the change to the metropolis especially in the new suburban districts as the railway network expanded. Booth's famous 'Descriptive Map of London Poverty' identified the income and social class of inhabitants in every street of the city through colour coding. Eight different colours were used to distinguish the different classes of society. A street coloured black represented 'The lowest class. Vicious and semi-criminal' while a yellow or gold street stood for 'Upper-middle and Upper classes. Wealthy'.

Right: LONDON: DRAWN AND ENGRAVED EXPRESSLY FOR THE POST OFFICE DIRECTORY, KELLY & CO., 1884

Overleaf: SECTIONS OF CHARLES BOOTH'S ORIGINAL HAND-COLOURED 'DESCRIPTIVE MAP OF LONDON POVERTY', 1888-91

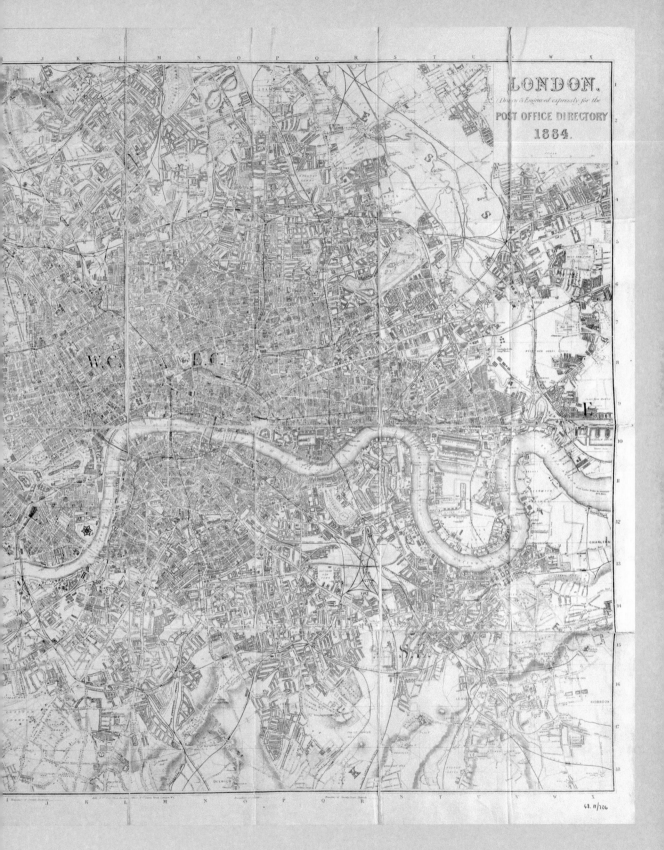

1. Charles Booth: Vicinity of Baker Street

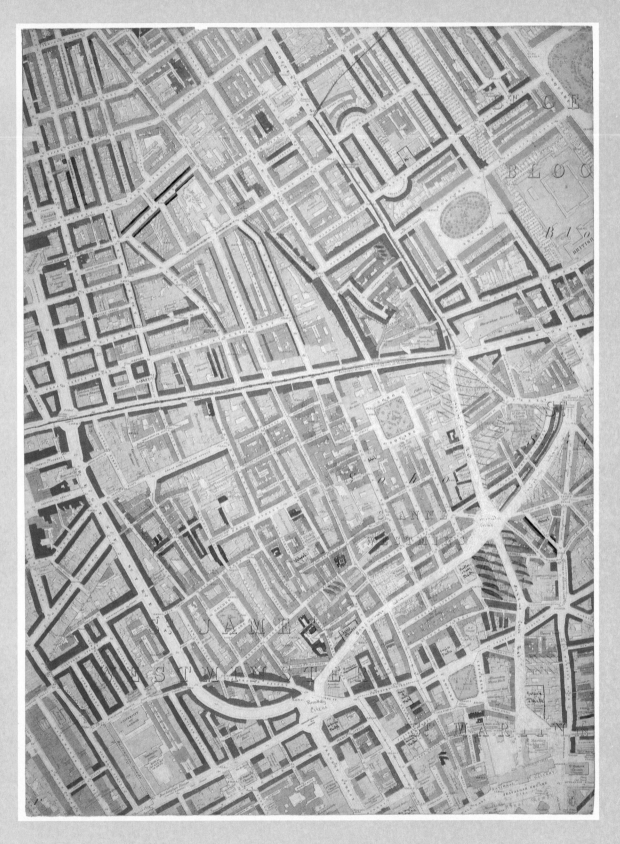

2. Charles Booth: Area around Piccadilly Circus

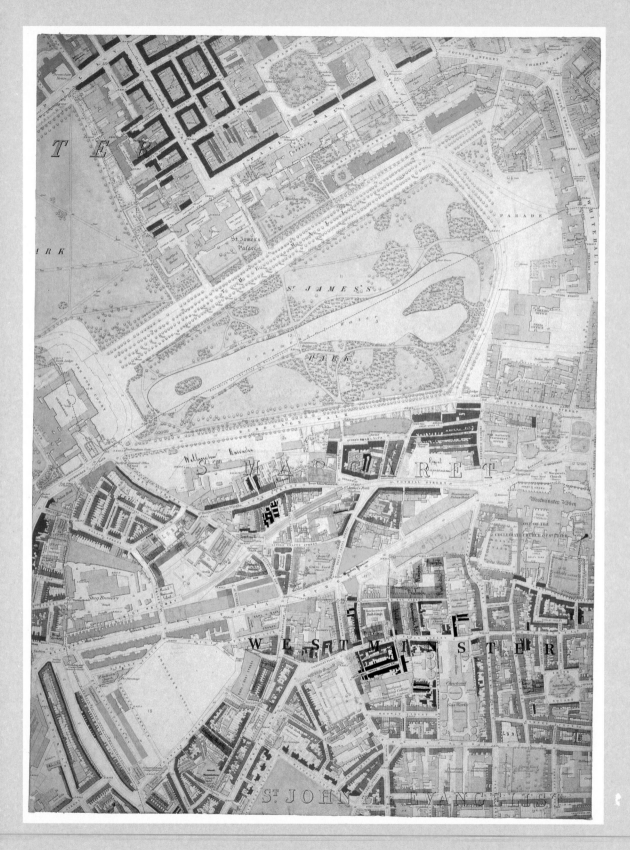

3. CHARLES BOOTH: WESTMINSTER

4. CHARLES BOOTH: LAMBETH AREA

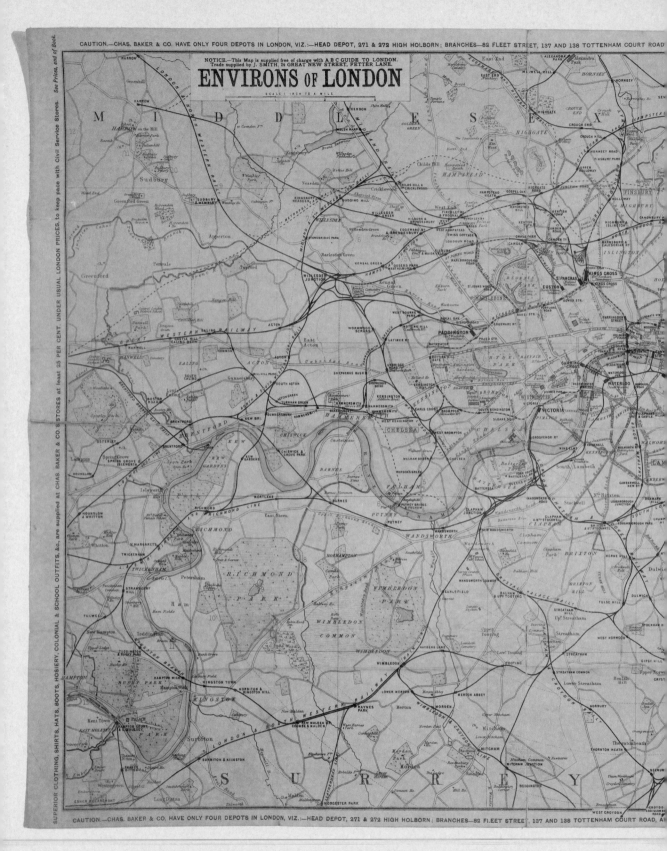

NOTICE.—This Map is supplied free of charge with A B C GUIDE TO LONDON.
Trade supplied by J. SMITH, 24 GREAT NEW STREET, FETTER LANE.

ENVIRONS OF LONDON

SCALE 1 INCH TO A MILE

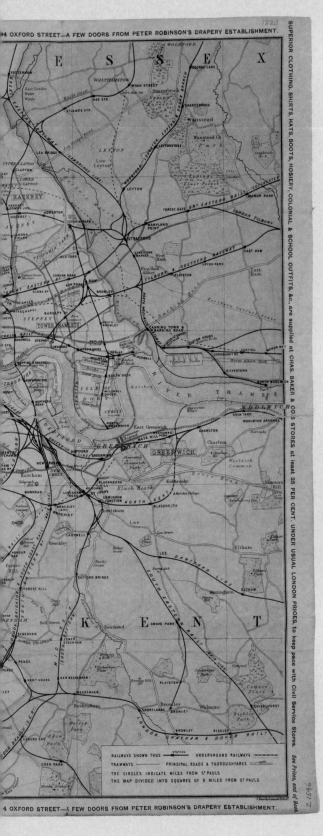

4 OXFORD STREET—A FEW DOORS FROM PETER ROBINSON'S DRAPERY ESTABLISHMENT.

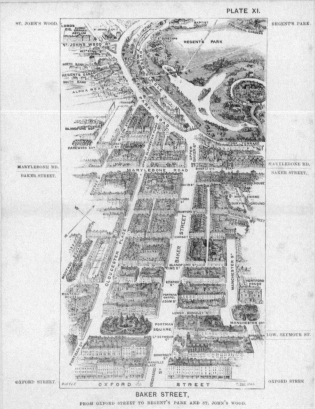

PLATE XI.

BAKER STREET,
FROM OXFORD STREET TO REGENT'S PARK AND ST. JOHN'S WOOD.

'It is a hobby of mine to have an exact knowledge of London.'

'The Red-Headed League'

Above right: 'BIRD'S-EYE VIEW OF BAKER STREET', 1887, FROM HERBERT FRY'S LONDON

Left: CHARLES BAKER'S MAP OF THE 'ENVIRONS OF LONDON', FROM THE *ABC GUIDE TO LONDON*, 1884

Overleaf: 'THE DISTRICT RAILWAY MAP OF LONDON', 5TH EDITION, c.1892

5TH EDITION.

THE "DISTRICT RAILWAY

PUTNEY BRIDGE & WIMBLEDON SECTION

DISTRICT RAILWAY MAP OF LONDON

District Railway Map of London

CHAPTER FIVE

Silent Sherlocks: Holmes and Early Cinema

NATHALIE MORRIS

THE SCREEN HAS ALWAYS loved Sherlock Holmes. To date there have been hundreds of Holmes film and TV adaptations, to say nothing of scores of theatre plays and radio programmes based on his exploits. As well as spanning media, the character has also crossed continents; he is an internationally recognised name and a significant cultural export. Recent big-screen outings, including *Sherlock Holmes* (2009) and *Sherlock Holmes: A Game of Shadows* (2011), and the popularity of the ongoing BBC series *Sherlock* (begun in 2010), which cleverly brings Holmes into the twenty-first century, demonstrate that more than 125 years after his first appearance in print, Sherlock Holmes is as appealing as ever.

Sir Arthur Conan Doyle, on the other hand, famously fell out of love with his greatest creation. In 1893, he tried to kill him off in 'The Final Problem', but was driven to resurrect him a decade later. By this time, Holmes had already taken on a life of his own on paper, stage and screen, which was quite independent of his progenitor. Sidney Paget's illustrations for the *Strand* Magazine fixed the popular image of Holmes early on and shaped subsequent portrayals, as did the performance of American actor William Gillette (1853–1937), who wrote and starred in the hugely successful *Sherlock Holmes: A Drama in Four Acts*, first performed in 1899. In the years between then and Conan Doyle's death in July 1930, the new medium of film evolved, and countless Sherlocks appeared in a wide array of adaptations, parodies and pastiches.

This chapter looks at Holmes's early on-screen outings, from his first film appearance up to the time of Conan Doyle's death. It considers the importance of Conan Doyle's original stories, Paget's *Strand* illustrations and the influence of Gillette on early screen portrayals of the great detective. It surveys a wide selection of international films, looking at some of the different ways in which film makers used the figure of Holmes, and how Conan Doyle occasionally responded to these. Authorised adaptations made during the author's lifetime are

Left: ACTOR EILLE NORWOOD WITH SIR ARTHUR CONAN DOYLE. THE AUTHOR DESCRIBED NORWOOD'S PORTRAYAL OF HOLMES AS 'MASTERLY'. PHOTO TAKEN AT THE STOLL FILMS CONVENTION DINNER AT THE TROCADERO BALLROOM, 27 SEPTEMBER 1921.

MR. WILLIAM GILLETTE AS SHERLOCK HOLMES.

IN HIS BIRD'S-EYE CLOUDS HE SEES HIS SWEETHEART, THE "BASHER," THE FRENCH MAID, HIS PAGE-BOY, THE
SCOUNDREL LARRABEE AND THE VILLAIN MORIARTY.

STAGE ACTOR WILLIAM
GILLETTE'S PORTRAYAL OF
HOLMES IN 1899'S *SHERLOCK
HOLMES: A PLAY IN FOUR
ACTS*, REMAINED HIGHLY
INFLUENTIAL THROUGHOUT
THE SILENT PERIOD. GILLETTE
HIMSELF PLAYED HOLMES
ON SCREEN IN 1916, A
PERFORMANCE WHICH IS
SADLY LOST.

vastly outnumbered by the host of films that simply took the character of Holmes and placed him in entirely new situations. These different approaches are examined, with a special focus on the later British (or Franco-British) works drawn directly from the original adventures and adapted with Conan Doyle's blessing. The most important of these were undoubtedly the two feature-length and forty-five short films produced by Stoll Picture Productions between 1921 and 1923, which created an iconic Holmes in the form of actor Eille Norwood, and also advanced methods of telling detective stories on screen.

Throughout the time Holmes was being adapted to the screen, Conan Doyle was continuing, albeit intermittently, to write Holmes stories. The last, 'Shoscombe Old Place', was published in 1927, forty years after Holmes's debut appearance in print. This meant that Conan Doyle was creating new, largely Victorian-set, adventures for his character while a host of other modern interpretations, which often shaped audiences' ideas of the look and personality of his detective, were being created all around him. Although he took pleasure in seeing a fine impersonation of his detective, Conan Doyle was not overly precious about how others presented Holmes, generally reserving his concern for adaptations of his more 'serious' fiction, such as *The House of Temperley* (filmed in 1913), *The Firm of Girdlestone* (filmed in 1915) and *Rodney Stone* (filmed in 1920). When William Gillette cabled him to ask if he could introduce an element of romance into his play and have Holmes marry, Conan Doyle famously replied: 'You may marry or murder or do whatever you like with him.'[1]

First films

THE FIRST KNOWN FILM to feature the character of Sherlock Holmes was the American Mutoscope and Biograph Company's *Sherlock Holmes Baffled* (c.1900). This trick film is less than a minute long and, pre-dating cinemas, was originally shown via coin-operated, peep-show devices to just one person at a time. It features an unknown actor as Holmes, and exploits the technical trickery of the still-new medium to confound the detective with a thief who breaks into Baker Street and appears and disappears at will. Via the detective's long and distinctive dressing gown, the film draws visually on the most famous Holmes adaptation to date at that time, William Gillette's stage impersonation in *Sherlock Holmes: A Drama in Four Acts*.

Another early parody was the Danish film *Sherlock Holmes at Elsinore* (1906), and many parodies and burlesques followed, such as *Hemlock Hoax, the Detective* (1910, Lubin), Pathé's *Charlie Combs* series (1912), *Sherlock Bonehead* (Kalem, 1914) and *The Mystery of the Leaping Fish* (1916, Triangle-Fine Arts) with Douglas Fairbanks as detective Coke Ennyday, referencing Holmes's infamous drug habit. But as film narratives developed and running times lengthened, a number of more serious Holmes films began to be made, primarily in northern Europe. In 1905, the American Vitagraph company made *The Adventures of Sherlock Holmes*, based loosely on *The Sign of Four*, with (it is generally thought) Maurice Costello as Holmes. From 1908 to 1911, the Danish Nordisk company, a major player during the early silent era, released a series of twelve Holmes films, none of which were based on the original stories. Two of these films feature Holmes facing off against gentleman burglar Raffles, a character originally created by

WILLIAM GILLETTE IN THE PLAY *SHERLOCK HOLMES* WITH ALICE FAULKNER (KATHERINE FLORENCE), ACT I, c.1900, SARONY

HOLMES RETURNING THE PACKET TO MISS FAULKNER—ACT I

Arthur Conan Doyle's brother-in-law, E.W. Hornung. It was a common device to pit the great detective against well-known fictional criminals created by other authors, a precursor to later twentieth-century adaptations, which have tested Holmes against the now almost mythical figure of Jack the Ripper, as in *A Study in Terror* (1965) and *Murder By Decree* (1979).[2]

Around the same time that Nordisk started making their series, the German Vitascope company produced the five-episode serial *Arsène Lupin Contra Sherlock Holmes* (1910–1911). This was based on author Maurice LeBlanc's *Arsène Lupin Contra Herlock Sholmes* in which Conan Doyle's detective faces LeBlanc's roguish burglar (Conan Doyle had refused LeBlanc permission to use his character's name but Vitascope had no such qualms over copyright). Holmes was also pitted against other fictional detectives, as in a 1912 French film (the original title of which appears to be lost, but which translates from German as something like), *Clever, Cleverer, Cleverest!*[3] In this film Holmes tests his wits against Nick Carter, Nick Winter and Nat Pinkerton, the detective heroes from series produced by the French studios Éclair, Pathé and Eclipse, respectively. Unfortunately, on this occasion, Holmes did not prove to be the cleverest and, in what now seems like an unthinkable conclusion, Nat Pinkerton triumphed over the great detective, perhaps a small revenge on the part of the French after the literary Holmes notoriously dismissed the skills of fictional French detectives Dupin and Lecoq in *A Study in Scarlet*.

The onset of the First World War did not halt the German obsession with the British Holmes. In 1914, Vitascope released *Der Hund Von Baskerville*, with Alwin Neuss as Holmes. Based on earlier stage adaptations rather than being taken directly from Conan Doyle's original, *Der Hund* takes various liberties with its source text. It is set in Scotland and, as Jay Weissberg notes, includes devices, such as secret pipelines and a watchful bust of Napoleon, that seem drawn from Louis Feuillade and French crime serials, such as *Fantômas* (1913–14) and *Les Vampires* (1915–16). *Der Hund* was so successful that a sequel with the same cast and crew was rushed into production, and a further five sequels were to follow before 1920.

The British are coming

EANWHILE, BRITISH PRODUCERS were finally getting in on the act. In 1912 the comic and semi-parodic *A Canine Sherlock Holmes* (Urban Trading Company), starring Spot the Dog, appeared, but at the same time the first authorised adaptations of Conan Doyle's stories by Éclair/Franco-British Films were being released. In 1911 Conan Doyle sold the Holmes film rights to French company Éclair for what the author himself recalled was 'a small sum'.* The issue of copyright around screen adaptations of literary works was, and for some time remained, unclear. As we've seen, throughout the 1900s and 1910s,

THERE WERE NUMEROUS PARODIES AND PASTICHES ON HOLMES DURING THE SILENT PERIOD SUCH AS THIS BRITISH TITLE, *A CANINE SHERLOCK HOLMES* (1912).

European and American film makers played fast and loose with the character of Holmes and – when they used them – with Conan Doyle's plots. Although this state of affairs would persist, the introduction of the 1911 Copyright Act widened the scope of copyright protection to include the moving image and recognised that the copyright in literary works could be infringed by an unauthorised film adaptation. Conan Doyle took advantage of this legislation to gain some financial benefit from film makers' obvious desire to put Holmes on the screen, and Éclair consequently produced the very first authorised Holmes film, *Les Aventures des Sherlock Holmes*, directed by Victorin Jasset with Henri Gouget as Holmes.

The following year, the company began a Franco-British co-produced series. This was directed by and starred French actor Georges Treville, but the rest of the cast were English and the films were shot in the south of England. It was a series of eight films with titles all taken directly from the original adventures. Of these, just two are known to survive, *The Copper Beeches* and *The Musgrave Ritual*. Keen to highlight their official status, advertisements for the films promoted the notion of Conan Doyle's involvement, even going so far as to say that some titles were made under the 'personal supervision' of the author. Whether or not this is true, it was clear that the films' authorised status was viewed as a strong selling point. It offered a way to differentiate these films from the more sensational crime serial style of most other Holmes films to date, thereby enticing a different, more literate, class of picture-goer into cinemas.[5]

Despite being authorised, the films nonetheless did not adhere rigidly to their sources. David Stuart Davies has pointed out that in *The Speckled Band*, for instance, Holmes apparently disguises himself as a wealthy foreigner in order to visit the formidable Dr Grimesby Roylott, to ask for permission to marry his step-daughter.[6] Likewise, *The Copper Beeches* differs significantly from the original by unravelling the series of events to present them chronologically, thereby removing all element of mystery from the story. In Conan Doyle's original, the adventure begins with Violet Hunter visiting Holmes to discuss an odd proposition with him. She has been asked to take up a position as governess on the condition that she cuts off her long hair. Holmes begins to investigate when other strange aspects of life at the Copper Beeches come to light. The film, on the other hand, starts by presenting the back story that is driving the whole mystery – Jethro Rucastle's imprisonment of his daughter to prevent her marrying. An intertitle immediately makes his reason for engaging Miss Hunter perfectly clear: 'Rucastle seeks, at the Westaway Agency, a governess resembling his daughter.' Holmes himself does not appear until halfway through the film and we, the audience, are in the unusual position of knowing more than he, until the mystery is solved at the very end. In this respect, *The Copper Beeches* treats its narrative in the same way as many early crime and detection films. As silent-film scholar Tom Gunning notes in an essay on the almost-contemporaneous French serial *Fantômas*, early crime narratives rarely withhold knowledge from their audience. Early film makers apparently had 'doubts about the ability of audiences to follow a non-chronological exposition of earlier events', especially as 'these could actually reconfigure the meaning of events already shown'.[7]

The narrative conundrum of how to tell a complex mystery story on the screen was one that continued throughout the teens. In 1914, *A Study in Scarlet*, the first British feature-length film to be based on Holmes's adventures, was released.[8] Sadly, the film is lost, but reviews and contemporary synopses of the story indicate that this, too, was re-ordered to show all events chronologically, instead of

presenting a mystery that is solved and then fully explained, as in the 1887 novella. The film therefore opens in the Utah Valley (filmed in the UK at Southport Sands) and follows the story of Lucy Ferrier and Jefferson Hope, and Hope's subsequent stalking of his enemies while he bides his time for revenge. Reviews consequently commented on the fact that Holmes appears in the film's final two reels only, after Hope finally closes in on his quarry.[9]

In *A Study in Scarlet*, Holmes was played by an unknown studio employee, James Bragington, cast for his physical resemblance to Holmes. George Pearson, the film's director, strongly believed that 'much depended upon his physical appearance, build, height, and mannerisms' and felt that even though Bragington was not an actor, he would be able to direct his performance effectively enough for the role.[10] Although Pearson professed himself pleased with the outcome, when he came to make *The Valley of Fear* two years later, Bragington did not feature. Instead, Holmes was played by the renowned stage actor H.A. Saintsbury. Saintsbury had already become synonymous with the part through theatre performances in the UK production of William Gillette's *Sherlock Holmes* and later in *The Speckled Band* (1910), adapted for the stage by Conan Doyle himself. Saintsbury's performance was

LIKE WILLIAM GILLETTE,
THE BRITISH ACTOR H.A.
SAINTSBURY PLAYED HOLMES
ON STAGE AND SCREEN IN
THE VALLEY OF FEAR (1916).
LIKE GILLETTE, HIS FILM
PERFORMANCE TOO, IS LOST.

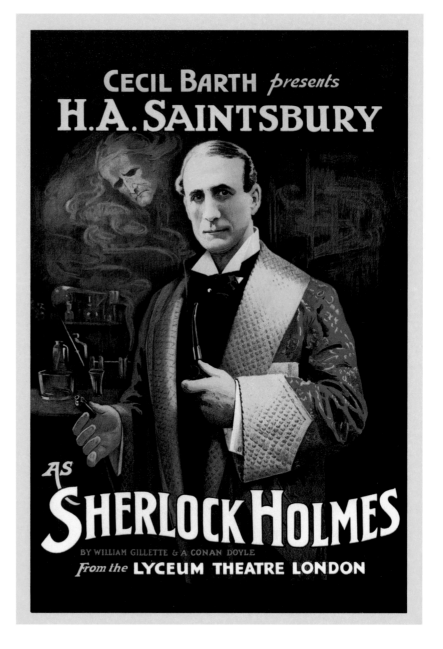

modelled on that of Gillette, who was still unquestionably the most influential personification of the great detective up to this time. In fact, in 1916, Gillette also finally committed his portrayal to the screen in Essanay's version of the play, *Sherlock Holmes*. As David Stuart Davis points out, this film was made at a time when many famous stage actors were being sought by Hollywood to recreate their most iconic roles on screen. Like *A Study in Scarlet* and *The Valley of Fear*, however, *Sherlock Holmes* is another lost film.

Stoll and Sherlock

SIGNIFICANT DEVELOPMENT in the history of Holmes on the screen occurred in 1920 when British company Stoll bought the rights to adapt the short stories and the two novellas, *The Hound of the Baskervilles* and *The Sign of Four*, with Eille Norwood as Sherlock Holmes. Conan Doyle had bought back his copyright from Éclair at, he claimed, 'exactly ten times' what he had received in the first place,[11] and his new deal with Stoll would net him ten per cent of the films' gross takings.[12] Stoll Picture Productions had been set up by variety theatre impresario Sir Oswald Stoll with the intention of making quality British films that could compete with Hollywood on home territory. Key to Stoll's strategy was the adaptation of popular, middlebrow literature, and the company produced a number of feature-length films that were marketed under the blanket series title of 'Eminent British Authors'. The Sherlock Holmes films became the jewel in the crown of this programme. Starting in 1921 with *The Adventures of Sherlock Holmes* series, fifteen two-reel films were released each year for three years – *The Further Adventures* in 1922 and *The Last Adventures* in 1923. Complementing these were the two features, *The Hound of the Baskervilles* in 1921 and *The Sign of Four* in 1923.

Adapting the Holmes stories as a series of short films (each ran for around half an hour) was a sound idea for many reasons. The two-reel format meant that the adventures did not need to be padded to stretch their running time to feature length. By releasing them as shorts on a regular weekly basis, Stoll was able to capitalise on the very strategy that had popularised Holmes with the reading public upon his first appearance in the *Strand* Magazine in 1891. At this time, Conan Doyle had astutely perceived that the serialised fiction published in many popular magazines at the time could be as much hindrance as help to a publication seeking a dedicated readership 'since, sooner or later, one missed a number and afterwards it … lost all interest'.[13] A series, however, with self-contained narratives but with an engaging central character who was a steady presence throughout, could help tie a reader to that particular publication. As Reginald Pound, historian of the *Strand*, puts it, readers could 'share the linked excitements of a serial without being committed to following every instalment'.[14] Stoll's films would have been shown as part of a typical 1920s changing, mixed programme, which would have included newsreels, cinemagazines, advertisements, cartoons and other short films, as well as the main feature/s. While the company sought to capture a regular dedicated audience by implementing a weekly release schedule and advertising individual titles with their own posters and

Right: Ellie Norwood and Hubert Willis on location with director Maurice Elvey filming *The Priory School*. Stoll's films made strong use of real locations both in London and the countryside.

news items, the self-contained nature of each meant that it did not matter if a viewer missed the occasional episode – they would be able to jump straight back in the following week to catch the detective's next thrilling case.

Taking the part of Holmes was theatre actor Eille Norwood. Although nearing sixty, Norwood proved to be an inspired choice for the role. He took the part extremely seriously. As well as immersing himself in the stories themselves, he studied Sidney Paget's original drawings for visual cues. He shaved his head to achieve Holmes's characteristic high forehead and took great pleasure in devising disguises suitable for the screen. As he remarked in an interview with (appropriately enough) the *Strand* Magazine, 'disguises which are excellent for the theatre are impossible for the screen. The searching eye of the camera finds out and reveals every join, line and trick of the actor.'[15] In addition to this, he had to build disguises that could be removed to reveal not the actor Eille Norwood, but the character of Sherlock Holmes, as played by Eille Norwood. Despite these challenges, the Stoll films do not shrink from using disguise and masquerade and, in fact, foreground it as a narrative device and a source of visual pleasure – a type of showmanship that had long been recognised in the context of the theatre.[16] During the course of the whole series, Norwood impersonated a vicar, a Cockney taxi driver, a stage actor, a Japanese

opium smoker, a news vendor and a bearded foreign spy, to say nothing of numerous tramps and pedlars.

Stoll's films also recognised the importance of another crucially important element of the original stories – the relationship between Holmes and Watson. In earlier Holmes films, the presence of Watson was sketchy and erratic. In contrast, he features in every one of Stoll's films, although series regular Hubert Willis was replaced by the younger Arthur Cullin in *The Sign of Four* in order to be a more convincing love interest for the glamorous Mary Morstan (played by Isobel Elsom). The consistent inclusion of Watson allows Holmes's abilities and character to shine more effectively – as we all know, Holmes and Watson are at their best when working together, with Watson's warmth and humanity off-setting Holmes's often coldly logical demeanour. The presence of Watson also gives the film makers the option of telling the story, or at least parts of it, through Watson's eyes, as with the original stories. In fact, Stoll's films offer a sophisticated set of narrative and cinematic devices through the way in which the stories are told and Holmes's deductive powers are demonstrated. Stoll's films are the first screen adaptations that really capture the intensely cinematic essence of Conan Doyle's original stories. The earliest Holmes stories preceded the emergence of cinema, but like some other authors of the nineteenth century, such as Charles Dickens and Thomas Hardy, Conan Doyle's writing can be described as 'cinematic' in its structure and use of language.

In his essay 'Dickens, Griffith and the Film Today', first published in 1944, film maker and theorist Sergei Eistenstein traced a line from Dickens's writing through to director D.W. Griffith and the techniques of narrative cinema. He asserted that Dickens's writing had an amazing 'nearness to the characteristics of cinema in method, style and especially in viewpoint and exposition', finding in his work literary equivalents of montage, close-ups, the point-of-view shot and even dissolves.[17] The same can be said of Conan Doyle, who was writing later than Dickens and closer to the emergence of cinema at the end of the nineteenth century. Within the Holmes stories we see evidence of Conan Doyle's cinematic sensibility in numerous ways. Like Dickens, Conan Doyle utilises the urban setting of London to create a series of highly cinematic scenes and moments that use light and motion in vivid and highly dramatic ways. Settings and objects are frequently described with strong visual detail, like establishing shots and close-ups in film, and characters are also introduced in ways that can be clearly visualised in cinematic terms. Watson as narrator functions like the camera; he is the lens through which the stories are (almost always) told. His perception and telling of the story shapes what we see and what we can know, in the same way that the camera shows some things but withholds others to control our understanding of the narrative. This is something that the Stoll adaptations heavily exploit, especially because they largely forsake the simplification and linearisation of the stories seen in earlier adaptations.

Maurice Elvey, who directed the first Stoll series and the two features, took a great deal of care to preserve the structure of the originals as much as possible, despite being nervous about how audiences would respond to an 'inverted' method of storytelling that worked backwards from a crime to unravel its causes.[18] On the whole, the results are extremely successful, with the films frequently using clever and occasionally complex flashbacks and elements of restricted narration. In *The Dying Detective* (1921), for example, an event is partially shown and then retold twice in flashback. Each retelling extends the sequence, showing more of what really happened, challenging the viewer's understanding of events and revealing the real extent of Holmes's cleverness when he initially appears to have been outsmarted by the villainous Culverton Smith.

Rather than being a disadvantage, the silent medium and its use of intertitles help place the viewer in the position of active spectator, being encouraged to act as detective and read the clues as presented. In *The Man With the Twisted Lip* the intertitles punctuate the deductive process. Intertitles announcing clues, such as bloody fingerprints and coat pockets weighed down with copper coins, label the shots as Holmes describes to Watson the police investigation of the room where Neville St Clair (played by Robert Vallis) was last seen. While being narrated to Watson, they also function as a direct address to the spectator, pulling us into the world of the film.

Although William J. Elliott, the writer of the first Stoll series, suggested that the audience 'would be profoundly bored if the exact process, as outlined in the stories, were shown – there is not much interest for the average picture-goer in

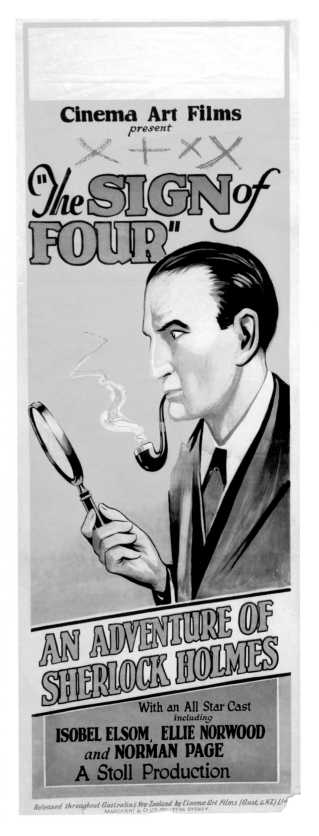

seeing a man examining mud or cigar ash under a magnifying lens',[19] there are, in fact, many scenes in which we see Holmes crawling around on his hands and knees, inspecting the evidence. When his observations and thought processes are presented, however, this is often done in highly visual and cinematically inventive ways. In *The Copper Beeches*, a series of flashback superimpositions show Holmes mentally running over the clues that Violet Hunter's testimony has just provided. In *The Beryl Coronet* (1921), superimposition is used to visualise Holmes's imagining of how a series of footprints were created on the night of the attempted theft. The camera enables us to see what Holmes's mental processes deduce as we cut between shots of Holmes and shots of both what he sees and what he reads from this.

The films benefited from extensive location shooting. Holmes's investigation in *The Beryl Coronet* actually took place in Eille Norwood's own garden in Little Ealing (a fact of which was made much of in Stoll's promotion of the episode), but other episodes capitalised on more recognisable locations, as well as a wealth and variety of urban, suburban and rural settings, which serve to provide a rich backdrop to the stories. Early on, director Maurice Elvey instituted a high-profile search for the 'real' 221B (he temporarily decided it was number 144) and some scenes were shot in Baker Street. Soon, though, the problems of using the thoroughfare as a regular location became too much for the director: 'As soon as one or two cars are gathered together ... word goes round that the "picture people" are there. Quicker than wireless the news travels down street after street – and in the twinkling of an eye all the office boys for miles around are on the spot. And they will not go away! Their first idea is to find the camera, and then their one ambition is to get right in its way, and to stay there at all costs.'[20]

Efforts to hide the camera with an overcoat thrown over the top were not successful and Elvey soon resorted to having art director Walter Murton build a full-scale façade of 221B at Stoll's Cricklewood studio. The long duration of the series justified this large expense and the set remained *in situ* until 1923.

The film makers had more success in other locations. The 'coat over the camera' trick seemingly worked for *The Man With the Twisted Lip*, for instance, which features brief scenes of its titular mendicant plying his trade at Piccadilly Circus. Interiors and exteriors for *A Scandal in Bohemia* were shot at the Ambassadors Theatre on St Martin's Lane. These scenes, in which Holmes goes to watch Irene Adler perform on stage, were not in the original story but demonstrate something of silent British cinema's close links to, and obsession with, the theatre. As always, Stoll's publicists capitalised on this stunt and made sure that the story got into both the trade and popular press. *The Times* reported in advance that audience members for the matinée of Lennox Robinson's comedy *The White-Headed Boy* would be invited 'to remain in their seats for half an hour after the curtain had fallen, and to participate in the film production which will follow'.[21] The scenes as shot are very effective, showing Holmes and Watson as audience members and, later, Holmes posing as an actor taking a role in the production itself. Although Stoll's films capture a distinctly 1920s London (*The Times* was keen to point out that the Ambassadors hadn't even been built at the time the first Holmes stories were written), they nevertheless help place Holmes firmly within his natural habitat, the great modern metropolis. This reaches its apotheosis in the 1923 feature, *The Sign of Four*, which reconfigures the final river chase as a dramatic Hollywood-style pursuit with Holmes criss-crossing the river by motor car, taking in key London landmarks along the way.

Conan Doyle was impressed with Stoll's films. He thought them 'excellent'[22] and even agreed to attend Stoll's annual convention dinner in October 1921 to congratulate the film makers and speak warmly of his admiration for Norwood's performance, which he placed as the latest in a line of distinguished interpretations of his character via illustrator Sidney Paget and actors William Gillette and H.A. Saintsbury.[23] In the same month, 'The Mazarin Stone' appeared in the *Strand* Magazine. It was the first new Holmes story since 'His Last Bow' in 1917 and was adapted by Conan Doyle from his play *The Crown Diamond*, which had opened just a few months before, in March 1921. It's possible that Stoll's new series of adaptations had re-awakened his interest in his creation, or at least in his detective's commercial possibilities. Bringing this intermediality full circle, Stoll adapted 'The Mazarin Stone' for the screen in 1923. Conan Doyle's only criticism of Stoll's films, which he voiced in his memoirs a few years later, was that, as mentioned above, the films were set in modern-day London and 'introduced telephones, motor cars and other luxuries of which the Victorian Holmes never dreamed'.[24] But no films up to this point, and indeed for some time to come, would attempt to recreate Holmes's Victorian London. This did not happen for another fifteen years, until Twentieth Century Fox's *The Hound of the Baskervilles*, starring Basil Rathbone, in 1939.

Sherlock Holmes (1922), an American film, also used a contemporary setting. It starred John Barrymore as a young Holmes, whom we see to begin with as an undergraduate at Cambridge, where he first encounters Moriarty's nefarious criminal web. The film was produced by the Goldwyn Pictures Corporation and was based on the only Holmes property they could license at the time, William Gillette's still popular play, *Sherlock Holmes*. It was released in the UK in the middle of Stoll's series and in between Stoll's two Holmes feature releases (*The Hound of*

JOHN BARRYMORE AS HOLMES CONFRONTS PROFESSOR MORIARTY (GUSTAV VON SEYFFERTITZ) IN ALBERT PARKER'S 1922 *SHERLOCK HOLMES*

the Baskervilles in 1921 and *The Sign of Four* in 1923). It benefited from location shooting in London but was not well received critically, being seen as a little dull and ponderous, with too many intertitles.[25] The film also caused friction between Conan Doyle and William Gillette due to an attempt made by the Goldwyn Corporation to bring legal action against Stoll because of its Holmes films. This was based on the fact that Goldwyn claimed rights in the name of Sherlock Holmes, having purchased the film rights to Gillette's play.[26] Conan Doyle was called to give evidence and, although the courts found in Stoll's favour, the legal wrangle soured their long and productive relationship.[27]

Brook and beyond

HE FIRST HOLMES SOUND FILM was released in 1929, just a year before Conan Doyle's death in July 1930. The suave British actor Clive Brook starred in Paramount's *The Return of Sherlock Holmes*, a story that features the characters of Holmes, Watson, Moriarty and Colonel Sebastian Moran, but is not based on a Conan Doyle story. Brook went on to play Holmes twice more, but in the 1930s and 1940s two other actors, Arthur Wontner and Basil Rathbone, took on and defined Holmes for their era in the same way that Gillette and Norwood had done earlier. During the silent era, screen portrayals of Holmes had developed in all sorts of ways, from short trick films and pastiches to extended narratives that explored the richness of film as a storytelling (particularly detective storytelling) medium. Essentially, this period established templates for two main types of film – those that use the

CLIVE BROOK AS HOLMES IN THE 1932 FILM *SHERLOCK HOLMES*

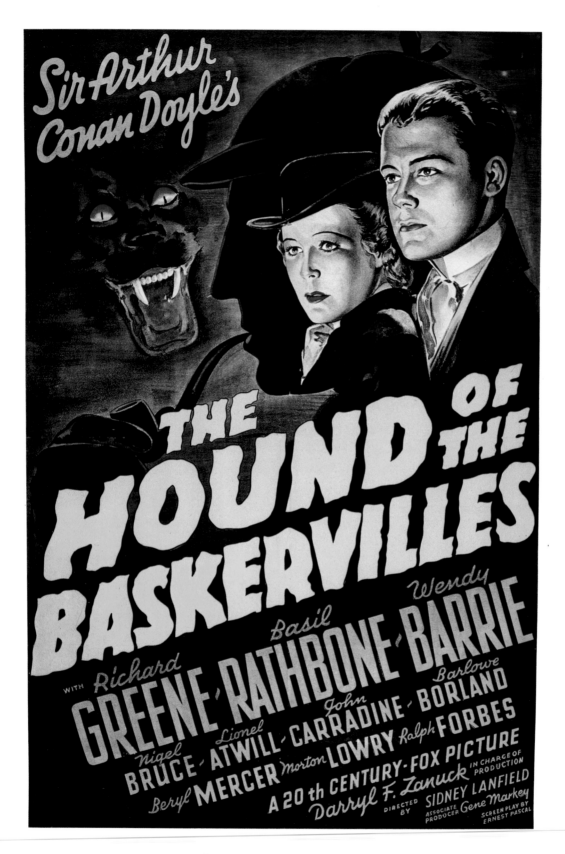

bare bones of the Holmes character, or of Conan Doyle's tales, as the basis of a new and exciting story, and those that, in contrast, stay as close and as faithful to the originals as possible.

All of these permutations continued into the sound period, and, as the Victorian era receded ever further into the past, attention to period detail added a new dimension and element of pleasure to screen adaptations to the extent that it eventually became unthinkable to imagine Holmes without frock coat and November fog. Granada's 1984–1994 television series essentially followed the strategy adopted by Stoll over sixty years before, by producing several series of individual episodes, which stayed close to the originals while making some minor adjustments to stretch out running times, or cope with the practical demands of screen adaptation. Whereas Stoll's films had a contemporary 1920s setting, Granada's series prided itself on its detailed recreation of Holmes's Victorian world, as well as its close adaptation of Conan Doyle's stories.

With the recent modern settings of *Sherlock* and also the American series *Elementary*, however, film and programme makers have come full circle. Holmes is being treated as a contemporary figure once again, albeit in a more deliberate and self-conscious way. In *Sherlock*, for instance, we are invited to take pleasure in the ingenious ways that elements of Conan Doyle's plots and characters, as well as Victorian features, such as telegrams and horse-drawn hansom cabs, are updated to the present day. What Conan Doyle would think of Benedict Cumberbatch's portrayal of Holmes as a text messaging 'high-functioning sociopath' is open to debate, but what is clear is that Holmes has outlived and outgrown his creator, something he had promised to do from the earliest days of his career on screen.

Holmes at the Cinema
and on TV

From the earliest films through to the most recent
TV productions, Sherlock Holmes and Dr Watson
have been played by an incredible range of
actors. Each one has interpreted the roles in their
own distinctive way. However, there seems to be a
common thread running through them all,
especially when it comes to Holmes in his 'thinking gaze' pose. Even if not dressed in tweed
or holding a pipe, there remains an intrinsic
Sherlock Holmes persona that always seems to
shine through.

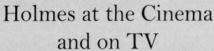

Above: RAYMOND MASSEY AS SHERLOCK HOLMES IN THE
FILM *THE SPECKLED BAND* (1931)

Above right: ARTHUR WONTNER AS SHERLOCK HOLMES
IN THE FILM *SHERLOCK HOLMES AND THE MISSING
REMBRANDT* (1932)

Right: REGINALD OWEN AS SHERLOCK HOLMES IN THE
FILM *A STUDY IN SCARLET* (1933)

Left: BASIL RATHBONE AS SHERLOCK HOLMES C.1939

Above left: BASIL RATHBONE AS SHERLOCK HOLMES AND NIGEL BRUCE AS DR WATSON C.1939

Above: PETER CUSHING AS SHERLOCK HOLMES IN THE FILM *THE HOUND OF THE BASKERVILLES* (1959)

Left: ROBERT STEPHENS AS SHERLOCK HOMES IN THE FILM *THE PRIVATE LIFE OF SHERLOCK HOLMES* (1970)

Above right: ROGER MOORE AS SHERLOCK HOLMES IN THE TV FILM *SHERLOCK HOLMES IN NEW YORK* (1976)

Right: ROBERT DUVAL AS DR WATSON AND NICOL WILLIAMSON AS SHERLOCK HOLMES IN THE FILM *THE SEVEN-PER-CENT SOLUTION* (1976)

Above: James Mason as Dr Watson and Christopher Plummer as Sherlock Holmes in the film *Murder by Decree* (1979)

Left: Peter Cook as Sherlock Holmes in the spoof film *The Hound of the Baskervilles* (1978)

Above right: Ian Richardson as Sherlock Holmes in the TV Film *The Hound of the Baskervilles* (1983)

Right: Nicolas Rowe as Sherlock Holmes and Alan Cox as John Watson in the film *Young Sherlock Holmes* (1985)

BRENT SPINER AS THE ANDROID DATA IN THE episode 'ELEMENTARY DEAR DATA' (1988) FROM THE TV SERIES *STAR TREK: THE NEXT GENERATION*

DAVID BURKE AS DR WATSON AND JEREMY BRETT AS SHERLOCK HOLMES IN THE EPISODE 'THE FINAL PROBLEM' (1984) OF THE TV SERIES *THE ADVENTURES OF SHERLOCK HOLMES*

CHRISTOPHER LEE AS SHERLOCK HOLMES IN THE TV FILM *SHERLOCK HOLMES AND THE LEADING LADY* (1991)

Martin Freeman as John Watson and Benedict Cumberbatch as Sherlock Holmes in the BBC TV series *Sherlock* (2010)

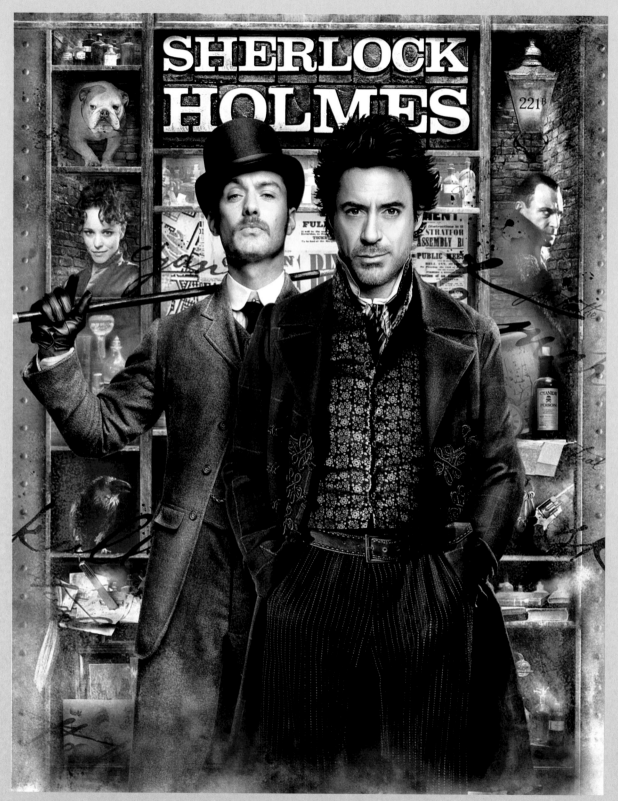

ROBERT DOWNEY JR AS SHERLOCK HOLMES AND JUDE LAW AS DR WATSON IN THE FILM *SHERLOCK HOLMES* (2009)

NEW HOLMES. NEW WATSON. NEW YORK.

JONNY LEE MILLER   LUCY LIU
ELEMENTARY

JONNY LEE MILLER AS SHERLOCK HOLMES AND LUCY LIU AS DR WATSON IN THE US TV SERIES *Elementary* (2012)

NOTES

'A Case of [Mistaken?] Identity'
DAVID CANNADINE

1 I am grateful to Linda Colley, Patricia Hardy, Maya Jasanoff, Mervyn King, Emma Rothschild, Quentin Skinner and Martha Vandrei for help and for comments on an earlier draft of this essay. Throughout the notes, I have used the following abbreviations:

Left: 'THE BAYSWATER OMNIBUS (DETAIL), 1895, GEORGE WILLIAM JOY'

ACD Sir Arthur Conan Doyle
CASH *The Penguin Complete Adventures of Sherlock Holmes* (Harmondsworth, 1984 edn.)
CD A.Lycett, *Conan Doyle: The Man Who Created Sherlock Holmes* (London, 2008)
LiL J. Lellenberg, D. Stashower and C. Foley (eds.), *Arthur Conan Doyle: A Life in Letters* (London, 2008)
SACD J. Dickson Carr, *The Life of Sir Arthur Conan Doyle* (New York, 2003 edn.)

2 A. Briggs, *Victorian Cities* (London, 1963), pp. 320–31. For the same description applied at an earlier time, see C. Fox (ed.), *London – World City, 1800–1840* (London, 1992).

3 J. Martin, 'Reinventing the Tower Beefeater in the Nineteenth Century', *History*, xcviii (2013), pp. 730–49; T.B. Smith, 'In Defence of Privilege: The City of London and the Challenge of Municipal Reform, 1875–1890', *Journal of Social History*, xxvii (1993), pp. 59–83.

4 G. Stedman Jones, *Outcast London: A Study in the Relationship between the Classes in Victorian Society* (Harmondsworth, 1976); W.J. Fishman, *East End 1888* (London, 1988); J.R. Walkowitz, *City of Dreadful Delight: Narratives of Sexual Danger in Late-Victorian London* (London, 1992); P.L. Garside, 'West End, East End: London, 1890–1940', in A. Sutcliffe (ed.), *Metropolis, 1890–1940* (London, 1984), pp. 221–35.

5 A. Service, *Edwardian Architecture: A Handbook to Building Design in Britain, 1890–1914* (London, 1977), pp. 43-44; C. Booth, *Life and Labour of the People in London* (2 vols, London, 1889–1891).

6 D. Rodgers, *Atlantic Crossings: Social Politics in a Progressive Age* (Cambridge, Mass., 1998), pp. 132–42; A. Lees, 'The Metropolis and the Intellectual', in Sutcliffe (ed.), *Metropolis*, pp.75–77, 79–81.

7 *CASH: A Study in Scarlet*, p. 15; ACD, 'On the Geographical Distribution of British Intellect', *The Nineteenth Century* (August 1888), p. 185; *CD*, p. 146.

8 M. Girouard, *Cities and People, A Social and Architectural History* (London, 1985), pp. 343–49; T. Hunt, *Building Jerusalem: The Rise and Fall of the Victorian City* (London, 2004). For contemporary views of the city as both the betrayer and redeemer of mankind, see G. Gilloch, *Myth and Metropolis: Walter Benjamin and the City* (Cambridge, 1996), pp. 1–5.

9 J. McLaughlin, *Writing the Urban Jungle: Reading Empire in London from Doyle to Eliot* (Charlottesville, 2000), p. 51.

10 There is a great deal of 'Sherlockian' pseudo-scholarship outlining the career and dating the cases of the great detective, as if he was a 'real' person, among which are: W.S. Baring-Gould, *Sherlock Holmes: A Biography of the World's First Consulting Detective* (London, 1963); M. Harrison, *The World of Sherlock Holmes* (London, 1973); H.F.R. Keating, *Sherlock Holmes: The Man and His World* (New York, 1979); D.A. Redmond, *Sherlock Holmes: A Study in Sources* (Montreal, 1982).

11 *CASH*: 'Greek Interpreter', p. 435; 'Musgrave Ritual', p. 387; ACD, *Memories & Adventures* (London, 1988 edn.), p. 99.

12 *CASH*: *His Last Bow*, preface, p. 869; 'Creeping Man', p. 1080; 'Lion's Mane', p. 1083.

13 J.G. Cawelti, *Adventure, Mystery and Romance: Formula Stories as Art and Popular Culture* (Chicago, 1976), p. 140; J. Conlin, *Tales of Two Cities: Paris, London and the Birth of the Modern City* (London, 2013), p. 175.

14 *CASH*: 'Empty House', p. 489; A. Welsh, *The City of Dickens* (Oxford, 1971); F.S. Schwartzbach, *Dickens and the City* (London, 1979); Briggs, *Victorian Cities*, pp 355–67.

15 ACD, *Memories & Adventures*, pp 95–97; *LiL*, p. 291.

16 *SACD*, pp. 276, 280.

17 Girouard, *Cities and People*, p. v; *LiL*, pp 63–71, 101–07; *CD*, pp. 42–43, 122; O. Dudley Edwards, *The Quest for Sherlock Holmes: A Biographical Study of Arthur Conan Doyle* (Edinburgh, 1983), pp. 39–40, 150–51.

18 *CASH*, *The Sign of Four*, p. 126; Dudley Edwards, *Quest for Sherlock Holmes*, pp. 202–03, 249–50.

19 *CASH*, 'The Priory School', p. 540; 'The Copper Beeches', p. 323; 'The Reigate Puzzle', p. 398.

20 P.D. James, *Talking about Detective Fiction* (London, Oxford, 2009), p. 40; *CASH*, 'The Copper Beeches', p. 317.

21 F.J. Brodie, 'On the Prevalence of Fog in London During the 20 Years 1871 to 1890', *Quarterly Journal of the Royal Meteorological Society*, xviii (1892), pp. 40–45; idem, 'Decrease of Fog in London During Recent Years', *Quarterly Journal of the Royal Meteorological Society*, xxxi (1905), pp. 15–28; H.T. Bernstein, 'The Mysterious Disappearance of Edwardian London Fog', *The London Journal*, i (1975), pp. 189–206; P. Brimblecombe, *The Big Smoke: A History of Air Pollution in London Since Medieval Times* (London, 2011), pp. 108–35.

22 H. James, *Essays on London and Elsewhere* (London, 1893), pp 1, 9; G. Seiberling, *Monet in London* (Seattle, 1988), p. 55. See also S.F. Khan, 'Monet at the Savoy Hotel and the London Fogs, 1899–1901' (unpublished PhD dissertation, University of Birmingham, 2011).

23 F.M.L. Thompson, 'Nineteenth-Century Horse Sense', *Economic History Review*, new ser., xxix (1976), pp. 62–63, 77.

24 Briggs, *Victorian Cities*, p. 331; G.M. Young, *Victorian England: Portrait of an Age* (Oxford, 1977 edn.), p. 92.

25 *CASH*, 'The Dying Detective', p. 933; *The Sign of Four*, p. 138; A. Service, *London 1900* (London, 1979), pp. 1–7.

26 *CASH*, 'The Naval Treaty', p. 451; M.H. Port, *Imperial London: Civil Government Building in London, 1850–1915* (London, 1995), pp. 198–210; Dudley Edwards, *Quest for Sherlock Holmes*, pp. 249–50.

27 *CASH*, 'The Blue Carbuncle', p. 251; *The Sign of Four*, p. 99.

28 There is also much 'Sherlockian' pseudo-scholarship on Holmes's London, which contains a great deal of valuable information but is wholly lacking in historical awareness or perspective, for which see, among others: M. Harrison, *The London of Sherlock Holmes* (Newton Abbot, 1972); T. Kobayashi, A. Higashiyama and M. Uemura, *Sherlock Holmes's London: Following in the Footsteps of London's Master Detective* (San Francisco, 1983); D. Sinclair, *Sherlock Holmes's London* (London, 2009); D. Sinclair, *Close to Holmes: A look at the connections between historical London, Sherlock Holmes and Sir Arthur Conan Doyle* (London, 2009); T. Bruce Wheeler, *The London of Sherlock Holmes* (London, 2011); J. Christiopher, *The London of Sherlock Holmes* (Stroud, 2012).

29 J. Summerson, *Georgian London* (London, 2003 edn.), pp. 179–224; J. Mordaunt Crook, *London's Arcadia: John Nash & the Planning of Regent's Park* (London, 2001); R. Porter, *London: A Social History* (London, 1994), pp. 313–14; *CASH*, 'The Bruce-Partington Plans', p. 915.

30 D.J. Olsen, *The Growth of Victorian London* (London, 1976), p. 81; J. White, *London in the Nineteenth Century: 'A Human Awful Wonder of God'* (London, 2007), p. 477.

31 Briggs, *Victorian Cities*, p. 335; H. Pelling, *Social Geography of British Elections, 1885–1910* (London, 1967), p. 27.

32 G. Grossmith and W. Grossmith, *The Diary of a Nobody* (Bristol, 1892).

33 *CASH*, 'The Six Napoleons', p. 588.

34 *SACD*, pp. 84, 236; *LiL*, p. 343; N. Pevsner, *An Outline of European Architecture* (Harmondsworth, 1963), pp. 397–98, 444–46; K.T. Jackson, 'The Capital of Capitalism: the New York Metropolitan Region, 1890–1940', in Sutcliffe (ed.), *Metropolis*, pp. 321–24; Girouard, *Cities and People*, pp. 319–24.

35 J. Schneer, *London 1900: The Imperial Metropolis* (London, 1999), pp. 184–226; D. Cannadine, 'The Context, Performance and Meaning of Ritual: The British Monarchy and the 'Invention of Tradition', c. 1820–1977', in E.J. Hobsbawm and T. Tanger (eds.), *The Invention of Tradition* (Cambridge, 1983), pp. 108–38.

36 S. Ledger and R. Luckhurst, 'Introduction: Reading the 'Fin de Siècle'', in idem (eds.), *The Fin de Siècle: A Reader in Cultural History, c. 1880–1900* (Oxford, 2000), pp. xvi–xviii; R.A. Kaye, 'Sexual Identity at the Fin de Siècle', in G. Marshall (ed.), *The Cambridge Companion to the Fin de Siècle* (Cambridge, 2007), pp 53–72.

37 L. McKinstry, *Rosebery: Statesman in Turmoil* (London, 2005), pp 348–68; R.F. Mackay, *Balfour: Intellectual Statesman* (Oxford, 1985), p 8.

38 Briggs, *Victorian Cities*, pp. 342–55; P. Thompson, *Socialists, Liberals and Labour: The Struggle for London, 1885–1914* (London, 1967), pp 80–82, 90–111; K. Young and P. Garside, *Metropolitan London: Politics and Urban Change, 1837–1981* (London, 1982), pp. 64–101; S. Pennybacker, *A Vision for London: Labour, Everyday Life and the LCC Experiment* (London, 1995), pp 1–32.

39 J. Walkowitz, *City of Dreadful Delight: Narratives of Sexual Danger in Late-Victorian London* (Chicago, 1992), pp 81–120, 191–228; D. Gray, 'Gang Crime and the Media in Late Nineteenth-Century London: The Regent's Park Murder of 1888', *Cultural and Social History*, x (2013), pp 559–75.

40 V.A.C. Gatrell, 'The Decline of Theft and Violence in Victorian and Edwardian England', in V.A.C. Gatrell, B. Lenman and G. Parker (eds.), *Crime and the Law: The Social History of Crime in Western Europe since 1500* (London, 1980), pp. 240–41, 280–86, 290–93; M.J. Wiener, *Reconstructing the Criminal: Culture, Law and Policy in England, 1830–1914* (Cambridge, 1990), pp. 216–17.

41 D. Cannadine, 'Gilbert and Sullivan: The Making and Un-Making of a British Tradition', and C. Emsley, 'The English Bobby: An Indulgent Tradition', both in R. Porter (ed.), *Myths of the English* (Cambridge, 1993), respectively p. 22, p 120; James, *Detective Fiction*, pp 18–19.

42 C. Emsley, *Crime, Police and Penal Policy: European Experiences, 1750–1940* (Oxford, 2007), pp. 142–59, 181–214; V.A.C. Gatrell, 'Crime, Authority and the Policeman State', in F.M.L. Thompson (ed.), *The Cambridge Social History of Britain*, vol. iii, *Social Agencies and Institutions* (Cambridge, 1990), pp. 306–10; Wiener, *Reconstructing the Criminal*, pp 224–56.

43 *SACD*, pp. 48–49; *LiL*, pp 267–68, 407–507, 566; ACD, *Memories & Adventures*, pp. 200–09; ACD, *The Great Boer War* (London, 1900); ACD, *The War in South Africa – Its Cause and Conduct* (London, 1902).

44 *SACD*, pp. xiv, 56–60, 163, 263–64, 276, 283; Schneer, *London 1900*, pp. 106–13; McLaughlin, *Writing the Urban Jungle*, pp 27–78.

45 *CD*, p. 44; Dudley Edwards, *Quest for Sherlock Holmes*, pp. 185–86, 189–90; *LiL*, pp 313, 357–58, 532–33, 579–60, 623, 637; *CASH*, 'The Second Stain', p. 650.

46 *CASH*, 'The Devil's Foot', p. 968; ACD, *Memories & Adventures*, pp. 78–79; Dudley Edwards, *Quest for Sherlock Holmes*, pp. 15–17; *SACD*, pp. 101–12; *CD*, pp. 242–46, 253–55, 259, 264–65, 277, 308–13, 320–21; *LiL*, pp. 412–18, 522.

47 *LiL*, pp 365–66, 562–63; ACD, *Memories & Adventures*, pp. 55–56; ACD, *The Story of Mr George Edalji* (London, 1907); ACD, *The Case of Oscar Slater* (London, 1912); ACD, *The Crime of the Congo* (London, 1909); C. Wynne, *The Colonial Conan Doyle: British Imperialism, Irish Nationalism and the Gothic* (London, 2002), pp. 101–08.

48 James, *Detective Fiction*, p. 31; *CASH*, *The Sign of Four*, pp. 89, 96, 129; 'The Red-Headed League', p. 190; 'The Abbey Grange', pp. 642, 646; *The Hound of the Baskervilles*, p. 754; 'The Bruce-Partington Plans', p. 927.

49 *CASH*, 'The Bruce-Partington Plans', p. 913; 'The Illustrious Client', p. 999; 'The

Three Gables', p. 1032; 'The Retired Colourman', p. 1120; Wiener, *Reconstructing the Criminal*, p. 222; Dudley Edwards, *Quest for Sherlock Holmes*, pp. 127–28, 132–33; *LiL*, pp. 78–79; W.O. Aydelotte, 'The Detective Story as a Historical Source', in F.M. Nevins (ed.), *The Mystery Writer's Art* (Bowling Green, Ohio, 1970), pp. 323–24.

50 R. Hill, 'Holmes: The Hamlet of Crime Fiction', in H.F.R. Keating (ed.), *Crime Writers* (London, 1978), p. 22–24.

51 *CASH*, 'The Greek Interpreter', p. 435; *The Sign of Four*, pp 89–90; 'The Priory School', p. 547.

52 *CD*, p. 358; *CASH*, *The Sign of Four*, p. 13; 'Scandal in Bohemia', p. 170; *The Valley of Fear*, pp 776, 809; 'The Dying Detective', p. 941; *The Hound of the Baskervilles*, p. 689; 'The Bruce-Partington Plans', p. 920; 'The Mazarin Stone', pp. 1012–13, 1022.

53 *CASH*, 'The Empty House', p. 488; 'Wisteria Lodge', p. 879; 'The Norwood Builder', p. 496; 'The Resident Patient', p. 423; 'The Cardboard Box', p. 888; 'The Blue Carbuncle', p. 245.

54 Gatrell, 'Crime, Authority and the Policeman-State', pp 264–65, 270; J. Walkowitz, *Prostitution and Victorian Society: Women, Class and the State* (Cambridge, 1980), pp. 13–14, 29–31.

55 *CASH*, *A Study in Scarlet*, p. 25; *The Sign of Four*, pp. 89–90, 93; 'The Red-Headed League', p. 190; 'A Case of Identity', p. 197; 'The Copper Beeches', p. 317; 'Wisteria Lodge', p. 870.

56 *CASH*, 'The Empty House', p. 496; 'The Blue Carbuncle', p. 245; 'The Priory School', pp. 543, 545, 555–56; 'Charles Augustus Milverton', p. 582; 'The Three Students', p. 596; 'The Missing Three-Quarter', pp. 629–30, 635; 'The Abbey Grange', p. 640; 'The Second Stain', pp 663, 666; *The Hound of the Baskervilles*, p. 695; 'The Problem of Thor Bridge', p. 1055; Wiener, *Reconstructing the Criminal*, pp. 219–20, 244–50; S. Knight, *Form and Ideology in Crime Fiction* (Bloomington, 1980), p. 88; Cawelti, *Adventure, Mystery and Romance*, pp. 95–96.

57 *CASH*, 'The Norwood Buiilder', p. 510; 'Charles Augustus Milverton', p. 572; 'The Second Stain', pp 651–53; 'The Bruce-Partington Plans', p. 916.

58 Dudley Edwards, *Quest for Sherlock Holmes*, pp. 117–18; *LiL*, p. 595; *CD*, pp. 24, 35, 364–65, 383; *CASH*, 'His Last Bow', p. 973.

59 J.A. Hobson, *Imperialism: A Study* (1965 edn.), pp. 48, 51, 59; idem, 'The General Election: A Sociological Interpretation', *Sociological Review*, iii (1910), pp. 112–13; P.J. Cain, 'J.A. Hobson, Financial Capitalism and Imperialism in Late Victorian and Edwardian England', *Journal of Imperial and Commonwealth History*, xiii (1985), pp. 8–9; P.J. Cain and A.G. Hopkins, *British Imperialism*, vol. i, *Innovation and Expansion, 1688–1914* (Harlow, 1993), pp. 16–17, 199–200.

60 Hobson, *Imperialism*, p. 54.

61 H. Orel, *Sir Arthur Conan Doyle: Interviews and Recollections* (New York, 1991), p. 126; *LiL*, pp 336–44; *CD*, pp. 21, 60, 82, 218–19; *CASH*, 'The Noble Bachelor', pp. 299–300.

62 *CASH*, 'The Five Orange Pips', pp. 226–27; *The Valley of Fear*, pp. 832–33; 'The Dancing Men', p. 523; 'The Three Garridebs', p. 1051; 'The Problem of Thor Bridge', pp. 1055–61.

63 *CASH*, *The Hound of the Baskervilles*, p. 676; 'The Boscombe Valley Mystery', pp. 203, 208; 'A Case of Identity', p. 193.

64 *CASH*, 'The Devil's Foot', pp 961, 970; 'The Priory School', p. 558; 'The Three Students', pp. 606–07; 'The Copper Beeches', p. 332.

65 J.A. Kestner, *Sherlock's Men: Masculinity, Conan Doyle, and Cultural History* (Aldershot, 1997), p. 7; *CD*, p. 325; *CASH*, The *Sign of Four*, pp. 138–39; 'The Disappearance of Lady Frances Carfax', p. 947.

66 *CASH*, 'The Speckled Band', pp. 260, 268, 272.

67 McLaughlin, *Writing the Urban Jungle*, p. 51; Hobson, *Imperialism*, p. 51. Hobson and ACD (and, indeed, Joseph Conrad in *Heart of Darkness*) also shared views about Belgian involvement in the Congo: Hobson, *Imperialism*, p. 198.

68 Dudley Edwards, *Quest for Sherlock Holmes*, p. 128.

69 *CASH*, *Case-Book*, preface, p. 983; Hill, 'Holmes: The Hamlet of Crime Fiction', p. 22.

70 *LiL*, p. 514.

71 *CASH*, 'The Empty House', p. 489; Dudley Edwards, *Quest for Sherlock Holmes*, p. 143; Conlin, *Tales of Two Cities*, pp. 194–209.

72 Hill, 'Holmes: the Hamlet of Crime Fiction', pp. 28–31; A. Hennegan, 'Personalities and Principles: Aspects of Literature and Life in Fin de Siècle England', in M. Teich and R. Porter (eds.), *Fin de Siècle and its Legacy* (Cambridge, 1990), pp. 173, 184; M.D. Stetz, 'Publishing Industries and Practices', in Marshall, *Cambridge Companion to the Fin de Siècle*, pp. 113–30.

73 *CD*, pp. 155–56, 173.

74 Thompson, 'Nineteenth-Century Horse Sense', p. 65.

75 Gatrell, 'Crime, Authority and the Policeman State', p. 261; Service, *Edwardian Architecture*, pp. 43–44; Hill, 'Holmes: the Hamlet of Crime Fiction', p. 33

76 Kestner, *Sherlock's Men*, pp. 6, 88; *CASH*, 'The Musgrave Ritual', p. 386.

77 *CASH*, 'The Naval Treaty', pp. 456–57; 'The Yellow Face', pp. 361–62; Dudley Edwards, *Quest for Sherlock Holmes*, pp. 273–76, 286–87.

78 *CASH*, 'The Red-Headed League', pp. 186, 189; 'The Beryl Coronet', pp. 304, 313; 'The Noble Bachelor', pp. 288–89; Dudley Edwards, *Quest for Sherlock Holmes*, pp. 65–66.

79 *SACD*, pp 159–61; *LiL*, pp. 494–507; *CASH*, 'The Three Garridebs', p. 1044.

80 *CASH*, 'The Abbey Grange', p. 148; 'The Devil's Foot', p. 968; 'The Second Stain', p. 653; 'The Six Napoleons', p. 588; 'The Golden Pince-Nez', p. 619; 'Wisteria Lodge', pp. 884–85; 'The Red Circle', pp. 908–09; 'The Devil's Foot', p. 955; Kestner, *Sherlock's Men*, pp. 165–76.

81 Service, *Edwardian Architecture*, pp 140–69; idem, *London 1900*, pp. 109–29, 141–53, 217–45; Port, *Imperial London*, pp. 18–19.

82 Service, *London 1900*, pp 60–71; Emsley, *Crime, Police and Penal Policy*, p. 187.

83 N. Barratt, *Greater London: The Story of the Suburbs* (London, 2012), pp. 343–56; Thompson, 'Nineteenth-Century Horse Sense', p. 61.

84 D.S. Davies, 'Introduction' to ACD, *The Best of Sherlock Holmes* (Ware, 1998), p. xi; ACD, *The Lost World & The Poison Belt* (San Francisco, 1989 edn.), p. 242; *LiL*, pp. 586–87.

85 ACD, *The New Revelation* (London, 1918); ACD, *The Vital Message* (London, 1919); ACD, *The Wanderings of a Spiritualist* (London, 1921); ACD, *The Coming of the Fairies* (London, 1922); ACD, *The Case for Spirit Photography* (London, 1922); ACD, *The History of Spiritualism* (London, 1926); ACD, *The Edge of the Unknown* (London, 1930).

86 *CD*, pp. 424–25, 439–40; *CASH*, 'The Sussex Vampire', p. 1034; 'The Creeping Man', pp. 1082–83; 'The Veiled Lodger', pp. 1101–02; 'The Illustrious Client', p. 998; 'The Three Garridebs', p. 1053.

87 C. Clausen, 'Sherlock Holmes, Order and the Late-Victorian Mind', *The Georgia Review*, xxxviii (1984), p. 122; Dudley Edwards, *Quest for Sherlock Holmes*, pp. 17–19, 113–14; Kestner, *Sherlock's Men*, pp 176–200.

88 *CASH*, 'The Retired Colourman', p. 1113; 'The Creeping Man', p. 1083.

89 Service, *London 1900*, pp. 228–29, 250–51; Port, *Imperial London*, p. 19.

90 Barratt, *Greater London*, pp. 357–76; Porter, *London*, pp. 316–18; Thompson, 'Nineteenth-Century Horse Sense', p. 76.

91 H. Clunn, *London Rebuilt, 1897–1927* (London, 1927), pp. 9–10; A. Sutcliffe, 'Introduction: Urbanization, Planning and the Giant City', in Sutcliffe (ed.), *Metropolis*, pp. 7, 11.

92 *LiL*, p. 596; *CD*, p. 368.

93 A. Sutcliffe, 'The Metropolis in the Cinema', in Sutcliffe (ed.), *Metropolis*, pp. 168–69.

94 ACD, *Memories & Adventures*, p. 106; *CD*, pp. 336, 406–07; R.W. Pohle and D.C. Hart, *Sherlock Holmes on the Screen: The Motion Picture Adventures of the World's Most Popular Detective* (South Brunswick, NJ); C. Steinbrunner and N. Michaels, *The Films of Sherlock Holmes* (Secaucus, NJ, 1978).

95 ACD and J. Dickson Carr, *The Exploits of Sherlock Holmes* (New York, 1954).

96 C. James, 'The Sherlockologists', *New York Review of Books*, 20 February 1975,

pp. 15 –18.

97 James, *Detective Fiction*, p. 31; ACD, *Sherlock Holmes: The Major Stories with Contemporary Critical Essays* (ed. J.A. Hodgson, Boston, 1994), pp. 437–41.

98 T.S. Eliot, 'Books of the Quarter', *Criterion*, viii (1929), p. 553.

99 CD, p. 455; Cawelti, *Adventure, Mystery and Romance*, p. 19; Brimblecombe, *Big Smoke*, pp. 161–78.

100 McLaughlin, *Writing the Urban Jungle*, p. 29.

101 Cannadine, 'Gilbert and Sullivan', pp 12–32; idem, 'Another "Last Victorian"?: P.G. Wodehouse and His World', *South Atlantic Quarterly*, lxxvii (1978), pp. 470–91.

CHAPTER ONE

The 'Bohemian Habits' of Sherlock Holmes
JOHN STOKES

Bibliography

Bratton, Jacky, *The Making of the West End Stage. Marriage, Management and the Mapping of Gender in London, 1830–1870* (Cambridge, 2011).Brooker, Peter, Bohemia in London. The Social Scene of Early Modernism (Basingstoke, 2007).

Clayton, Antony, *Decadent London. Fin de siècle city* (London, 2005).

Cottom, Daniel, *International Bohemia. Scenes of Nineteenth-Century Life* (Philadelphia, 2013).

Graña, César and Marigay Graña, *On Bohemia. The Code of the Self-Exiled* (New Brunswick and London, 1990).

Nead, Lynda, *Victorian Babylon. People, Streets and Images in Nineteenth-Century London* (London and New Haven, 2000).

Ransome, Arthur, *Bohemia in London*, Introduced by Rupert Hart-Davis (Oxford, 1984, first published in 1907).

Wilson, Elizabeth, *Bohemians. The Glamorous Outcasts* (London, 2000).

1 C.J. Wills, *In and About Bohemia. Being Forty-One Short Stories*, (London,1892).

2 At times other areas took on Bohemian associations. Justin McCarthy's *Reminiscences* (London, Second Edition, 1899), vol. 1, pp. 308–24, has a chapter entitled 'A Fitzroy Square Bohemia' in which he compares the Aesthetic movement of the 1870s with earlier manifestations.

3 S.J. Adair Fitzgerald, *Sketches from Bohemia. Stories of the Stage, the Study and the Studio* (London, 1890), p. 150. For the Strand in general, see Michael Harrison, *The London of Sherlock Holmes* (Newton Abbott, 1972), pp. 140–67.

4 See Antony Clayton, *Decadent London. Fin de siècle city* (London, 2005), pp 18, 56–7; Lynda Nead, Victorian Babylon. *People, Streets and Images in Nineteenth-Century London* (London and New Haven, 2000), pp. 161–2, 165, 229–30; Michael Harrison, *In the Footsteps of Sherlock Holmes* (London, 1958), p. 62.

5 Harry Furniss, *My Bohemian Days* (London, 1919), pp. 1–2.

6 Nead, *Victorian Babylon*, pp. 161–62.

7 See Christopher Kent, 'The Idea of Bohemia in Mid-Victorian England', *Queen's Quarterly*, vol. 80, no. 3, autumn 1973, pp 360–69. Reproduced in *Bohemia. The code of the self-exiled*, eds. by César Graña and Marigay Graña (New Brunswick and London, 1990), pp. 158–67, 158.

8 Henri Murger, *The Bohemians of the Latin Quarter* (London, 1888), pp xxv–xxix.

9 [Justin McCarthy], 'The Literature of Bohemia', *Westminster Review*, January 1863, n.s. 23, pp. 32–56, 52.

10 George Saintsbury, 'Henry Murger', *Fortnightly Review*, No. CXL, n.s., August 1, 1878, pp. 230–49, 230.

11 Michael Harrison, *In the Footsteps of Sherlock Holmes* (London, 1958), p. 150.

12 Arthur Ransome, *Bohemia in London*, Introduced by Rupert Hart-Davis (Oxford,

1984, first published in 1907), pp. 129–30.

13 [Justin McCarthy], 'In its essence, Bohemia is or was a protest against the subjection of human life to money-making, and of human intellect to conventional rule.' The Literature of Bohemia', p. 33.

14 The opera was composed by Michael William Balfe, libretto by Alfred Bunn. See Richard Schoch, 'Performing Bohemia', *Nineteenth Century Theatre and Film*, 30:2, Winter 2003, 1–13. This important article concentrates on the representation of theatrical Bohemia in plays such as Tom Robertson's *Society* (1865), memoirs such as J.G. Bertram's *Glimpses of Real Life* (1864) and parody burlesques of Balfe's opera.

15 Jacky Bratton, *The Making of the West End Stage. Marriage, Management and the Mapping of Gender in London*, 1830–1870 (Cambridge, 2011), p. 96.

16 London, 1898.

17 Sir Arthur Conan Doyle, *Memories and Adventures* (London, 1924), pp. 61, 71.

18 London, 1921.

19 London, 1926.

20 London, 1882.

21 London, 1883.

22 Arthur Symons, *Selected Letters 1880–1935* (Iowa City, 1989), p. 79.

23 Joseph Hatton, 'Stories of Famous Men. 1. – The Boyhood of Henry Irving', *The Idler*, 1895, pp. 669–85, 681.

24 London, 1884.

25 Elizabeth P. Ramsay-Laye, *The Adventures of a Respectable Bohemian* (London, 1907), p. 39.

26 E.P. Thompson, 'Time, Work-Discipline, and Industrial Capitalism', *Past and Present*, No. 38 (December 1967), pp. 56–97, 95.

27 Fitzroy Gardner, *More Reminiscences*, p. 107. See Christopher Kent 'British Bohemia and the Victorian Journalist', *Australasian Victorian Studies Journal*, vol. 6, December 2000, pp. 24–35.

28 Jeffrey Richards, Sir Henry Irving. *A Victorian Actor and his World* (Hambledon and London, 2005), p. 158.

29 'The Tragic Generation', *Autobiographies* (London, 1966), pp. 304, 309.

30 E. Beresford Chancellor, *Wanderings in Piccadilly, Mayfair and Pall Mall* (London, 1908), p. 81.

31 See 'Wilde at Bay: the diary of George Ives' in John Stokes, *Oscar Wilde. Myths, Miracles and Imitations* (Cambridge, 1996), pp. 65–88.

32 See Carolyn Steedman's discussion of the 'bedsitter land' that provides the background for novels about young women in the 1890s: 'Fictions of Engagement' in *Eleanor Marx (1855–1898). Life – Work – Contacts*, ed. John Stokes (Aldershot, 2000), pp. 23–39.

33 Adair Fitzgerald, *Sketches from Bohemia*, p. 84.

34 Bratton, *The Making of the West End*, p. 110.

35 Sir Arthur Conan Doyle, *Memories and Adventures* (London, 1924), p. 265.

36 London: Remington and Co., 1876, p. 6. Also see Ransome, *Bohemia*, pp. 67–98.

37 Adair Fitzgerald, *Sketches from Bohemia*, p. 147.

38 Adair Fitzgerald, *Ballads of a Bohemian* (London, 1893), pp. 163–66, 166.

39 A Journalist [i.e. William Mackay], *Bohemian Days in Fleet Street* (London, 1913), p. 221.

40 Adair Fitzgerald, *Sketches from Bohemia*, p. 154.

41 Beresford Chancellor, *Wanderings*, p. 76.

42 For London restaurants, see Clayton, *Decadent London*, pp. 86–94.

43 Glasgow, 1898, pp. 39–40.

44 Fitzroy Gardner, *More Reminiscences*, pp. 165–66.

45 Fitzroy Gardner, *Days and Ways of an old Bohemian* (London, 1921), p. 171.

46 Dan Farson, *Marie Lloyd and the Music-Hall* (London, 1972), p. 94.

47 Adair Fitzgerald, *Ballads of a Bohemian*, pp. 180–81.

48 'St. George's Day', *Fleet Street Eclogues*, 2nd series (London, 1896), p. 81.

49 Andrew Lycett, *Conan Doyle. The Man who Created Sherlock Holmes* (London, 2007), p. 184.

50 Peter Toohey, Boredom. A Lively History (New Haven and London, 2011), p. 187.

51 Patricia Meyer Spacks, Boredom. *The Literary History of a State of Mind* (Chicago and London, 1995), p. 12; Charles Palliser, introduction to *The Valley of Fear and Selected Cases* (Harmondsworth, 2001), p. xv.

52 In his discussion of Holmes's cocaine habit (*Emperor of Dreams. Drugs in the Nineteenth Century* (Sawtry, Cambs, 2000)), Mike Jay connects the detective with 'the bohemian stereotype', p. 175.

53 Adair Fitzgerald, *Ballads of a Bohemian*, p. 3.

54 Ransome, *Bohemia*, p. 251.

55 Ransome, *Bohemia*, p. 283.

56 London, 1882, vol. 1, pp. 3–4.

57 London, 1888, p. 53.

58 London, 1899, p. 1.

59 Furniss, *Bohemian Days*, pp 1–2.

60 George R. Sims, *My Life. Sixty Years' Recollections of Bohemian London* (London, 1917), p. 338.

61 Orlo Williams, *Vie de Bohème. A Patch of Romantic Paris* (London, 1913), p. 5.

CHAPTER TWO

Sherlock Holmes, Sidney Paget and the *Strand* Magazine

ALEX WERNER

1 There is a suggestion that Sherlock Holmes was better known in the United States than in Britain at this time, largely because of the circulation of cheap editions that took advantage of the lack of any copyright law. Conan Doyle noted that he had seen 'some of his early American editions . . . printed on the paper that shopmen use for parcels' and that his 'Holmes book had met with some American success'. Sir Arthur Conan Doyle, *Memories and Adventures* (Oxford, 1989), pp. 77–78.

2 Peter McDonald, *British Literary Culture and Publishing Practice 1880–1914* (Cambridge, 1997), pp. 135–37.

3 Conan Doyle, *Memories and Adventures*, pp. 95–96.

4 Conan Doyle had also been struck down by a 'virulent attack of influenza' at this time which he suggested nearly killed him. *Memories and Adventures*, p. 96.

5 See McDonald, *British Literary Culture*, pp. 144–157 and Kate Jackson, *George Newnes and the New Journalism in Britain, 1880–1901 Culture and Profit* (Aldershot, 2001), pp. 53–117.

6 The *Strand* Magazine, Vol. IV August 1892, pp. 182–88.

7 G.R. Sims, *Tales of To-Day* (London, 1889).

8 Alex Werner, 'The *London Society* magazine and the influence of William Powell Frith on modern life illustration of the early 1860s', in Mark Bills and Vivien Knight (eds) *William Powell Frith painting the Victorian Age* (New Haven and London 2006), pp. 94–109.

9 Edgar Allan Poe, *The Fall of the House of Usher and Other Writings* (London, 1986), p. 193.

10 The *Strand* Magazine, Vol. II July 1891, p. 62.

11 *The Idler* Magazine, Vol. I May 1892, pp. 413–24.

12 Conan Doyle, *Memories and Adventures*, p. 106.

13 Dusan C. Stulik & Art Kaplan, *Halftone* (Los Angeles, 2013).

14 The drawing is in the Allen Mackler Collection, University of Minnesota.

15 Jon Lellenberg, Daniel Stashower & Charles Folly (eds), *Arthur Conan Doyle, A Life in Letters* (London, 2007), pp. 394–95.

16 Quoted by Philip Pullman 'Words and Pictures', *The Author*, Autumn 2013, pp. 90–93. Powell also wrote: 'I am convinced that Holmes and Watson would never have been household heroes without pictures. For the first time, and all over the world,

a storyteller's images, as well as his words, were known and recognised. Sidney Paget and Arthur Conan Doyle were the parents of the silent film, the sound film, the colour film, TV, video tape, of all the audio-visual storytelling inventions of the next 90 years.' Michael Powell, *A Life in Movies* (London, 1986), pp. 45–47.

CHAPTER THREE
The Art of Sherlock Holmes
PAT HARDY

1 Lynda Nead, *Victorian Babylon* (London and New Haven, 2000), pp. 13–14.
2 B. Guinaudeau, 'La Décennale anglaise', *L'Aurore*, 22 August 1900.
3 Tristram Ellis, *Art Journal*, 1880, p. 121.
4 Jonathan Ribner, 'The Poetics of Pollution', in *Turner, Whistler, Monet*, exh. cat. Tate, 2004, pp. 51–53.
5 S.F. Khan, 'Monet at the Savoy Hotel and the London Fogs, 1899–1901', (unpublished PhD dissertation, University of Birmingham, 2011).
6 Daniel Wildenstein, *Claude Monet: Biographie et catalogue raisonné*, (Lausanne, 1974–91), Vol. III, letter 1511.
7 Octave Mirabeau, Preface to *Claude Monet, Vues de la Tamise à Londres (1902–1904)* exh cat. Paris: Galeries Durand-Ruel, 1904.
8 René Gimpel, *Diary of an Art Dealer*, trans. John Rosenberg (New York, 1966) p. 129.
9 E. Billet Maconommies, 'The sculptor working hard as a painter', *The Eagle*, 8 September 1901.
10 G. Geffroy, *Claude Monet, sa vie, son temps, son oeuvre*, two volumes (Paris 1922), pp. 130–31.
11 'Alvin Langdon Coburn, Artist-Photographer by Himself', *Pall Mall Magazine*, 51 (June 1913), p. 762.
12 Elizabeth Pennell, *Life and Letters of Joseph Pennell* (London, 1930).
13 Mark Bills, 'Atkinson Grimshaw in London', in Jane Sellars (ed) *Atkinson Grimshaw, Painter of Moonlight*, exh. cat, Mercer Art Gallery (Harrogate, 2011), p. 76.
14 Sidney Dark, *London with Illustrations by Joseph Pennell* (London, 1924), p. 1.
15 Jon Lellenberg, Daniel Stashower and Charles Foley, *Arthur Conan Doyle A Life in Letters* (London, 2007) p. 101.
16 *Ditto.*
17 HOL/42 1886 Holden Papers, Bradford University, J.B. Priestley Library.
18 Antoine Proust, 1882, p. 534 in John House, *Impressions of France, Monet, Renoir, Pissarro and their Rivals* (Boston, 1995), p. 39.

CHAPTER FOUR
Throwaway Holmes
CLARE PETTITT

1 Letter from Conan Doyle to Mary Doyle (11 November 1891); MS facsimile in John Dickson Carr, *The Life of Sir Arthur Conan Doyle*, (London, 1949), facing p. 64; quoted Peter McDonald, *British Literary Culture and Publishing Practice 1880–1914* (Cambridge, 1997), p. 170.
2 *The Adventures of Sherlock Holmes* (July 1891 to December 1892) was followed by *The Memoirs of Sherlock Holmes* (December 1892 to November 1893).
3 Herbert Greenhough Smith, 'Some Letters of Conan Doyle', *Strand*, (October 1930): 393; quoted Peter McDonald, p. 144.
4 Reginald Pound, *Mirror of the Century*, The *Strand* Magazine, *1891–1950*, (London, 1966), p. 64.
5 W.T. Stead 'Preface' to the 'Index to the Periodical Literature of the World. Covering the Year 1891', *Review of Reviews*, (1892), pp. 5–6, p. 5. Stead is talking

specifically about 'the phenomenal success of the *Strand*' here.

6 Nicholas Dames complains that, '[m]ore precision is needed in terms of both novelistic form and cultural norms of attentiveness, in order to determine ... how certain genres managed readerly attention and how those generic formations of readerly attention related to wider cultural notions of what qualified as mental alertness.' Nicholas Dames, *The Physiology of the Novel: Reading, Neural Science, and the Form of the Novel* (Oxford, 2007), p. ix.

7 Matthew Arnold held W.T. Stead responsible for the 'feather-brained' New Journalism in his article, 'Up to Easter', *Nineteenth Century* 21 (May 1887): p. 638.

8 Laurel Brake, 'The "Trepidation of the Spheres": The Serial and the Book in the Nineteenth Century' in Robin Myers and Michael Harris (eds.), *Serials and Their Readers 1660–1914* (Winchester, 1993), pp 83–102, p. 88; on the practice of skimming see Leah Price, *The Anthology and the Rise of the Novel. From Richardson to George Eliot* (Cambridge, 2000).

9 Conan Doyle to Smith (4 March 1908) quoted from Cameron Hollyer, 'Author to Editor: Arthur Conan Doyle's Correspondence with H. Greenhough Smith' *A.C.D.: The Journal of the Arthur Conan Doyle Society* 3 (1992): 11–34, p. 19; quoted in Peter McDonald, p. 144.

10 Arthur Conan Doyle, *Memories and Adventures* (London, 1924), pp. 95–96; quoted in Peter McDonald, p. 138.

11 Alexander Pollack Watt, ALS to ACD, (11 April 1891) *Letter–Books: March–June 1891*, vol. 25, ts. And ms. Berg Collection, New York Public Library, New York, p. 165; quoted Peter McDonald, p. 139.

12 James Mussell, 'The Spectacular Spaces of Science and Detection in the *Strand* Magazine' Chapter 2 in *Science, Time and Space in the Late Nineteenth-Century Periodical Press: Movable Types*, (Aldershot, 2007), p. 62.

13 Alex Werner discusses the cover of the *Strand* Magazine in this volume, and he suggests that the title picked out in lights is there to remind us of Newnes's electric sign on top of his Southampton Row office building.

14 Steven Marcus, 'Introduction', *The Sherlock Holmes Illustrated Omnibus* (New York, 1976), pp. vii–xii, p. ix.

15 Jennifer Phlegley, *Courtship and Marriage in Victorian England* (Santa Barbara, 2012), p. 78.

16 The *Leader* (5 January 1856), p. 10; quoted in Jennifer Phlegley, p. 78.

17 For more on personal advertisements in the nineteenth century, see Matthew Rubery, 'The Personal Advertisements: Advertisements, Agony Columns, and the Sensation Fiction of the 1860s', Chapter 2 in *The Novelty of Newspapers. Victorian Fiction after the Invention of the News* (Oxford, 2009), pp. 24–47.

18 Mr William G. Fitzgerald, 'The Lost Property Office', The *Strand* Magazine (Christmas Edition, December 1895): 641–653, p. 650.

19 See Ronald R. Thomas, *Detective Fiction and the Rise of Forensic Science* (Cambridge, 1999).

20 Alice Clay (ed.), *The Agony Column of The Times, 1800–1870* (London, 1881), p. viii.

21 *Ibid*, p. viii.

22 *Ibid*, p. xvi.

23 Edgar Smith, 'Foreword', *Profile by Gaslight: An Irregular Reader About the Private Life of Sherlock Holmes* (New York, 1944), n.p.; quoted in Michael Saler, *As If: Modern Enchantment and the Literary Prehistory of Virtual Reality* (Oxford, 2012), p. 126.

24 The media theorist, Marshall McLuhan, claimed that Holmes stood against the narrow instrumental reason of the bureaucrats of Scotland Yard with 'tidy desk[s] ... whose technique is serial, segmented and circumstantial. They conclude effect from preceding cause in linear and chronological order.' McLuhan enjoyed Holmes's ability instead to see the 'major relevance of details' and therefore to swerve out of a sequential logic if something odd caught his eye. Marshall McLuhan, 'The Artist and the Bureaucrat' in eds. Eric McLuhan and Frank Zingrone, *The Essential McLuhan* (New York, 1995), p. 193; quoted in Michael Saler, p. 119. Saler himself

argues that '[Holmes] re-enchanted modernity without compromising the central tenets of modernity: rationalism, secularism, urbanism and mass consumerism.' *As If* (Oxford, 2012), p. 117.

25 Matt Hill, 'Sherlocks for the Twenty-first Century' in *Barthes' Mythologies Today: Readings of Contemporary Culture*, eds. Pete Bennett and Julian McDougall (New York and Abingdon, 2013), pp. 41–44, p. 41 and p. 44.

CHAPTER FIVE
Silent Sherlocks: Holmes and Early Cinema
NATHALIE MORRIS

1 Daniel Stashower, *Teller of Tales: The Life of Arthur Conan Doyle* (London, 2000), p. 214.

2 Holmes shown in context of real-life characters (Jack the Ripper, Sigmund Freud in *The Seven Per Cent Solution*) says something about how he has expanded beyond being a fictional character and has taken on the status of a real historical figure.

3 Jay Weissberg, 'Sherlock and Beyond', catalogue for Le Giornate del Cinema Muto 2009, p. 31. I am indebted to Weissberg's 2009 festival programme for the opportunity to view so many early, and often rare, Sherlock Holmes films.

4 Arthur Conan Doyle, *Memories and Adventures* (Ware, 2007, first published London, 1924), p. 90.

5 According to the American *Motion Picture World*, 'That these reproductions on the screen of some of the more important incidents in the career of the mythical detective-scientist will bring to the picture houses a new clientele goes without saying'. 23 November 1912.

6 David Stuart Davis, *Starring Sherlock Holmes* (London, 2001), p. 14.

7 Tom Gunning, 'A Tale of Two Prologues: Actors and Roles, Detectives and Disguises in *Fantômas*, Film and Novel', *The Velvet Light Trap*, Number 37, Spring 1996, p. 32.

8 Note un-official American version at virtually the same time.

9 *Kinematograph Monthly*, November 1914, n.p.

10 George Pearson, *Flashback* (London, 1957).

11 Arthur Conan Doyle, *Memories and Adventures*, p. 90.

12 Andrew Lycett, *Conan Doyle: The Man Who Created Sherlock Holmes* (London, 2007), p. 417.

13 Arthur Conan Doyle, *Memories and Adventures*, p. 81.

14 Reginald Pound, The *Strand* Magazine *1891–1950* (London, 1966), p. 46.

15 Fenn Sherie, 'Sherlock Holmes on the Film, The *Strand* Magazine, July 1921, p. 76.

16 Tom Gunning discusses this in relation to *Fantômas*, p. 33.

17 Sergei Eisenstein, 'Dickens, Griffith and the Film Today', *Film Form: Essays in Film Theory* (Harcourt, 1949), pp. 195–255.

18 *Stoll's Editorial News*, 17 February 1921, p. iv.

19 *Kinematograph Weekly*, 17 March 1921, p. 68.

20 'Stories for Programmes and Papers', *Stoll's Editorial News*, 26 May 1921, p. viii.

21 'Theatre as Film Studio', *The Times*, 18 December 1920, p. 8.

22 *Stoll's Editorial News*, 6 October 1921, p. 20.

23 *Kinematograph Weekly*, 6 October 1921, p. 59.

24 Arthur Conan Doyle, *Memories and Adventures*, p. 90. Of course, Holmes does use the telephone, and is even pictured by illustrator Howard Elcock doing so, in 1924's 'The Three Garridebs'.

25 For many years the film was believed lost but was rediscovered and restored by film historian Kevin Brownlow in 1976.

26 Andrew Lycett, *Conan Doyle*, pp. 417–18.

27 The Goldwyn Corporation had long been antagonistic towards Stoll since a spat over the British company's distribution of Goldwyn films in 1919.

BIOGRAPHIES

Sir David Cannadine FBA is Dodge Professor of History at Princeton University. He is the author of fourteen books, including *The Decline and Fall of the British Aristocracy, Class in Britain, Ornamentalism, Mellon*, and *The Undivided Past*, and has just completed a short biography of King George V. Sir David is a Trustee of the Wolfson Foundation, the Royal Academy, the Library of Birmingham, the Rothschild Archive, the Gladstone Library and the Gordon Brown Archive. He is also the Editor of the Oxford Dictionary of National Biography, Vice Chair of the Westminster Abbey Fabric Commission and the Editorial Board of Past and Present, a Vice President of the Victorian Society, and a member of the Royal Mint Advisory Committee and the Editorial Board of the History of Parliament. He is a former Chair of the Trustees of the National Portrait Gallery and of the Blue Plaques Panel, and has also served as a Commissioner of English Heritage, a Trustee of the Kennedy Memorial Trust, and a Trustee of the British Empire and Commonwealth Museum. Sir David makes frequent appearances on radio and television in the UK and is a regular contributor to BBC Radio 4's 'A Point of View' programme.

John Stokes is Emeritus Professor of Modern British Literature at King's College London. He has written widely on the culture of the 'fin de siècle' and, together with Mark W. Turner, has edited two volumes of Oscar Wilde 's journalism, *Complete Works*, (Oxford University Press, 2013).

Alex Werner is Head of History Collections at the Museum of London. He has curated a number of major displays including Dickens and London (2011–12), the Expanding City gallery (2010) and Jack the Ripper and the East End (2008–9). His publications include *Dickens's Victorian London* (co-authored with Tony Williams, Ebury Press, 2011) and *Dockland Life* (co-authored with Chris Ellmers, Mainstream Publishing, 2000).

Pat Hardy is Curator of Paintings, Prints and Drawings at the Museum of London and Curator of the exhibition on Sherlock Holmes. Having obtained a PhD at the Courtauld Institute on nineteenth-century British Art, she was an Assistant Curator at the National Portrait Gallery where she worked on the critically acclaimed Sir Thomas Lawrence exhibition and then took up the position of Curator of Works on Paper at National Museums Liverpool. Most recently at the Museum she has worked on the exhibition Dickens and London (2011–12) and Drawing the Games: London 2012 and Nicholas Garland and is currently researching corporate art for an exhibition about this for the Museum of London Docklands in 2015. She is published widely and is currently writing a book on the imagery of nineteenth-century migration.

Clare Pettitt is Professor of Nineteenth-Century Literature and Culture at King's College London. Her first monograph, *Patent Inventions: Intellectual Property and the Victorian Novel* (Oxford University Press, 2004) investigated the status of creativity in an industrialising world. Her second book, *Dr. Livingstone, I Presume?: Missionaries, Journalists, Explorers and Empire* (Profile and Harvard University Press, 2007) was about the clash of African and European modernities in the nineteenth century. From 2006–2011, she was a Research Director on the Cambridge Victorian Studies Project, and she is now working on 'Scrambled Messages: The Telegraphic Imaginary 1857–1900', a four-year AHRC-funded project on the aesthetics of the Atlantic Telegraph.

Dr Nathalie Morris is Senior Curator of the BFI National Archive's Special Collections. She has written and presented on various aspects of silent and British cinema including women working the British film industry, particularly before 1930; film marketing and publicity; and the early career (and London connections) of Alfred Hitchcock and his wife Alma Reville. Her current research interests include food and cinema, British cinema costume design, and the films of Michael Powell and Emeric Pressburger.

INDEX

(the initials ACD refer to Arthur Conan Doyle)

ACKNOWLEDGEMENTS

Special thanks firstly to all the authors, also to Geraldine Beare, Catherine Cooke, David Hay, Jenny de Gex, Michael Gunton, Roger Johnson, Jon Lellenberg, Glen Miranker, Randall Stock, Mark Turner, Jean Upton and Nicholas Utechin for their help at critical moments in the book's development; all colleagues at the Museum, particularly Nikki Braunton, John Chase, Sean O'Sullivan, Maria Rego, Roz Sherris, Anna Sparham, Richard Stroud and Sean Waterman; the book's designer, Peter Ward who has brought it all together; Nicki Crossley and Carey Smith and all the team at Ebury Press, and last but not least, to my wife Ann.

PICTURE CREDITS

Primrose Hill Park

ZOOLOGICAL GARDENS

REGENTS PARK

CAMDEN TOWN

Marlboro Rd Sta

ST JOHN'S WOOD

St John's Wood Road Sta

Lords Cricket Ground

London & North Western Railway Terminus

Cumberland Market

Clarence Gardens

St Pancras Church

Metropolitan Rly Kings Cross

Munster Square

University College

Gower St Sta

Catholic Apostolic Church

Foundling Hospital

H. Alfred Theatre

Pr. of Wales Th.

BISHOP'S ROAD STATION

Metropolitan Music Hall

Gt Western Railway Terminus and Hotel

PRAED ST STA

BAYSWATER

Museum

Bazaar

Langham Hotel

Princess Theatre

Oxford Music Hall

Crystal Palace

Queens Rd Bayswater Sta

Marble Arch

OXFORD STREET

Grosvenor Gallery

University of London

Hanover Chapel

St George's Church

National Gallery

CHARING CROSS

NOTTING HILL GATE

KENSINGTON GARDENS

HYDE PARK

THE SERPENTINE

Apsley House

GREEN PARK

Duke of York's Column

Grand Hotel

Marlborough House

Kensington Palace

Achilles

St James's Palace

Buckingham Palace

Treasury Buildings

Westminster

HIGH ST KENSINGTON STA

Albert Memorial

Kensington Museum

St George's Hospital

BIRDCAGE WALK

GT GEORGE ST

Westminster Hospital

Westminster Bridge

KENSINGTON

INTERNATIONAL EXHIBITION

Natural History Museum

National Portrait Gall

GLOUCESTER RD BROMPTON STA

SOUTH KENSINGTON STA

Buckingham Palace Hotel Westminster Palace Hotel

Victoria Sta

BELGRAVIA

VICTORIA STREET

Houses of Parliament

Lambeth Bridge

DISTRICT RAILWAY

Victoria Sta

Regent Square Church

Millbank

Consumption Hospital

St James's Royal Court Theatre

BROMPTON

Guards Barracks

Penitentiary

CHELSEA

Chelsea Hospital

BRIGHTON & SOUTH COAST RAILWAYS

LAMBETH

Vauxhall Rail Sta

GREAT WESTERN CHATHAM & DOVER RAILWAY

GROSVENOR ROAD

LONDON & SOUTH WESTERN

BATTERSEA PARK

C. SMITH & SON, 63 CHARING CROSS SW